The Senator's Son

The Senator's Son

The Shocking Disappearance, The Celebrated Trial, and The Mystery That Remains A Century Later

Charles Oldham

BEACH GLASS
BOOKS

Copyright © 2018
by Charles Oldham

All rights reserved, including the right to reproduce this book or portions thereof in any form whatsoever. For information, address Beach Glass Books, P.O. Box 72672, North Chesterfield, VA 23235.

Published by Beach Glass Books, 2018
Manufactured in the United States of America
First Printing September 2018

Front and back cover photographs courtesy of Samuel Walker
Front cover photo modification by Matt Stanton
Author photograph supplied by the author
Book and jacket design by Ray McAllister

Charles Oldham, 1974-
The Senator's Son: The Shocking Disappearance, The Celebrated Trial, and The Mystery That Remains A Century Later / by Charles Oldham
ISBN 978-0-9987881-4-2

This is for the family,
Mom, Dad, Eric, and Pamolu,
who thought this was a story worth telling,
and who encouraged me to make it happen.

And for my nephew,
Hemingway.
I wish for you a world where politics is not
a matter of life and death for children.

Contents

Foreword by Ray McAllister   *ix*

Introduction   *1*

PART I   THE DISAPPEARANCE
Chapter 1   The Scene, Set   *7*
Chapter 2   Shadows Descend   *17*
Chapter 3   An Aggressive Breed   *27*
Chapter 4   Will-o'-the-Wisp Clews   *37*

PART II   THE TIMES
Chapter 5   The Charley Ross Case   *47*
Chapter 6   The Eddie Cudahy Case   *59*
Chapter 7   Delayed Reckoning   *71*
Chapter 8   A Culture of Lynching   *79*
Chapter 9   Race and Politics   *87*
Chapter 10   The Anti-Liquor Crusade   *103*

PART III   THE TRIAL
Chapter 11   Battle Lines Drawn   *115*
Chapter 12   Revenge on Him or His Family, One   *131*
Chapter 13   Laying Out the Alibis   *139*
Chapter 14   Was the Answer in Norfolk?   *151*
Chapter 15   One Lady Must Be Lying   *159*
Chapter 16   Eloquent Machinations   *171*

Contents

PART IV RESOLUTIONS
Chapter 17 At His Own Hands *185*
Chapter 18 Theories of Lost Boy Cases *193*
Chapter 19 All Misgivings Relieved *203*

PART V RECKONINGS AND REASSESSMENTS
Chapter 20 History in Transition *217*
Chapter 21 To the Four Winds *229*

Acknowledgments *241*

Endnotes *247*
Bibliography *283*
Illustration Credits *295*
Index *299*
About the Author *307*

Foreword

You hold in your hands a gem.

It is the fascinating true story of the disappearance and presumed murder of a state senator's eight-year-old son in 1905; of the lengthy search and investigation that led to the arrest of the senator's sworn political enemy; of the riveting courtroom drama that ensued, a drama given star power by the presence of two former governors on one legal team and prosecutors who would be elevated to the positions of congressman and judge on the other, but a drama marred by unruly spectators and freely tossed—and sadly successful—racial epithets; of a press and public from two states so captivated that they clamored for each new bit of information, whether true or not; and of an aftermath that not only led to a suicide and damaged families for generations but fueled an ongoing mystery that is now more than one hundred years old.

Fortunately, this is also a detective story.

Charles Oldham, an attorney by trade, has set about retracing every step of the tragedy, visiting the site of the young boy's schoolyard disappearance, the North Carolina courthouses, and even the Norfolk, Virginia, boardinghouses that played an important role in the case. He studied every available newspaper from the day, every available transcript from the trial and other proceedings, and every other writing of the day. He talked with historians and even offspring of the long-dead participants. Along the way, for fuller context, he detours into the country's two previous major kidnapping-for-ransom cases, so that you, like those who lived in the time of young Kenneth Beasley's disappearance, will know what everyone knew. Oldham even takes us through North Carolina's histories of politics, liquor, race relations, and lynching, which as you might surmise, are not unrelated. These histories, too, factor in. So very much does.

Then Oldham sets about analyzing it all. The result is a guided tour of what, had it occurred in a major city with competing newspapers rather than in far-flung North Carolina, surely would have been labeled one of the first "trials of the century." As it was, newspapers from Norfolk to Elizabeth City, from Richmond to Raleigh, and even in New York and Washington, D.C., reported on the events.

It is quite a story and quite a book. With the aid of first-person accounts, vintage photographs and newspapers, and Oldham's storytelling, it transports readers to the remote North Carolina backwoods of the early twentieth century. It takes us into that schoolyard and into those dense, swampy woods, lets us stand in a remote cabin, in those city boardinghouses, and in that raucous courtroom. Oldham leads us back over the events with exceptional research, back over the evidence, back over the clues gathered and missed, back over the alibis and the lies, dissecting it all with an attorney's eye to show what mattered, what didn't, what didn't happen but should have—and likely what it all means. In the end, he establishes a more-than-plausible theory of what befell little puppy-loving Kenneth on that fateful day behind the schoolhouse.

Nowadays, this Carolina tidewater region may be better known for its pass-through highway of vacationers. Few whizzing by on their way to the beaches of the famed Outer Banks know this story of Kenneth Beasley, though I suspect this book may help change that.

But the most surprising part of this book may be this: it is a joy to read. It is an important book, yes, and at times a shocking book, but it is also an entertaining book.

I confess to initial misgivings. One of my pre-author training

Foreword

grounds was as a newspaper reporter covering courts. I read countless lengthy briefs and petitions, pondered too many obtuse contracts, and listened to so many long-winded legal arguments that I began looking at my watch the moment a lawyer stood up.

All of this is to say Charles Oldham doesn't write like a lawyer.
He writes like a writer.
And a darned good one.
Enjoy.

Ray McAllister
Richmond, Virginia

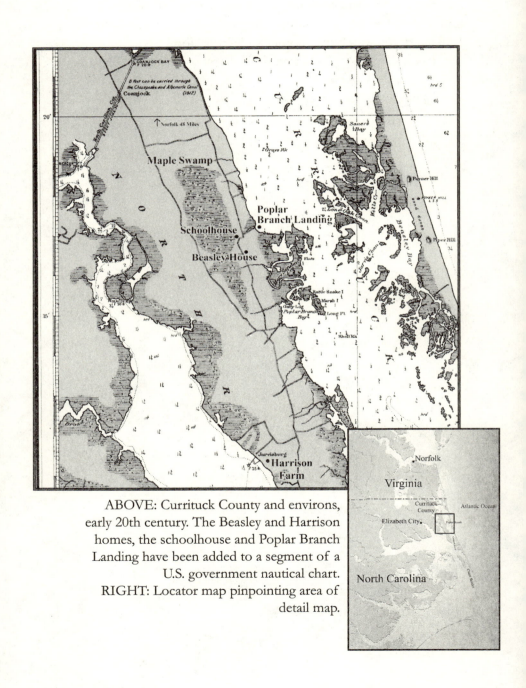

ABOVE: Currituck County and environs, early 20th century. The Beasley and Harrison homes, the schoolhouse and Poplar Branch Landing have been added to a segment of a U.S. government nautical chart.
RIGHT: Locator map pinpointing area of detail map.

INTRODUCTION

Currituck County is an old place, almost as old as Jamestown and Plymouth Rock. Naturally, it has seen a lot of changes. And as with most parts of the North Carolina coast, the biggest changes have been the most recent.

Driving down the Currituck peninsula on Highway 158, the main thoroughfare between the Hampton Roads of Virginia and North Carolina's Outer Banks, you don't see much that is old. The most conspicuous sights are convenience stores, surf shops, fast food outlets—the sorts of things that make travel easier for tourists as they head down to Kill Devil Hills and Nags Head on summer weekends. As easy as possible, at least. Those beaches are getting more and more popular all the time, and the traffic congestion shows it.

If ever there were a road that screamed to be called a "Beach Highway," 158 would be it. But all of that is relatively new.

Until a couple of generations ago, there were no waterfront condominiums or marinas and not many convenience stores in Currituck. Most folks still made their living as their forebears did—which is to say, from the land and the water. It was a region of small farms, where everyone worked hard to squeeze harvests of corn, potatoes, and soybeans out of the damp, sandy soil. And the soil is still damp today because it is surrounded by water. In any direction, you cannot go far without coming across a swampy, black-water creek that leads out into the briny waters of Currituck and Albemarle Sounds. It's not surprising that when the farmers were not working the fields, they were working the sounds, fishing and hunting the ducks and geese that used to flock there en masse.

But venture off the highway on to one of the side roads, as few beachgoers do, and it does not take long to find that Carolina tidewater as it once was. You can still see old white farmhouses surrounded by fields, the fields surrounded by woods. There are wide front yards, most of them with a big oak tree or two, and many of them with a small family cemetery nearby. In the old days, farm families held on to the land and to each other. Few people cared to venture too far afield, even after death.

One of those side roads leads a couple of miles to the tiny crossroads of Poplar Branch. Off the highway, back in the woods, the sounds of the traffic die away quickly. The road dips into the bottomland of the Maple Swamp, where dark water licks up against the trunks of sweetgum, maple, and cypress trees so thick that it is a challenge to see even ten feet ahead.

All around are shadows. Not just in the summer, when the leaves grow thickly on the trees and the sunlight barely filters down to dapple the ground. Even on an overcast winter day, the light creates illusions. The gray tree bark casts its reflection onto the water, and you have to watch your step carefully. What you see might actually be a fallen limb, and it might be solid enough to support you. Or it might not. It might also be one of the poisonous snakes that abound in the area.

If you wanted to get lost in the woods, this would be an easy place to do it. Especially if you were an eight-year-old boy. Or just as well, if you wanted a boy to get lost in the woods and leave no trace, this spot could serve your purpose.

This story does not lack for adjectives. It is a sad, heart-wrenching, human drama. It is also a confounding tale. Of course, there have always been clues, but they lead in different directions, usually into blind alleys. Theories, but they fail to satisfy. Even a trial and a verdict, yet doubts have remained. For years, it seemed as if the case were written on ice and all the details had melted away with time, until one tiny, overlooked clue finally brought resolution in the minds of some people, but by no means all.

It's the kind of mystery that you want, with all your heart and soul, to solve. So many people suffered, and you want them to rest in peace. But a solution remains elusive, even after a lot of digging through the swamps, the woods, attics, books, and repressed recollections.

And maybe most of all, through a history of brutal, dirty politics that most folks with twenty-first-century sensibilities would rather forget. And for a long time *did* forget.

Some folks will think, at first, *I'm surprised I haven't heard this story before.*

And then, with some reflection about how long it takes for painful memories to re-emerge, they will think, *Oh, yeah. That's why I haven't heard it.*

History, like a tall tree, casts a long shadow.

Part I

The Disappearance

Sam Beasley, owner of the Poplar Branch Landing and soon to become a state representative and then a state senator, with his wife, Cassie, circa 1890.

CHAPTER 1

THE SCENE, SET

Poplar Branch is still on all the maps, just as it has been since the early 1800s. But as a place where folks live, not much remains. Pay a visit, and then delve into local history, and you have a wonderful locale for contemplating the ebb and flow of time.

When it comes to communities, few stay the same for a century or more. Most places grow, a few shrink, but none remains unchanged, although Currituck County did a good job of remaining the same size for a long time. In every ten-year federal census between 1800 and 1970, the population of the county never fell below five thousand or rose above eight thousand.[1] There were some ups and downs, reflecting major upheavals such as the Civil War and the Great Depression, but the social rhythm of the area remained basically the same. Farming, fishing, and hunting were the order of the day.

Then, in the 1970s, Norfolk and Virginia Beach began to fill up and spill over the state line down Highway 158. Every year, new subdivisions have cropped up on old farm fields like mushrooms after a spring rain. By 1980, Currituck County had more than eleven thousand people. Thirteen thousand by 1990, eighteen thousand by 2000, and more than twenty-three thousand by 2010.[2] For that story, one needs only two words: suburban sprawl.

With all that transformation, it is hard to believe that Poplar Branch, separated though it is from the main highway by the swamp, was actually a busier place a century ago than it is now.

Today, it is fields, some houses, and little else. The main road, Poplar Branch Road, runs north and south, roughly paralleling the shore of Currituck Sound, about a half-mile to the east. At the intersection, one crossroad heads west toward the highway, through the woods on a raised causeway above the swampy water. The other heads east to the sound, to a recreational boat landing that is especially popular on summer weekends. The landing accounts for much of the traffic in Poplar Branch today. People from all over bring their bass boats and Jet Skis to access the sound, with its gentle waves that are more challenging than a lake, not as rough as the ocean.

If you could step back to 1905, you would find most community activity centered around that boat landing, but in a different way. Back then, Poplar Branch Landing was a commercial boat dock, not one for pleasure boats. The landing was opened shortly before the turn of the twentieth century by Samuel M. Beasley, a local farmer and landowner. He operated it—sometimes in partnership with his brother-in-law, William H. Walker, who lived on a farm adjoining his—as a place where locals could buy and sell the fish and birds they harvested in the local waters.[3]

Those were the days of the working coast, when on any day that the fish or birds were in season, the sound teemed with small wooden boats. Fishermen would be scraping the shallow bottom for oysters or casting nets for flounder, mullet, bass, or anything else with fins. At the same time, the "gunners" would cast their decoys onto the water to attract the ducks and geese. Sometimes, they would take aim from their boats, but more often they would conceal themselves in wooden duck blinds they built on the marshy islands scattered

The Scene, Set

through the sound. The more ambitious hunters would erect the blinds on pilings over the water.

Back on shore, the landing was the foundation for a commercial community that prospered for as long as the landing did, and for not much longer than that. Starting in the late 1800s, Wilson Woodhouse operated a grocery store and Ella Williams had an adjacent dry-goods store. S. J. Young had a watch-making, locksmith, and gunsmith shop, and J. C. Brown operated a machine shop that opened around 1910.[4]

With all the farming and harvesting going on, there had to be a way to move the area's produce, and especially seafood, quickly to market in those horse-and-buggy days. The main road through Poplar Branch was long, sandy, and not much use for transporting large quantities of anything. The locals needed another means to move their goods to Norfolk, fifty miles away, a rapidly growing seaport and industrial center. Just as an illustration, by 1905 the city had thirty oyster-shucking plants.[5]

Not surprisingly, the locals turned to the water for their transportation. Each week, several commercial vessels docked regularly at Poplar Branch Landing. They included the *Comet*, which steamed three times weekly between there and Munden's Point, Virginia, just up the sound, where goods could be loaded onto the recently completed Norfolk Southern Railway and hauled into the city. There was also the *Currituck*, a 115-foot vessel that traveled the same route and included a saloon, dining room, and staterooms for passengers.[6]

Today, Poplar Branch shows no visible reminders of any of that. Some of the old farmhouses still stand, but there is no sign of the commercial enterprise that gave the community its lifeblood. Over time, the fish were overharvested and the oysters decimated by pollution and disease. As the inlets leading to the ocean opened and closed with passing storms, affecting the salinity of the water, waterfowl shifted north toward Chesapeake Bay.[7] Poplar Branch Landing went through a series of owners until finally it was closed and the land sold to the North Carolina Department of Wildlife. In 1969, the state called in the local volunteer fire department to burn the wharf and warehouse structures down to the waterline, and then it completed the boat ramp in its place.[8]

The working coast was transformed into the pleasure coast. It is a pattern encountered frequently in North Carolina, and is probably inescapable in light of economic reality. Fishing and farming just are not as viable as they once were. If someone owns a parcel of land on a scenic tidewater creek, in an area where the population is growing and tax rates are rising, it is not realistic to grow soybeans on it. It is going to be subdivided into residential lots with houses, tennis courts, and private boat docks.

Not that the trend is in itself a bad thing. There is a human tendency to view the past through rose-tinted glasses, although, to be objective, it is fair to ask what exactly was so good about "the good ol' days." For that point, a nondescript, yet ineradicable, reminder stands just slightly north of the crossroads in Poplar Branch. It is a building that dates back to the early 1900s, the same time period as Poplar Branch Landing.

The building is a simple frame house. Single story, surely no more than four rooms, frame construction with a small brick chimney at one end and a rickety covered porch—and yet no foundation, as it rests on short pilings of bricks stacked three or four high. It is now painted lime green, although that could not have been the original

The old schoolhouse, originally the Odd Fellows Hall, as it stands today.

color. Driving past, you would not look at the house twice, or have any reason to guess the lamentable tale that began there on a February day in 1905. Nor would you guess its original purpose. It was built as a meeting place for a fraternal order, the Independent Order of Odd Fellows of North Carolina, and so it was usually known as "the Odd Fellows Hall." But it was also used as the local school.[9]

Few American myths are as deeply cherished as that of the one-room schoolhouse. Reading stories of the sorry state of public education, one grows nostalgic for *Little House on the Prairie* and *Anne of Green Gables*. One pictures a selfless young teacher dressed in a long skirt, white blouse, and cameo brooch standing beside her wooden desk with the Stars and Stripes and a framed picture of George Washington on the wall. And the students, even if they are poor kids off the farm, are sitting at their desks, listening politely and attentively.

The reality was different. Currituck County in the late 1800s and early 1900s provides an appalling example, although it was not markedly worse than other places in North Carolina. In 1885, every Currituck schoolhouse consisted of one room. The county had twenty-one schoolhouses for white children and eleven for African-American children, referred to in polite language as "colored." The county apportioned the money to be spent based upon a school census, and it was to be no more than $.71 per child per year. White teachers were paid an average of $27.14 per month and colored teachers an average of $21.36.[10] The county had discretion on those expenditures because it, not the state, provided the funding. It was raised primarily through local property taxes, which were optional for towns and counties, many of which simply made no attempt to establish or fund schools. The state, for its part, had not issued any appropriation at all for schools since 1869.[11]

Over the next few years, and starting especially with the new century, North Carolina did make a sincere effort to improve its schools. In the 1898 election, the Democratic Party won control of the state's General Assembly, and one of the elements of its platform was educational reform. In 1899, it passed an appropriations bill that earmarked one hundred thousand dollars to support schools, which led to construction of nearly seven hundred new schools within four years. The following year, Charles B. Aycock was elected governor, completing the Democratic takeover of state government. Aycock made educational advancement his political crusade and urged school districts to adopt local-option taxes to supplement the state's spending on schools. By the end of Aycock's term in 1905, some 229 districts had voted to adopt such taxes, while only 30 had done so previously.[12]

For many years afterward, Aycock would be remembered as North Carolina's foremost educational statesman, and it is true that he set in motion a new commitment to progress in education. By some counts, the state built a new schoolhouse for each day of his four-year term. And it would continue after he left office. In 1907, the General Assembly passed a statute providing for establishment of rural high schools, and within one year 160 of them opened, including one in Currituck County. By 1920, North Carolina's spending on its public schools had increased by 1,200 percent over 1898, although its per-student spending was still only half the national average.[13]

So change was coming to Currituck County in the early years of the twentieth century. But as anyone at the time would have noticed, it was coming slowly, and the improvements were rudimentary at best.

Carrie Parker, just out of school herself at the age of seventeen, was recruited to move to Currituck County in 1908 to teach in one of the newly established schoolhouses. Parker decided to settle permanently in Currituck and taught there for forty-eight years, most of them in the school at Poplar Branch. However, she began her first assignment at the Long Point School near Jarvisburg, just a few miles down the shore.

The conditions Parker found at Long Point would have deterred all but the most enthusiastic and dedicated. She and one other teacher had to share one room with more than seventy-five students ranging from kindergarten to eighteen years of age. They had only eight long, homemade desks. For chairs, they had freshly cut, resin-saturated pine blocks. "The turpentine almost glued the pupils down sometime, so they were easily kept in place," she wrote.

And when Parker arrived at the schoolhouse for her first day, she saw several men gathered in the yard, filling buckets with water from an iron hand pump. As each bucket was filled, the men tossed water into the crawlspace underneath the school. Parker "asked one of the men what was happening as I noticed many children's heads sticking out of the windows. The man told me they were drowning fleas that had been left there by hogs, that ran loose, and slept under the school building during warm weather. This was my first experience in finding out what to do with fleas under a house." [14]

Carrie Parker later married into the Walker family of Poplar Branch, who were related by marriage to Samuel M. Beasley, who, as the owner of the Poplar Branch Landing, was one of the most respected local leaders. As in most small communities, landowners and merchants held the positions of civic authority, and Sam Beasley clearly fit the bill. In 1893, at age thirty, he was appointed justice of the peace for Poplar Branch township, and in 1895 was popularly elected to the post. He was appointed a notary public in 1897 and was active in the local Masonic lodge as well as the Independent Order of Odd Fellows, who elected him the "Grand High Priest of the Great Encampment."[15] In that position, he presumably had some role in choosing to locate the school in the Odd Fellows Hall.

No one could have been surprised when Sam Beasley, a loyal Democrat, was nominated and elected to the North Carolina House of Representatives in the Democratic landslide year of 1898. He was re-elected in 1900 and 1902, and then in November 1904 won Currituck County's seat in the State Senate. Although Republican Theodore Roosevelt won the presidency in a landslide that year, North Carolina, like all of the South, was a different story. The Democrats were firmly in control, and Sam Beasley had established himself in the legislature as a staunch party man, a loyal ally of Charles Aycock and his progressive agenda.

By early 1905, Senator Beasley had been married for almost twenty years to the former Cassie Walker, the daughter of Nathan Walker, a prominent area landowner. They had settled near the landing on a forty-three-acre tract of farmland formerly owned by the Walkers and bordering land still owned by Cassie's brothers and their families.[16] Their home, bordered on the northern end by a thick cedar tree, was a stately white frame farmhouse two stories high with a tall brick chimney. The house is no longer there. Age and termite damage finally overtook it in the 1980s, and it had to be demolished.[17] Yet the cedar tree survives, marking the spot where the house stood facing Poplar Branch Road, less than a half-mile south of, and almost within sight distance of, the crossroads and Odd Fellows Hall.

Senator and Mrs. Beasley had two sons and a daughter. Their older son, Louis Moran, whom everyone called Moran, was eighteen by 1905. He was away from home most of the time, attending Atlantic Collegiate Institute, a private boarding school in Elizabeth City, the largest town in the area, about twenty-five miles to the west.[18] Their daughter, Ethel, was ten, and their younger son, William Kenneth, also known by his middle name, was eight.

And so on the morning of February 13, 1905, when Kenneth Beasley trudged off to school on foot, there could not have been much anxiety weighing on his mind. True, he lived on a rural

The Beasleys' home, no longer standing.

farm, and farm life could be tough in those days when electricity had barely begun to make an impact in the countryside. No doubt, he and his sister would have some chores to do later in the day—maybe gathering eggs or milking the cow, as farm kids usually did. But Kenneth had a stable, materially secure family with devoted parents. He had a school to attend, crude though it was, which he could easily walk to without encountering anything more than a passing buckboard wagon or buggy. And he had friends his age to play with; on that particular day, he was probably looking forward to recess, when he and his buddies could go out and throw a few snowballs. It had snowed the day before, and on this cold, cloudy day there was still slush on the ground.

And of course, he was only eight years old. A third-grader, by today's definition.

Later, when every event of that day was the subject of legal inquiry, Kenneth's mother would remember, almost in passing, the last thing her son said as he left the house that morning. Or at least other people remembered Cassie Beasley mentioning it, although it was not part of the testimony she or anyone else gave in court.

Not surprisingly for a boy his age, Kenneth had pets on his mind.

"I've seen some mighty pretty puppies, and I want one."[19]

Nina Harrison, "Miss Nina," was Kenneth Beasley's teacher and Joshua Harrison's daughter.

CHAPTER 2

SHADOWS DESCEND

Kenneth's father was not around, as the General Assembly was starting a new session that very Monday. Senator Beasley had left early on Saturday, before his two younger children had woken up. He had to get an early start, as his journey would take him on a long, cold, horse-drawn trip up the snowy road to Suffolk, Virginia, where he would board the train to Raleigh, two hundred miles away. So on Monday morning, it was his mother who got Kenneth up and dressed in his usual attire for a cold, wet day. He put on a dark gray suit, a blue cap, and brown stockings of a "country knit" type.[1]

As he went out the door, Kenneth was also wearing gloves, which, in the manner of so many boys before and since, he probably did not wear for long. The gloves would later be found in his coat, hanging in the closet of the schoolhouse two days later. Senator Beasley would be the one to find them.[2]

Kenneth probably was also carrying his new pocketknife, intending to show it to his buddies at school. Later, Sam Beasley would remember the pocketknife because it featured in the last talk he had with Kenneth the Friday before. As the senator was preparing for his trip to Raleigh and an absence of several weeks, Kenneth came up to him in the living room, jumped on his lap, and proudly showed him the knife. The senator recalled it as a two-bladed knife of pretty good quality, worth maybe a dollar or seventy-five cents. He did not know where Kenneth had gotten it, and the boy did not say, but it seemed of no importance at the time. As he would recall, there was "no correction or reprimand administered" to his son, aside from a routine fatherly admonition to be careful with the knife and not cut himself or any of his friends.[3]

Arriving at the Odd Fellows Hall, Kenneth would have been met by the two teachers who shared responsibility for the school. Professor Minuard P. Jennings, whom press reports later described as slim, smooth-shaven, bespectacled, and tall "above the medium," was the supervising teacher at only twenty-two years old. He taught one of the classes, consisting of grades five through twelve.[4] The lower four grades, including Kenneth and his fellow third-graders, were taught by Nina Pocahontas Harrison.

Miss Nina, also just twenty-two, had the title of assistant teacher. She was Currituck County born and bred, having grown up on a farm owned by her father, Joshua Harrison, located in Jarvisburg, six miles south of Poplar Branch, down the main road that ran the length of the Currituck peninsula. Her mother was the former Ann Caroline Jarvis, and through her Miss Nina could lay claim to the most distinguished lineage in the county.

Ann Harrison's brother, and Nina's uncle, was Thomas J. Jarvis, whom everyone knew as "Governor." He was a wounded Confederate veteran who parlayed his military record into success in legal practice as well as politics. He worked his way up through the legislative ranks to become lieutenant governor, then governor of North Carolina from 1879 to 1885. As a Democrat, Jarvis was later appointed by President Grover Cleveland to serve as the U.S. minister to Brazil. After returning in 1889, he served in the U.S. Senate for two years, filling a vacancy left by the death of Zebulon

B. Vance, North Carolina's former Civil War governor. Later, Jarvis established a legal practice in Greenville, North Carolina, and was instrumental in persuading the General Assembly to establish a teachers' training school there, which would grow into today's East Carolina University.[5]

Miss Nina was fairly new to the Poplar Branch school; she had been hired to teach there just months before, in September 1904. As was the custom for unmarried schoolmarms of the day, she boarded not far from where she worked. She lived in the home of a Mr. Lindsey, about a quarter-mile from the school.[6] Senator Beasley was a member of the school committee that agreed to hire her, and considering the prominence of her family, she would have seemed an obvious candidate for a teaching job. The senator would eventually testify that Miss Nina obtained the job through his influence, although in light of other revelations, many thought it strange that he would want her teaching his children.[7]

Walking through the school door, Kenneth would have seen several friends who lived on neighboring farms, among them Ernest Wright, Edward Meggs, Irving Gallop, and Kenneth's cousin Bennett "Benny" Walker, who lived on the farm adjacent to the Beasley homeplace.[8] Benny would recall later that Kenneth had gotten his shoes wet while walking through the slush on the way to school, so he took them off and set them to dry in front of the fireplace in the corner of the schoolroom.[9] Miss Nina then led the students through various lessons during the morning class session. By the noontime recess, though, the sun had come out and the temperature had warmed enough to run loose outside. Kenneth hung his suitcoat in the school closet and went out to play in his shirtsleeves, apparently still wearing his blue cap. The Odd Fellows Hall had nothing in the way of playground equipment, but there was an open space behind the building where boys could run, play, and maybe toss a softball, if anybody had one.

At about 1:15, the school bell rang to summon the children back inside for afternoon classes. Kenneth, however, did not return and was nowhere to be seen. Miss Nina asked the other children if anyone knew where he might be, and Benny Walker spoke up. He said that he and Kenneth had been playing together down by the edge of the schoolhouse's backyard, near the woods. Just as the bell started to ring, Kenneth turned to his cousin and said, "I'm going back farther." Then Kenneth stepped off into the woods, quickly disappearing into the trees, and Benny did not see him again.[10]

In later years, as time passed and the story was retold countless times, there was some confusion about where exactly Kenneth was last seen. Some people had the impression he had walked back to his parents' house for lunch, intending to return after recess, and some of the newspaper coverage did in fact give that impression.[11] But if Kenneth had started home and either did not reach it or failed to return to school after eating lunch, then he would have come to grief somewhere between the school and the house, located south of the school. The neighbors in Poplar Branch had no doubts about the general area where Kenneth had wandered off. All sources agree that in the next few hours, they quickly focused their search on the woods and swampy terrain behind the Odd Fellows Hall, to its north and northwest.

When Miss Nina heard Benny tell of Kenneth's walking into the woods, she reported it to Professor Jennings. They then dispatched Ernest Wright, another of Kenneth and Benny's friends, to go find Kenneth and bring him back to class. Ernest went but came back within a few minutes, saying he did not see Kenneth anywhere. Professor Jennings then sent Benny to go back to where he had last seen Kenneth, search in the woods, and, if he could not find him, walk to the Woodhouse store, just up the Aydlett Road to the northeast. There, at least, Benny could make a phone call to Mrs. Beasley at home to see if Kenneth had returned there.[12]

Apparently, the Odd Fellows Hall had no telephone, but the Woodhouse store did, and the Beasleys had one at home. If so, the Beasleys were among the privileged few. Phone service was new at the time, and not everyone had easy access, an important thing to remember when considering the speed of communication with an emergency such as a missing child. Less than two years earlier, in October 1903, the Currituck Telephone Company was chartered and began stringing lines among the farming communities in the area.[13] Coverage was scattered, and even many of those living near a phone line could not afford the luxury of their own phone.[14] For them, the best option was to share a neighbor's or to use a phone in a central location such as a country store to send or leave messages. Several people, as they later recounted their comings and goings during the week of February 13, would remember doing just that.

Benny Walker had a look through the woods behind the hall but did not see any sign of his cousin, so he trudged up the road to the store, arriving there at about two in the afternoon. Around that time, the always unpredictable coastal weather took a turn. The skies clouded and a cold rain began to fall. At the store, Benny met the owner, Daniel W. Woodhouse, and also Deputy Sheriff John W. Poyner, who listened to the boy's story and sensed an urgent situation. Whether they were able to reach Kenneth's mother by phone is not known, but Woodhouse and Poyner returned with Benny to the schoolhouse, where they spoke with Professor Jennings.[15]

A quick look into the school closet revealed Kenneth's overcoat, still hanging there since before recess. Kenneth had never been a troublesome student, so it seemed unlikely he would have skipped school. Even had he planned to do so, his teachers did not think he would have left his coat.[16] If he had gotten lost in the woods in the cold rain while not warmly dressed, then he was certainly in danger. It was definitely time to call the neighbors and make a systematic search for the boy.

In those days, gathering the neighbors was the only practical way to deal with an emergency. There was no rescue squad and no concept of calling the police, as people now would. No one would think of relying on the government to deal with a disappearance, especially in Currituck, where there was little government to begin with. There were not, and still are not today, any incorporated towns or villages in the county. There was an elected sheriff, who had the authority to deputize men to assist him; J. W. Poyner had probably been so designated at some previous time. Each township also had a justice of the peace, a position Sam Beasley once held for Poplar Branch. But these people were not full-time government employees; they had their regular occupations, mostly farming. And of course, it took time to send a message to summon the sheriff.

So, as quickly as they could, Poyner and Woodhouse went around to the local houses, sounding the alarm and asking everyone else to do the same. By four that afternoon, nearly fifty people had gathered at the Odd Fellows Hall to form the search party. And there was not a moment to lose, for the weather continued to deteriorate. The temperature was dropping, the rain turning to snow.[17]

Behind the hall was an open field that extended back about fifty to seventy-five yards to the edge of the woods where Benny had last seen Kenneth. Beyond that point, the woods continued north and west for three-hundred-plus yards to the Maple Swamp, which still exists in a condition little changed. Then as now, the swamp stretched north and west about six miles to Parkers Creek, on the sound side of the Currituck peninsula. It also branched off to the northeast to the North River, the inland bay that separates Currituck from Camden County.[18] The swamp ranged from one to one and a half miles wide, bounded on the west by the main road running the length of the peninsula and on the east by the Aydlett Road, which paralleled the sound shoreline. Roughly five miles north of Poplar Branch, the Aydlett Road made a ninety-degree turn to the left, crossing the swamp to join the main road.[19] In between were a few wagon paths and timber trails leading from one dry spot to another, with a few rickety wooden bridges "two to three feet wide."[20]

When the searchers described it later, they used terms including *woods*, *swamp*, and *pocosin* almost interchangeably because that was the nature of the terrain. Parts of the woods were flooded at certain times, dry at others. One witness recalled that part of the swamp had sustained a forest fire in the dry preceding summer but was flooded at the time of the search.[21]

As far as the search party could tell, a child had gone missing into an approximately eight-square-mile expanse of dark, swampy woods. Searching that nasty terrain in the cold, raw weather was going to be miserable, but the child needed to be found quickly. The searchers thought that if the boy was lost, at least he could not have ventured far. So they plunged into the woods and the mud calling Kenneth's name, without any real organization. After darkness fell, with nothing yet found, they kept searching with lanterns into the early-morning hours.[22]

The following day, Tuesday, was Valentine's Day. As Sam Beasley sat in the North Carolina Senate chamber at the State

Capitol in Raleigh, the holiday turned sorrowful when he received a telegram notifying him of his son's disappearance. Immediately, he left for home by train, taking the same route he had traveled only four days previously. Passing through Elizabeth City, he picked up his older son, Moran. When they reached Suffolk, they boarded a special train provided to the senator in the emergency by the Norfolk and Southern Railway, which conveyed them down to Snowden station, the nearest point on the railroad to Poplar Branch. Also in Suffolk, they were joined by "Hurricane" Branch, a local detective who had a team of sharp-nosed bloodhounds to bring to the search. They all arrived in Poplar Branch at around one o'clock Wednesday morning.[23]

The searchers had continued combing through the woods all day Tuesday, still with nothing to show. By Wednesday morning, between 150 and 200 men were on the scene. Senator Beasley went to the school, talked with Professor Jennings, and found his son's coat hanging in the schoolhouse closet with his gloves and handkerchief in the pocket. Everyone hoped that Hurricane Branch's dogs might pick up Kenneth's scent, but they could follow it no farther than the edge of the woods.[24]

The search continued through Thursday and Friday, although by that time the local men realized their mission was more recovery than rescue. They were experienced woodsmen and hunters and knew that if Kenneth had gotten lost, he would be dead by then from hypothermia. They looked to the sky, thinking a flock of buzzards might lead them to the body, but saw none. By Friday morning, three hundred men were taking part. They had organized a dragnet, forming themselves into lines between five and eight feet apart, combing the woods north and west of the schoolhouse. Some of them waded through the swamp itself in water up to their knees, poking with sticks in hope—if one can call it that—of finding the drowned body.[25]

But all along, even while the search was ongoing, there was talk among the locals about whether Kenneth had really, and just by chance, gotten lost in the woods behind his schoolhouse. The newspapers were speculating within days that the disappearance was not accidental. On Wednesday, the Raleigh *News & Observer* printed that "it is thought that [Kenneth] was made a prisoner by some parties to be held for ransom."[26] The following day, the paper continued its speculation: "The mystery deepens. If [Kenneth] was kidnapped, who are his abductors and for what reason is he being held? If he has met with foul play and is now dead, where is his body concealed?" As the paper put it, "These are the questions being asked many times." No one, however, was yet speaking for attribution.[27]

Over the next week, the shortcomings of communication, and of newspaper coverage, were made plain by some wishful but badly mistaken reporting. Several papers carried rumors that Kenneth had been found alive and unharmed in an unoccupied lumberman's log cabin nestled deep in the woods behind the schoolhouse. Supposedly, Kenneth had been discovered "locked in with a white man, who was in a semi-conscious condition from drinking whiskey or taking morphine or both."[28] The report was completely untrue but was notable for a couple of reasons. First, it introduced the specter of illicit drunkenness, which would be a recurring feature in the story. Second, it posited a man in the lumber cabin. His name is still unknown, although he would be referred to variously as a "Yankee," a "foreigner," and a "hermit" as the story unfolded.[29]

And then on February 24, 1905, the *News & Observer* carried its most provocative piece yet. The story, which was reprinted in several other papers throughout North Carolina, is steeped in anonymity and implicit in its assertions—understandable, perhaps, in a time when it was easier to sue for common-law defamation than it is now.[30]

The story quoted several excerpts from a letter written to "a gentleman of Raleigh" from "a party living near the home of Senator Beasley." No one has ever identified who sent or received the letter, or how it came into the hands of the *News & Observer*—or, indeed, whether the "letter" actually existed or was just a euphemism for anonymous gossip. It described how the search for Kenneth had continued for several days, through all of the "potato houses and hills and wells, under the hall and houses, every outhouse, fodder loft, barn, woods and swamp." It also referenced the Yankee in the cabin, stating that, contrary to previous reports, the bloodhounds had followed Kenneth's scent to the cabin, and the searchers then coerced the unwilling Yankee to let them search his cabin, but found nothing.[31]

The letter writer also claimed to have some insight into the Beasley home and the sorrow Kenneth's parents were enduring: "They think that Mrs. Beasley will die. She neither eats nor sleeps, only as they give her medicine to make her sleep, and the minute her eyes are open she is crying, 'Give me the body of my boy.'"[32]

The letter asserted that, on the afternoon of Kenneth's disappearance, "there was a strange man seen up about Barco post office [twelve miles north of Poplar Branch] and two more places by three different men. He was in a buggy drawn by a black mule, and had the boy down between his knees, but the people saw him before they heard that the boy was missing. The men say that saw him that the boy was crying and seemed to be dissatisfied, but the man was talking to him roughly." The three witnesses were identified as Caleb Barco, Mack Griggs, and W. E. Ansell, the elected clerk of court for Currituck County, all of whom were suspicious to see a man riding in his buggy with a small child in such cold and rainy weather.[33]

And finally, the anonymous author left this hint pointing to the identity of the alleged strange man: "Mr. Joshua Harrison went off Tuesday morning and never got back until Sunday. He claimed he had been to Pasquotank."[34]

Anyone in Currituck County would have picked up on the significance. Joshua Harrison was the well-known landowner and farmer from Jarvisburg. And the father of Kenneth's teacher, Miss Nina. And the brother-in-law of the former diplomat, governor, and U.S. senator.

The home of Joshua Harrison. The home is no longer standing.

CHAPTER 3

AN AGGRESSIVE BREED

After more than eleven decades, it is no simple thing to pick up the trail of a missing child. Aside from newspaper clippings and court documents, not much source material is to be found. Most folks who live in Currituck County today have never heard of Kenneth Beasley, which owes to the many newcomers who have arrived over the past generation. But even among the descendants of families who have lived and farmed there since the 1800s or beyond, one finds a certain reluctance to talk about it. People live as neighbors today, but they had ancestors in 1905 who may have been witnesses on one side of the case or the other. In a small community, that can be a big deal, and any researcher has to be mindful of the fact when he goes digging into the past.

For those who do know the story today, if they did not grow up in the area and hear it from whispers that filtered down through their families, they probably learned it from a single written source dating to the 1950s. It comes from an eccentric author with an exotic background, whose works range from serious history to rural folklore to science fiction, and plenty else in between.

Manly Wade Wellman was born in 1903 in, of all places, the village of Kamundongo in Portuguese West Africa, present-day Angola. His father worked there as a missionary doctor. His family returned to the United States when he was a boy. Wellman attended schools in New York and Salt Lake City, then college at Wichita State University before receiving a law degree at Columbia University in 1927. Part of his ancestry was Native American, which spurred in him an interest in folk legends of the Appalachian and Ozark regions.[1]

From the beginning, it seems Wellman intended to be a writer, and his eclectic personal life is reflected in his work. He started out contributing Buck Rogers–style sci-fi stories to the pulp fiction magazines popular in the 1930s and 1940s, such as *Weird Tales and Astounding Stories*. One of Wellman's recurring characters was Judge Keith Hilary Pursuivant, a retired jurist from the Appalachians who was also a World War I veteran and an "occult scholar" who spent his spare time solving bizarre crimes. Pursuivant investigated crime scenes while carrying his mystical silver-headed cane, which was useful for slaying beasts such as vampires and werewolves.

After serving in World War II, Wellman moved to the town of Pinebluff in Moore County, North Carolina, and later to Chapel Hill. The focus of his writing changed from sci-fi to history. In the 1960s, he wrote historical fiction in the Robert Louis Stevenson mold, much of it adventure drama intended for the teen and young-adult audience. Afterward, Wellman focused on local history, writing detailed, well-sourced works including *The Story of Moore County* (1974) and *The Kingdom of Madison* (1971), a history of Madison County, high in the mountains just north of Asheville.

In the meantime, in 1954, Wellman completed *Dead and Gone:*

AN AGGRESSIVE BREED

Classic Crimes of North Carolina. It was a collection of ten true-crime cases that occurred between the early nineteenth and early twentieth centuries, each described in a chapter of twenty pages or so. One of those stories was the disappearance of Kenneth Beasley, and although it is valuable as the only account of the case written since the actual event, it must be taken with several grains of salt. It lies somewhere between fiction and serious history. The author's purpose was to recount interesting tales, focusing on their elements of local folklore, rather than to perform detailed journalism or historical research. And nowhere does he address the underlying political dynamics one now suspects were involved in the Beasley story.

Wellman had at his disposal the newspaper accounts from 1905. And since he was writing just forty-nine years after the event, it was still within living memory. He probably spoke with some Currituck residents who were there at the time, although if he did, he does not name them. But *Dead and Gone* provides just a thumbnail sketch of the events. Wellman summarizes the disappearance of Kenneth Beasley and recounts the theories and the rumors behind them but does not fully explore them.

For example, when introducing Joshua Harrison, the sixty-six-year-old local farmer who was fingered as a suspect in the disappearance, Wellman says the Harrisons were known as "an aggressive breed." For that assertion, he provides no details regarding Harrison's family. But he claims that, remarkably, Joshua Harrison had been charged with homicide on two occasions in his younger years, and had been found not guilty both times.[2]

What does the historical record show? The Harrisons were definitely not new to the area; they had been there since at least the eighteenth century. Joshua's grandfather Zorababel Harrison had lived in the Harbinger area, on the southern tip of the Currituck peninsula. He died there in 1812 and was buried in a small family cemetery surrounded by a few dozen relatives. His intricately carved tombstone can still be seen today. Zorababel had at least two daughters and four sons, one of whom, William, was the father of Joshua, who was born in 1839.[3]

It was in February 1866 that Joshua Harrison married Ann C.

Jarvis, whose father, Bannister H. Jarvis, was a respected Methodist minister and the owner of a three-hundred-acre Currituck plantation.[4] Clearly, Harrison married into a good family. Ann's brother Thomas had recently returned home from the Civil War and was beginning to make his mark as a local businessman and politician. In 1867, Thomas received his law degree and went into business with a dry-goods store in Tyrell County, across the Albemarle Sound from Currituck. He won his first term in the North Carolina House of Commons in 1868 and was elected its speaker in 1872.

One must wonder if the Jarvis family would have welcomed Harrison if they had known how his alleged "aggressive" tendencies would assert themselves, as they soon did. The legend is in fact true. Joshua Harrison was charged with two different murders, and each time was found not guilty at trial.

The legal records from Currituck County in that time period are vague and sparse. They are found in superior-court "Minute Dockets": thick, leather-bound volumes maintained by the clerk of court's office, in which the clerk made handwritten notes recording the bare details of cases that were heard. The handwriting changed from year to year, depending on who was filling the clerk's part-time job. Often, it was barely legible. And the clerks were not always consistent in the details they wrote down. Sometimes, a clerk would note that a defendant was tried by a jury and found guilty or not guilty but would fail to record the offense charged.

One persistent rumor is that Harrison was accused of killing another young boy thirty years before Kenneth Beasley went missing. Charles Griggs, a longtime Poplar Branch resident whose family later purchased the Beasley homeplace, and who still lives on the property now, recalls it as the "oyster shell" incident. As Griggs and his neighbor and longtime friend Roy Sawyer heard the story retold, Harrison supposedly had a young black boy working for him. One day, the boy was tasked with carrying a load of oyster shells, possibly for building a jetty or a breakwater on the sound. The boy was moving too slowly to suit Harrison, who lost his temper and shot him.[5] Years later, one press report recalled that Harrison was put on trial, "but the jury found that the gun was accidentally discharged and he was very much devoted to the child."[6]

The legal records tell in thusly: In the fall 1867 term of Currituck Superior Court, when he was about twenty-eight, Harrison was indicted for the murder of one Caleb Owens. Curiously, the act was alleged to have occurred more than two years earlier, on July 1, 1865. The reason for the time lapse is not clear, but at that point in 1865, with the Civil War barely ended and the countryside desolate and chaotic, anything was possible. The indictment alleged that the defendant, "not having fear of God before his eyes, but being moved and seduced by instigation of the Devil," used a pistol of approximately five dollars' value to shoot the victim in the forehead with a lead ball, causing a wound with the "breadth of one inch, depth of five inches," from which he "instantly died."[7]

Placed under arrest, Harrison was released on a five-thousand-dollar bond, which was pledged by his brother Walter and someone named James M. Woodhouse as sureties. The case was bound over for trial in the spring 1868 term, at which time the jury was selected. It was a lengthy process. The state dismissed thirty-six potential jurors with peremptory challenges, and the defense dismissed twenty. Apparently, it was not easy to find twelve county residents with whom both sides were comfortable. Beyond that, aside from listing the names of the jurors, the record states only that Harrison was found not guilty.[8]

Many questions remain. In addition to the time gap between 1865 and 1867, one might wonder why the killing of a black child, either free or slave, by a white man in that time and place would even result in prosecution. The likelihood is that it would not have, and so the victim was almost certainly white. According to the 1860 federal census, there was indeed a Caleb Owens in Currituck County. He was four years old in 1860, and therefore by 1865 he was about the same age as Kenneth Beasley when he disappeared. Caleb lived in Powells Point with his parents, Patrick and Lydia Owens. Patrick was listed as a "seaman" by trade, and he and his wife and four children were clearly shown among the white residents of the county.[9] But in later Currituck censuses, they do not appear. After the incident, they evidently did not stick around.

Harrison next found himself in court in the fall term of 1870, charged with another murder, for which he was tried in the winter term of 1871.[10] This time, the Minute Docket reveals even less about the allegations. It says nothing about the particulars of the crime, or even the victim's name. To fill in the gaps, researchers have little more than rumors, which the papers summarized nearly forty years later as follows: Harrison was accused of killing an elderly man, whose death was thought at first to have been accidental. But five years after the event, someone claimed to have seen "blood on the back of [the victim's] head, evidently from a bullet wound." However, Harrison's influential brother-in-law, legislator Thomas Jarvis, came along and had the body exhumed. The analysis revealed "no bruise anywhere except a little bruise where the old man had fallen down the steps at his mill," which apparently gave the jury reasonable doubt.[11]

Once again, Harrison was found not guilty of murder. Whether Thomas J. Jarvis actually played a role in the trial is unknown. But here again, the clerk made a point to record the names of the twelve jurors. Three of them stand out: Thomas B. Jarvis, John Newbern, and Isaac Forbes.[12]

Although Thomas B. Jarvis might have been a scrivener's error, it probably was not the same person as Harrison's brother-in-law, whose middle name was Jordan. But if there was another Thomas Jarvis in Currituck County at the time, he surely was at least an extended family member.[13] The same could be said of John Newbern: that was the name of a brother of Thomas E. Newbern, who was married to Joshua Harrison's first cousin, Sarah.[14] And Isaac Forbes had at least some family connection with Thomas Forbes, the husband of Julia Harrison Forbes, another of Joshua's first cousins.[15]

And to round out the familial nature of this 1871 trial, consider the identity of the alleged murder victim, which the clerk of court omitted from his notes but which can be found through some old newspaper records. The elderly man Joshua Harrison had allegedly shot in the back of the head was his own father, William S. Harrison.[16]

Perhaps that has something to do with a civil case mentioned in the Minute Docket. In the winter term of 1872, after Joshua was acquitted of his father's murder, apparently clearing him to share in the estate, his brother Benjamin Harrison filed a partition proceeding naming all his siblings including Joshua as respondents, seeking a distribution of the property. The records do not reflect exactly what actions were taken by the court leading to the property division, except that the case was continued numerous times over several years.[17]

However it transpired, there is no question Joshua Harrison came out quite well from the distribution of his father's property. The estate sale was held by the clerk on March 10, 1876.[18] In the Currituck deed registry are at least five deeds dated between 1878 and 1885, in which Joshua and his wife, Ann, sold a total of 429 acres to various people; the land was described as having been part of the William S. Harrison estate.[19] And by 1905, Joshua still owned at least the tract on which he lived and farmed, consisting of 170 acres.[20]

Therefore, one must ask how, exactly, Joshua Harrison managed to be acquitted of two murders within a four-year period. The simple fact that he was born into a major landowning family, and had married into an even more prominent one, likely played a role. As for the accusation of killing his father, that might be attributed to a squabble over the family land. Maybe one of Joshua's siblings wanted to exclude him from the inheritance and swore out a criminal warrant but wasn't able to back it up at trial.

But it is also useful to consider to what extent the court system was functioning at all in those years following the war. No battles were fought in Currituck County, but Reconstruction had brought about nothing less than the destruction of the economy and social structure, with many people killed, displaced, and impoverished. Whereas Currituck had a population of 7,415 in the 1860 census, it had dropped nearly a third to 5,131 people in 1870.[21] How was it possible to summon a jury pool for a trial under those circumstances? Frankly, the county was fortunate even to have a courthouse still standing intact. Just twenty-five miles away, in Elizabeth City, the Pasquotank County Courthouse was burned to the ground, along with most of the town's business district, by retreating Confederates when a Union army moved through in 1862.

Perhaps the rumors were true. Harrison may have been represented in court by his newly prominent brother-in-law, who perhaps was able to pack the juries with enough friends and relatives to ensure him a good outcome.

Harrison came out of the proceedings with his freedom and financial security, but he could not stay out of trouble in the following years. His name appears as frequently as any other single defendant in the Minute Docket. In winter 1874, a jury found him guilty of some offense, recorded as "A&B," which probably meant assault and battery. For that, he paid a ten-dollar fine and court costs. In July 1875, he was charged with another unspecified offense, but the charge was dismissed. Much later, in fall 1895, he was again found guilty of an assault and battery on an unnamed victim; judgment was suspended upon payment of costs, plus a "fine remitted to one penny."[22]

Through it all, Harrison and his wife raised a substantial family on their Jarvisburg farm. By 1905, he had reached age sixty-six, quite a long lifespan for the time. Press accounts would describe him as "of tall stature, standing six feet or more, and slender, weighing probably 150 pounds. His eyes are deep-set and shrewd, together with a firm jaw covered with a gray beard, which portrays resolution and firmness in every feature."[23]

They had eight children, five of whom grew to adulthood and were still living in 1905. Their three sons were still in the area and assisted their father on the farm. Their younger daughter, Miss Nina, was teaching school just up the road.

Only their older daughter, Maggie Harrison Gallop, had moved away. She had married a local fellow, Hodges M. Gallop, who was well known in the area as a surfman. He worked for the U.S. Life-Saving Service, a forerunner of the Coast Guard, which operated lifesaving stations at various points along the Outer Banks, the infamous "Graveyard of the Atlantic." Their harrowing job, whenever a ship would run aground offshore, was to row out through the pounding surf in their open boats to rescue survivors. By all accounts, Gallop was well regarded in his field. He rose to the rank of captain and was commander of the Whalehead Life-Saving

Station, located on the Currituck Banks just east across the sound and about a mile north of where the Currituck Lighthouse stands today.[24] Sadly, Captain Gallop passed away in 1902 of "an illness of short duration." He was only thirty-five, and he left his wife with three young sons to support, ages seven, four, and one.[25] With that, the Harrisons' daughter moved with her children to Norfolk and took up an occupation well suited for a young widow with children. She began to manage a boardinghouse.

That fact would come into play just a few years later.

Kenneth Beasley and his sister, Ethel, circa 1902.

CHAPTER 4

WILL-O'-THE-WISP CLUES

Toward the end of February 1905, there was no question about how Sam Beasley was going to approach the disappearance of his son. He believed Kenneth was still alive, and he was going to do all he could to get his boy back. Starting on February 28, the following notice began appearing regularly in the *News & Observer* and other papers throughout North Carolina and Virginia:

$500 REWARD for
LOST BOY!!

Mysteriously disappeared from Poplar Branch High School on Monday, Feb. 13, 1905, about the hour 12:30, my little son Kenneth, age 8 years, height about 4 feet, complexion light, eyes blue, a scar on the nose between the eyes, can be detected by close inspection. A reward of five hundred dollars[1] is hereby offered for the return of the boy alive, to his parents.

S. M. BEASLEY[2]

Poplar Branch, N.C.

The notice was essentially a classified ad, appearing in the section of the newspapers reserved for all sorts of solicitations: requests and offers for employment, items for sale, and the like. In those days, newsprint was still the most reliable means to communicate anything. In fact, classified ads seeking lost children were not unfamiliar to newspaper readers of the late nineteenth and early twentieth centuries. In 1887, for example, the police department in Boston, Massachusetts, recorded 1,572 children who were reported missing for any variety of reasons. Some may have been deliberately stolen or murdered. The vast majority, however, had just wandered off or were fleeing from real or perceived abuse; of those, most were located when someone turned them in to the police.[3]

But the ad lacked something notable. It does not have a photograph, which is surprising. Even in the pre-digital days, newspapers were capable of reproducing photos. Even if they lacked the half-tone technology required to print a photo, many papers had artists who could produce an engraving based upon it.[4] In this case, the Beasleys had a photo that could have been useful to them, and it is lucky it survives today.

Like any photo of the time, it tells only so much about the subject's personality. The facial expressions are a blank slate, not because no one smiled in the Victorian age but because the camera would not allow it. Even young children had to hold their poses for the film to expose completely, which Kenneth and his sister, Ethel, apparently were able to do. They are side by side, Kenneth appearing about five years old, which would put it around 1902, three years before he disappeared. It was probably taken in a photographic studio in Norfolk. They seem to be posed in front of some kind of artificial pastoral background. Kenneth, two years younger and a bit shorter than his sister, is sitting on what looks like a sawed-off wooden stump, specially designed for posing children. Ethel stands beside him, on his left.

Both children are dressed neatly, although not necessarily in their Sunday best. Ethel wears a pretty white dress, stockings, and a ribbon in her hair, while Kenneth has on short pants and a shirt with some sort of floral pattern on it. As for the poses, no one could have doubted they were brother and sister, as they looked so much alike—the same blond hair, the same wide-set eyes, the nearly identical curves to their mouths and chins.

But even without the release of Kenneth's photo, the story of his disappearance was poignant enough to keep the press and public interested. On February 26, the *News & Observer* reported that the senator and his neighbors believed the disappearance was a kidnapping. Although they had given up the search of the woods, they were "working on strong clues which indicate the boy is living, and hope to restore him to home and loved ones soon." Also, just two days after printing the story of the "strange man" with the child in his buggy, it reported a rumor that Kenneth was being "secreted" by his abductor(s) near Shiloh—a farming community in southern Camden County, thirty miles by road from Poplar Branch—and that Johnson Cartwright, a former Camden sheriff, was undertaking to "make investigation of every house in the neighborhood."[5] That rumor came to nothing, but it helped set a pattern for others.

Interestingly, the *News & Observer* story, in speculating about the identity of the kidnapper, reported that "Senator Beasley has no enemies of which he is aware."[6] That may or may not have been based on a direct statement from the senator, but it would be contradicted later by Beasley himself, who would testify that he had at least one enemy in the county.

In late March, the Beasleys were contacted by J. J. Pierce, a resident of Shiloh who apparently was an acquaintance of theirs, and who now had an interesting story to tell. On the first Sunday in March, he had been on a streetcar in Norfolk when he saw Kenneth riding in the company of two young men he did not recognize, one of whom appeared to have been drinking. Pierce recognized Kenneth after previously having seen him attending services with his family at the Methodist church in Poplar Branch. Pierce spoke to him, saying "Hello, Kenneth," but the boy did not answer.[7]

Unfortunately, at the time Pierce saw the boy he believed to be Kenneth, he had not yet heard about the disappearance. Shortly after, when he heard the news, he immediately got in touch with Senator Beasley.[8]

Eyewitness sightings are always tricky, as any investigator who works with missing persons cases can attest. The witness believes the person he sees is the same person he just heard about in a news report, not because of any intent to deceive but simply due to human nature. People have a tendency to focus on coincidences and disregard inconsistencies. But here, Pierce's story did not seem to have been tainted by prior knowledge of Kenneth's disappearance. The senator may have believed the report to be credible, as he quickly got into contact with the police in Norfolk and began to focus his attention there.

Early April brought rumors, reported breathlessly in the press but soon disproved and retracted, that Kenneth had been located alive and unharmed in Norfolk, and that the kidnapper—the son of a "prominent divine" or a "prominent preacher," depending on the source—was arrested, with "fear being entertained for his safety."[9] Then, in late May, another ruckus arose in Norfolk when police received a report that a white child who looked like Kenneth Beasley was seen playing in a "negro woman's yard." The Norfolk police chief, along with a crowd of people including a special representative of Elizabeth City's *Weekly Economist*, went to the scene and found the child playing in the yard with several other children "many times blacker than he," making him look white by comparison. The child was actually a "very light mulatto," which the police chief realized after examining the boy, shining a bright light in his face to reveal "the complexion of a russet apple, dark brown eyes, a nose that was decidedly African in its broadness, and hair that was greatly inclined to tangle itself into the proverbial kink."[10]

In the meantime, Senator Beasley increased his reward for Kenneth's safe return from $500 to $1,000 (roughly $26,000 in 2015 dollars),[11] a move that may have been prompted by an attempt to collect ransom for the boy. Senator Beasley recalled later that he received a letter from the purported kidnapper proposing a swap.

Whether the letter was genuine or not will never be known, but the senator appears to have acted upon it. As he stated, "The writer told me if I would place $500 under a trestle on the Atlantic Coast Line Railway, near Rocky Mount, N.C. at 5 o'clock on the evening of April 11th, my son would be returned to me at whatever place I desired him left, but that if I made any alarm his body would be sent to me in a keg of brine." The senator immediately withdrew the funds and went to Rocky Mount, more than a hundred miles away, accompanied by Detectives Cotton and Rose of the Norfolk police, intending to make the swap. However, no one appeared.[12] The kidnapper may have gotten wind of the detectives' presence, or of course the letter may have been a hoax.*

And yet the most intriguing—and maybe the most revelatory—"clew" had emerged back in February, although now it is hard to tell whether anyone recognized its value at the time. Just two weeks after Kenneth disappeared, in the article reporting that the Poplar Branch neighbors had given up their search and concluded he was kidnapped but still alive, the *News & Observer* also carried some personal recollections about Kenneth. It recounted that "Kenneth was a quiet, studious boy, and always knew his lessons well. He was fond of playing marbles, his favorite pastime, and was well liked by the children. He was not very talkative and did not bother anybody. The kidnapping clues are being run down as quickly as possible."[13]

The source of the quote is not clear from the article. Since it describes Kenneth's habits at school, some of it probably came from his teacher. At any rate, the article goes on to quote directly from the teacher, Nina Harrison. The wording suggests that she wrote the statement as a letter to the editors:

> Kenneth, the eight-year-old son of Senator and Mrs. S. M. Beasley, who so mysteriously disappeared on Monday, February 13, 1905, and of which the papers have already been notified, was a bright and lovely child in his parents' home and in the school room. His was a fine character, always retiring and unassuming, never hard to control but

---

* *The Roanoke Beacon*, of Plymouth, N.C., called such dead-end clues "Will-o'-the-Wisp Clews" in a subhead on the day's front-page article. There were to be many such clues.

gentle as a girl. He loved dearly to go to school and always tried hard to master his studies, which he did successfully, and to please his teacher, who was so fond of him, and whose disappearance from her room has saddened her heart. Would that we could call him back, and place him in the arms of his sad and loving parents, his dear brother and sweet sister, and to his teacher and schoolmates, who mourn his loss so deeply. May God, in his tender mercies help the parents who are bowed with grief, and the dear brother and sister, to bear their sorrow so that they may live for one another.

HIS TEACHER[14]

In his account, Manly Wade Wellman describes Miss Nina's words as "a touching tribute, even if the syntax was somewhat shaky for a schoolmistress."[15] In fact, the subject-verb agreement is the least suspicious thing about it. Even taking into account the formal, overwrought writing style of that Edwardian era, there are enough linguistic clues in that "tribute" to raise suspicions about the writer's motives, and how much she really knew about the disappearance.

When investigators are interviewing, or examining statements made by, witnesses or suspects, they are trained to look for a range of verbal cues that indicate deception. For example, when someone gives a truthful statement, he usually does so in the first person. He will refer to himself as "I," or at least to himself and others as "we." If someone is hesitant to use first-person pronouns, it suggests he is not committed to the story he is telling; he is trying to distance himself from his own words and from involvement in the scenario he is describing. Also, and especially when someone speaks about a missing person, verb tense is important. The normal way to describe someone is in the present tense. One of the neighbors searching for the boy might have said, for instance, "I just hope and pray that Kenneth is safe." When a witness slips into the past tense in describing a missing person, it suggests a knowledge that the person is no longer alive.[16]

Miss Nina, for all the sappy sentiment expressed in her letter, was not willing to sign her name to it. Nor could she even write as "I," but only as "his teacher." It suggests a lack of personal attachment to a student she supposedly liked so much, or at least a desire to keep her family name from being printed, in light of the aspersions being cast on her father.

Even more revealing is the description of Kenneth in the past tense. It is hard to believe Miss Nina was writing about someone who was still among the living.

Why would Kenneth's teacher write in this manner less than two weeks after his disappearance, when other folks in the community were convinced he was still alive and being held by abductors? It may have been a deliberate attempt to sway the neighbors, to get them thinking Kenneth had either gotten lost and died from the cold or stumbled into a creek and drowned. At best, it may have been a well-meaning attempt to deflect suspicion from her family; more likely, it revealed her knowledge that the boy would not be returning home.

For the press, the mystery continued unabated through the end of 1905. All the papers could do was speculate about what had befallen Kenneth. In September, Sam Beasley gave an interview stating that he believed his son was alive and being held captive, but "for what purpose he could not imagine."[17] Two months later, he said he and his family were still hopeful but most other folks had given up. Since there had been no ransom deal, they had settled into resignation that Kenneth was dead, either by accident or murder. But the senator was determined to keep searching for the answer, despite the devastating effect on his family. The press noted that the tragedy had "made an invalid of Mrs. Beasley" and "almost incapacitated Mr. Beasley from business."[18]

The paper concluded, "It is now and will be always likened to the Charley Ross case, an affair the whole country puzzled over for years."[19]

No further explanation was needed. In 1905, everyone in the United States knew who Charley Ross was. If Kenneth's disappearance really was a ransom kidnapping, it was almost unprecedented in American history.

Part II

The Times

"Abduction of Charles Brewster Ross" lithograph, second half of 1874. Artist unknown. Charley Ross was four years old when he was kidnapped on July 1, 1874. His abduction gained worldwide attention when his kidnappers demanded ransom.

CHAPTER 5

THE CHARLEY ROSS CASE

Philadelphia is one of the oldest cities in the country. As every schoolchild is taught, Independence Hall was the site of the signing of the Declaration of Independence on July 4, 1776, the date traditionally marked as the birthdate of the United States. But since the Declaration was signed in the midst of the Revolutionary War, it was not until after George Washington's victory at Yorktown in 1781 that American independence became an accomplished fact. In the meantime, many bloody battles were fought, and not all of them went well for the Patriots.

One of those battles, Germantown, took its name from a small community on the outskirts of Philadelphia. It had been settled around 1683, when William Penn sold a tract of former Delaware Indian land to a group of German immigrants, many of whom were Quakers and Mennonites fleeing religious persecution in the old country. Over time, these arrivals built a solid, prosperous community of tradespeople who specialized in shoemaking, weaving, and tailoring.[1] It was there that, in October 1777, Washington's army advanced toward Philadelphia in an unsuccessful attempt to dislodge William Howe's British troops from the city. Philadelphia, the birthplace of American liberty, had fallen embarrassingly to the British after the Battle of Brandywine the previous month, little more than a year after the Declaration was signed.[2]

After the war, Philadelphia continued to grow, eventually absorbing Germantown into its boundaries. Germantown grew along with it, becoming perhaps its most prosperous district. Many of the city's commercial elite built Victorian mansions, Colonial houses, and Gothic cottages along its leafy streets. And yet the place stayed true to its religious roots as it prospered. The Quakers and Mennonites had a strong social conscience, founding some of the first anti-slavery societies in the United States. Germantown also had Philadelphia's only known stop on the Underground Railroad.[3] By the post–Civil War era, most anyone would have counted Germantown a highly desirable place to live.

Then, on July 1, 1874, just as all of Philadelphia was preparing to celebrate the city's most cherished anniversary, Germantown became the scene of a transformative event in the annals of American crime. It began with two boys playing in their front yard.

Walter Ross, six, and his brother Charles, two years younger, were two of the seven children of Christian and Sarah Ross. Their home on Washington Lane, one of Germantown's main thoroughfares, was not literally a mansion, although the press would describe it as such. It was a spacious two-and-a-half-story house and had a wide front lawn that sloped downhill toward the street, which was separated from it by a low stone wall. The boys' father was the owner of a wholesale dry-goods business located ten miles away at the corner of Third and Market Streets. Their mother was away on a trip to Atlantic City with their older sister Sophia, and two of their older brothers were visiting their grandmother in central Pennsylvania. So, on this hot summer afternoon, the boys were home with just their two other sisters and the household staff—two nannies, a cook, and a groundsman.[4]

At some point that Wednesday afternoon, two men came down the street in their horse-drawn buggy. They stopped in front of the Ross house and, after some friendly chat, enticed Walter and Charley into the buggy with them. It was not difficult to do, since the men had acquainted themselves with the boys already. The previous Saturday, they had driven by, introduced themselves, and given the boys candy. The boys later mentioned this to their father, who wisely cautioned them about not talking with or taking gifts from strangers.[5] But on the following days, these same two men happened along two more times to talk with Walter and Charley, and on Wednesday they offered another inducement. They asked the boys to come with them to buy some firecrackers for the upcoming Independence Day festivities.[6]

Despite the warm day, the two men pulled open a canvas wagon cover to enclose themselves and the boys as they rode down the street. Walter was not able to see outside, but fortunately he proved to have a retentive memory for age six. He was able to recall the intersections where the buggy made turns. And one of the abductors had a distinctive appearance that would stick out in Walter's mind. He had a deformed nose; the cartilage between his nostrils appeared to have worn away, and the tip of his nose seemed to curl back and point toward his forehead. The index finger of his left hand also was disfigured, having "shriveled to a sharp point around his nail."[7]

After a while, the buggy made its way into Kensington, a north Philadelphia neighborhood seven or eight miles from Germantown. Four-year-old Charley, growing agitated at being taken with his brother so far from home, began to cry quietly. The two men placated him with candy until they stopped at a store on the corner of Palmer and Richmond Streets that had firecrackers and "torpedo" rockets in its window display. They gave Walter twenty-five cents and told him to go inside and load himself up with firecrackers, which he did. Minutes later, when he came back outside, the buggy containing the two men and his little brother was nowhere to be seen.[8]

By that time, it was late afternoon, and Christian Ross had returned home to Washington Lane. At first, he was not worried that his sons were not there awaiting him. The nannies reported that

Walter and Charley had been playing on the lawn, so Ross assumed they had fallen in with some of the neighborhood children but would wander back home in time for dinner. Not until the dinner hour came and passed did he grow concerned. He spoke to a neighbor across the street, a Mrs. Kidder, who recalled she had seen the two boys talking with a man on the street and then getting in a buggy with him. The neighbor had thought it slightly unusual but not alarming. After all, crime was not something to worry about in Germantown.[9]

At about eight that night, Ross made his way toward the nearest Philadelphia police station house, the Fourteenth Precinct, just blocks away on Germantown Avenue. But before he could get there on foot, he was met on the street by a man accompanied by Walter. The boy was rubbing his red and swollen eyes and clearly had been crying, but still he carried the bag of firecrackers in his hand. The gentleman identified himself to Ross and said he had found the boy standing outside the Kensington store, wailing in distress. Walter had been able to relate to the man his name and where he lived, and that "a man had put him out of a buggy and had then gone off and left him."

"Walter, where is Charley?" asked his father. The boy did not know.[10]

Continuing to the police station, Ross found a disturbing lack of interest in the story of his four-year-old son, who, it seemed clear to him, had been abducted. The police could not imagine any nefarious motive for strangers to abscond with a child in broad daylight, assuring Ross that it was some sort of prank, or at worst maybe a drunken frolic by holiday revelers.[11] They sent a telegraph message to central police headquarters, which in turn wired other precincts to inform it if anyone brought in a lost child matching Charley's description.[12] But surely the boy would turn up soon. There was nothing more the police could do, they said.[13]

Faced with such official indifference, Christian Ross did what little any father of a missing child could do in 1874. He placed a classified ad in the *Philadelphia Public Ledger*, using language strikingly similar to the ads seeking the return of Kenneth Beasley three decades later. It appeared in the paper's July 3 edition, along with other "Lost and Found" items seeking, for example, a missing pair of gold spectacles, a gold double-drop earring, and a pet cat named Dick whose owners promised a "liberal reward for his return."

The ad read, "Lost—A SMALL BOY, ABOUT FOUR YEARS of age, light complexion and light curly hair. A suitable reward will be given by returning him to L. JOYCE, Central Police Station."[14]

The following day, July 4, Ross followed up the ad in the paper's holiday edition with an expanded solicitation specifying three hundred dollars as the reward for his son's safe return.[15] Ross spent most of that morning at the police station, unsuccessfully urging the officers to take further action, when Joseph Lewis, Ross's brother-in-law, burst into the station shouting, "I have it! I have it!" He was bearing a handwritten letter someone had delivered to Ross's place of business that morning. The police officers gathered around Christian Ross as he took the letter from its envelope and began to read.

> July 3—Mr. Ros: be not uneasy you son charley bruster be all writ we is got him and no powers on earth can deliver out of our hand. you wil have two pay us before you git from us, and pay us a big cent to. If you put the cops hunting for him you is only defeetin yu own end. We is got him put so no living power can gets him from us a live. If any approach is maid to his hidin place that is the signil for his instant annihilation. If you regard his lif puts no one to search for him yu mony can fech him out alive an no other existin powers. don't deceve yuself an think the detectives can git him from us for that is imposebel. You here from us in few day.[16]

Later, Christian Ross would describe the sickening pall that fell over the room in those moments: "So overwhelming was the astonishment and indignation that for a time everyone was silent. Then followed varied expressions of horror, as each one realized that there existed a human being capable of committing an act so cruel, so full of unspeakable torment to its victims as that of child stealing. The disguised writing, the evident effort at bad spelling, the absence of any signature, and the revelation of the fact that my child had been taken away for money, indicated that the wretch who designed the plot had carefully prepared to guard himself and his vile accomplices from detection."[17]

Even the case-hardened policemen were left speechless. There was little doubt the letter was genuine. Few people knew Charley's middle name, Brewster, so the writer must have heard that detail from the boy himself. Here, for the first time in the United States, was a documented case of ransom kidnapping. As the *New York World* exclaimed in the following days, "If there is a crime viler, baser, more anti-social than ... blackmailing ... it is the crime that has been committed in Philadelphia ... blood-mailing."[18]

In the popular press, all hell broke loose. The kidnapping of Charley Ross became a national sensation, so much so that in 1876 Christian Ross would publish his own account of the crime and its aftermath. The very title of his book* is enough to provide a preview of the stunning events that followed.

Any parent in Christian Ross's position would seek the quickest, least risky means of getting the kidnappers to release his child. He would simply pay the ransom. But from the beginning, that was both impractical and controversial. Shortly after their first communication, the kidnappers wrote another letter to Ross, demanding a twenty-thousand-dollar ransom—a huge pile of cash, roughly four hundred thousand dollars in present-day figures.[19] Further, the kidnappers overestimated his ability to pay. Despite living in a fine house in an affluent neighborhood, Christian Ross was in financial straits. He had a wife and seven children to support, and his business was having serious cash-flow problems; the financial panic of 1873, sparked by the Franco-Prussian War and railroad over-speculation, among other things, had put a major strain on everyone's bank reserves.[20]

Ross had plenty of friends, relatives, and business associates in Philadelphia who could have loaned him funds to pay the ransom. He even had one extremely generous benefactor (whose name he

---

*   *The Father's Story of Charley Ross, the Kidnapped Child, Containing a Full and Complete Account of the Abduction of Charles Brewster Ross From the Home of His Parents in Germantown, with the Pursuit of the Abductors and Their Tragic Death; The Various Incidents Connected With the Search for the Lost Boy; The Discovery of Other Lost Children, Etc., Etc. With Facsimiles of Letters From the Abductors.*

never revealed) who was so appalled by the crime and so eager to help that he offered Ross a *gift* of twenty thousand dollars, with no expectation of repayment.[21] But even with those resources available, Ross had problems. Some of his "friends" placed a stipulation on the money; they would allow it to be paid not as a ransom but only as a reward for the capture of the kidnappers as well as Charley's release. "This proviso, of course, restricted how the money could be used since it necessarily involved setting a trap for the kidnappers, a trap the cagey kidnappers foresaw and effectively avoided by refusing to make a direct, simultaneous child-for-money exchange."[22]

And beyond all that was Christian Ross's sense of civic duty. As a responsible businessman, community leader, and Methodist Sunday-school teacher, he faced pressure not to make a deal with such reprehensible criminals. To do so would, some feared, encourage copycat crimes. In the words of George Washington Walling, superintendent of the New York Police Department, which was investigating possible local connections to the kidnapping, "any arrangements made with the kidnappers for the restoration of the child would be a public calamity; no child would be safe hereafter if it had parents or friends who could raise money."[23] Ross also had the Philadelphia political establishment, especially Republican mayor William Stokley, leaning on him. That establishment had a vested interest in upholding the city's reputation as a safe place to live and visit, especially during the upcoming centennial celebration.[24]

With a heavy heart, Christian Ross met again with the benevolent millionaire who had offered the twenty-thousand-dollar gift. "I thank you, sir," he said. "I cannot accept your generous offer; for having taken the position that I would not compound the felony, I prefer continuing to make efforts to find the criminals. Hoping, if successful in getting them, that I will recover my child and probably prevent a repetition of child-stealing for a ransom."[25]

Instead of paying the ransom, Ross began a bizarre series of communications with the kidnappers. Eventually, they would send him twenty-three letters, all written in the same stilted, disguised handwriting.[26] The only way for Ross to reply was by running classified ads professing his desire to deal with the kidnappers. For example, the July 9, 1874, edition of the *Philadelphia Public Ledger* ran this notice: "Ros is willing. Have not got it; am doing my best to raise it."[27] The problem was that Ross, at the insistence of his moneyed friends and advisers but against his own instincts, was stalling the kidnappers. He was trying to figure out a way to lure the kidnappers into a face-to-face meeting where they might be caught.[28]

All the while, the newspapers followed the story, breathlessly reporting every rumor. They tracked Ross's comings and goings, which newspaper offices he was visiting, and his contacts with the police. Inevitably, the kidnappers discovered through the press that the police were surveilling and advising Ross, thereby increasing their risks if they continued trying to collect the ransom. Then, on July 14, the *Philadelphia Inquirer* ran a story that detailed for the first time Christian Ross's financial difficulties. The kidnappers realized then that Ross did not have the twenty thousand and that they were being played.[29] Eventually, the ransom communications ceased.

The public also speculated about *why* Christian Ross was so stubborn about paying the ransom. Was it because he himself had engineered the kidnapping, hoping to profit from the publicity and reward offers? The Victorian penny press was not above printing such vicious nonsense, and worse. Some claimed that Sarah Ross was an adultress, that Charley was a bastard child, or that Christian had planned the crime to cover up his business losses. That, in fact, was the storyline of a hit Broadway play entitled *Pique*, by John Daly. The play's producers implied it was based on the Ross case, saying that "truth is stranger than fiction." Christian Ross ultimately was forced to initiate libel proceedings in court.[30]

Meanwhile, the police had some credible leads on the kidnappers. In New York, Superintendent Walling had a regular informer named William Westervelt, who previously had served on his police force. Westervelt had a despicable brother-in-law, William Mosher, whose career had included turns as a boat builder, carpenter, peddler of Bibles and fake insect repellents, thief, burglar, and river pirate. Mosher also had peculiar physical characteristics. His nose was deformed, and one of his fingers was crushed and withered.[31]

Walling discovered that the handwriting of the ransom letters was similar to Mosher's, and he tried to convince Westervelt to lead him to his brother-in-law. Westervelt pretended to cooperate but in fact alerted Mosher that the cops were on to him; Westervelt had his own designs on the reward money.[32]

The case was not cracked until a dark and rainy night in December 1874. Mosher and his accomplice, Joseph Douglass, were caught in the act of burglarizing a home in the Bay Ridge neighborhood of Brooklyn, on the eastern shore of Long Island. Upon hearing noise, some of the homeowner's neighbors came running with their guns, and both burglars were shot. Mosher died instantly, but Douglass, with a bullet through his stomach, survived two hours more.[33]

In fact, he lasted long enough to blurt out, while lying on the damp ground, "It's no use lying now. I helped to steal Charley Ross." When one of the startled neighbors then asked Douglass the whereabouts of the child, he claimed he did not know. "Mosher knows all about it. Inspector Walling knows, and the boy will get home all right. All I ask of you is that you give me a decent burial. Give me a decent burial, that's all I ask."[34]

Days later, two of Christian Ross's brothers-in-law made a trip to New York, bringing with them their six-year-old nephew, Walter. Their task was to accompany the boy to the city morgue to attempt an identification of the two men who had taken him and his brother into their buggy five months previously. Walter understandably was upset by the sight of Mosher's bullet-riddled corpse, but eventually the keen-eyed boy said, "That's the man who gave me candy in the buggy. I remember him by his nose. I never saw a nose like that before." Then the coroner led Walter to Douglass's body, showing him only the face, keeping the torso with its gaping gut wound covered. Walter said, "Oh, that's awful like him; he's the driver. He sometimes had candy too."[35]

Child witnesses are often forgetful, vague, and susceptible to leading questions. But the police were convinced. They were glad to have finally gotten their men, even if dead. And most of them expected Charley would soon be returned to his family. Surely, if the boy had been hidden away with some associate of Mosher and Douglass, that person would now release him after hearing of the kidnappers' deaths, maybe in hopes of gaining a reward for himself.

In fact, the authorities stepped in with a legal incentive for that very thing. On February 25, 1875, the Pennsylvania state legislature unanimously passed a new statute elevating kidnapping from a misdemeanor to a felony, punishable by up to twenty-five years' imprisonment. But the act also contained a provision granting immunity to anyone then concealing a kidnapped child. The provision, to expire on March 25, clearly was intended to encourage anyone holding Charley to release him. Additionally, Christian Ross offered his own five-thousand-dollar reward, as well as a personal proclamation that he believed Mosher and Douglass were the only guilty parties in the crime.[36]

But none of it worked. Charley was never found, and to this day no one knows what became of him. The police waited until April 1875, hoping William Westervelt would reveal the boy's whereabouts. When he failed to do so, Westervelt was charged with conspiracy to kidnap, harbor, and conceal. His trial lasted three weeks and was front-page news nationwide. But he maintained his innocence, claiming he knew nothing of where Charley might be, even after he was convicted and sentenced to seven years' imprisonment.[37]

The legal proceedings had come to a close, but not the personal heartbreak for the Ross family. For years afterward, freelance bounty hunters from all over the United States brought children to Christian and Sarah Ross's door, asking them to determine if the children were theirs. They met with so many children that they began issuing "Certificates of Inspection" to show that they already had examined a particular child and to prevent the child from being misidentified again. Christian and his relatives traveled as far away as Illinois in some cases, chasing especially promising-sounding leads of boys who looked like Charley. The press continued to cover all of it, of course, adding to the legend. Even P. T. Barnum, the circus impresario and America's most sensational showman, tried to horn in on the story. In 1877, he offered to advertise a new ten-thousand-dollar reward for Charley's return, and to publicize it in his traveling exhibition, if Christian Ross would agree for Charley to join the circus after being found. Christian agreed, with the provision that he could simply reimburse Barnum his ten thousand dollars plus expenses, rather than letting his son become a sideshow exhibit.[38] Again, none of it bore fruit.

The Charley Ross Case

But the name of Charley Ross became synonymous with ransom kidnapping, a new crime that was uniquely horrible and cruel and exceptionally rare. This was well before the Great Depression, when economic upheaval and Prohibition would turn the entire country into a gangsters' paradise and kidnapping became such an epidemic that Congress would make it a federal crime.

In fact, following the Ross tragedy, it was not until after the turn of the twentieth century that another ransom kidnapping would be documented.[39] By the day Kenneth Beasley disappeared in 1905, there had been only two of them.

Edward Cudahy, Jr. and his two sisters, circa 1900. In December 1900 two men kidnapped the 15-year-old son of millionaire Omaha meatpacker Edward A. Cudahy, and held him for a $25,000 ransom.

CHAPTER 6

THE EDDIE CUDAHY CASE

America's second ransom kidnapping occurred a quarter-century later and many miles away, in a city much newer than Philadelphia. Omaha, Nebraska, was a prairie boomtown. Just after the Civil War, the Union Pacific Railroad came passing through, part of the long-awaited transcontinental railway. As with Chicago and Kansas City, the railway provided Omaha with the energy and material for explosive growth. It was the transportation hub for farmers from miles around to get their goods to market.

The arrival of industry on the Great Plains brought about a new type of enterprise. Several local businessmen organized packinghouses, facilities where livestock from surrounding farms could be corralled, slaughtered, and processed on a massive scale, with the meat then shipped out on the rails. Much like John D. Rockefeller's Standard Oil was able to bring drilling, refining, and sale of petroleum under the umbrella of one business entity, the packinghouses streamlined the process for delivering beef to the nation's dinner tables. And just as Standard Oil put plenty of independent oil wildcatters out of business, the packinghouses shut down quite a few small butcher shops in Omaha and elsewhere.

Not surprising, then, that Omaha, like other cities in the late nineteenth and early twentieth centuries, saw its share of class division and labor unrest. The business-owning elite built huge Victorian mansions, while the masses of the city's industrial workers, many of them recent immigrants from Ireland and southern and eastern Europe, were sequestered in ethnic enclaves with names such as Little Italy and Little Bohemia. While it was possible for an immigrant laborer to advance to white-collar status, the odds were unfavorable; by 1900, only about 25 percent had a realistic shot at it.[1] Labor unions were beginning to organize, with predictable backlash from the establishment.[2]

Omaha's first big news story of the twentieth century was rooted, at least indirectly, in those economic and political tensions. It was a brazen crime targeting one of the city's most influential power brokers.

Edward A. Cudahy Sr. was the owner of the Cudahy Packing Company, one of the largest of Omaha's meat-packing houses. He lived with his wife and children on South Thirty-seventh Street in an ornate mansion decorated with a cupola and Tiffany windows. On the evening of December 18, 1900, Cudahy sent his fifteen-year-old son, Edward Jr., to return some books he had borrowed from a neighbor, a Mrs. Rustin, who lived three blocks away. Eddie set off with his collie dog beside him. An hour passed and Eddie did not return, although the dog came trotting down the sidewalk alone. After hearing from Mrs. Rustin that Eddie had left to return home just after delivering the books, Cudahy became apprehensive. By midnight, when his son still had not turned up, he contacted the police.[3]

The Omaha police, upon hearing of the disappearance of this wealthy scion, sprang into action much more quickly than had the Philadelphia police in 1874. The chief of police, J. J. Donahue, appears to have concluded immediately that Eddie was kidnapped. He and Cudahy put out alerts to hospitals and the railroad station to look out for the boy and sent a telegraphed request for assistance from the Pinkerton Detective Agency in Chicago. Cudahy also began organizing his packinghouse employees into search parties to comb the city if necessary to find his son.[4]

The following morning, Cudahy received an anonymous phone call suggesting that he look through the grass on his front lawn. There, he found a handwritten note tied to a stick. It informed him that his son had been kidnapped and demanded twenty-five thousand dollars in gold coins for his safe return. The kidnappers threatened that if they were not paid, they would blind Eddie by putting acid in his eyes, after which they would kidnap another "millionaire's child" until they got their money.[5]

To underline the threat, the kidnappers could not resist invoking the legend of the still-famous original "lost boy." Recalling the twenty-thousand-dollar ransom demand for Charley Ross, they told Cudahy that "old man Ross was willing to give up the money, but [the police] persuaded the old man not to give up the money, assuring him that the thieves would be captured. Ross died of a broken heart, sorry that he allowed the detectives to dictate to him. Mr. Cudahy, you are up against it and there is only one way out—give up the coin. Money we want and money we will get. If you don't give up the next man will, for he will see that we mean business, and you can lead your boy around blind the rest of your days."[6]

For Edward Cudahy, there was no agonizing over the ethics of paying the ransom. Although Police Chief Donahue and Cudahy's attorneys advised him not to do it because the kidnappers might refuse to release Eddie after being paid, Cudahy decided to take the chance. As he explained it, "I am determined to punish the people connected with the affair, but of course my first consideration is to get the boy back. What's $25,000 compared to my boy?"[7]

Cudahy went to his bank, withdrew the twenty-five thousand in gold coins, then set out to follow the instructions left by the kidnappers. He took the money, in five leather sacks loaded into a wagon, to the designated spot beside a lonely road on the outskirts of town and left it there. The Omaha police stood down and let Cudahy go through the maneuver without attempting to snag the kidnappers. In the following days, they would face criticism from other police departments, who accused them of abetting the extortion and encouraging more abductions. But Edward Cudahy got his desired result. The following day, only thirty hours after he was abducted, Eddie walked back up the front steps of the Cudahy mansion.[8] He was physically unharmed but rather shaken and had a heck of a story to tell. It was harrowing and traumatic, yet also absurd in a Buster Keaton sort of way.

As he was walking home from the Rustin house after delivering the books, Eddie had been approached by two men carrying revolvers and wearing masks. One of the men told the boy, "We're detectives, and you're a robber named McGee. We've been after you, McGee, and now we've got you! Come along with us." Eddie was taken aback by this and shouted at them, "You're crazy!" But the two men overpowered him and wrestled him into a nearby buggy, where they tied his hands and feet and threw a sack over his head.[9]

Nonetheless, Eddie was able to sense the direction in which he was being taken and the turns made by the buggy. They drove down Thirty-seventh Street, then onto Leavenworth Street, then made several more turns until Eddie's nose realized they had reached the grimy industrial district of South Omaha. "Two or three whiffs from the packing house district . . . assured me that my conjuncture was correct," he testified later.[10]

The abductors took Eddie to their "captivity house," where they led him, still blindfolded, into a room with no furnishings except a rickety bed. They chained him to the bed with leg irons, and there he stayed through the night, although he could hear the abductors in the adjacent room, drinking and yammering about this and that. He remembered one of the kidnappers, whose job it was to watch him, spoke with a thick Irish brogue. Eddie tried to sleep during the night but was too frightened.

Late the following day, Eddie heard one of the kidnappers become angry when his co-conspirator came in from picking up the ransom but claimed he had only five thousand dollars of it; he had fallen in a creek and lost the remaining twenty thousand, he said. The guard threatened to shoot his partner if he did not come up with the rest of the money so they could divide it equally. How they resolved that dispute was not clear, but soon afterward they hustled

Eddie into their buggy again and drove him back to within a block of his house. Once they let him out, he tore off his blindfold and ran home.[11]

Although the crime ended quickly and happily, it had a serious side. The men who took Eddie were the first kidnappers in American history to collect a ransom successfully. Many, especially among the wealthy class in Omaha, feared a dangerous precedent had been set. Edward Cudahy Sr. told the press that he took those concerns seriously and would work to apprehend the kidnappers. He offered a five-thousand-dollar reward for information leading to their capture and conviction.[12]

It did not take long for the police to get an idea of who had instigated the crime. On December 21, 1900, only three days after the abduction, the *Omaha World-Herald* and the *Omaha Daily News* each ran a story pointing the finger at Pat Crowe, a well-known local miscreant. Apparently, a "reputable citizen" remembered that, at some time prior to the kidnapping, Pat Crowe had talked about kidnapping a wealthy youngster and demanding ransom. Neither the loose talk nor the threatened act would have been out of character.[13]

Much like William Mosher, Pat Crowe was a habitual criminal who seized on the idea of kidnapping as a means to make money. After the Cudahy kidnapping, Crowe became known through the press as one of America's first celebrity criminals, an obfuscator who peddled shameless tales about himself to a curious public. He wanted to be seen as a modern-day Robin Hood, stealing from the robber barons because, well, they just deserved to have someone stick it to them. Crowe made no pretense of giving any of the proceeds to the poor. But many people were enthralled by his exploits, as shown by the adoring throngs who read his stories and cheered his ability to evade many of the legal prosecutions he faced.

Born on an Iowa farm in 1864, Crowe moved to Omaha at seventeen after the death of his mother. At that young age, he had enough entrepreneurial spirit to start an independent butcher shop with a partner, James Callahan. It went well for a couple of years, but then the Cudahy Packing Company began to expand from its wholesale operations into the retail market. The Crowe and Callahan shop was one of many small butcher operations that could not compete with Cudahy's mass production and had to close down. Crowe worked briefly in one of the Cudahy retail outlets, where he was caught pilfering from the till and was fired personally by the head man, Edward Cudahy himself. At that time, Crowe was only twenty, a young man whose business dreams had been squashed by the rich and powerful. He had a grievance weighing on his mind.[14]

After his falling out with Cudahy, Crowe took to the road and a life of opportunistic theft. He circulated from Chicago to Denver to Kansas City, burglarizing stores and homes. Jewelry was his favorite item; in Kansas City, he is believed to have stolen six thousand dollars' worth of diamonds from one store. Later, he moved to Philadelphia and the seaside resorts on the New Jersey shore, where he found plenty of well-to-do visitors to rob. Afterward, in 1897, he found himself back in Chicago, where the law finally caught up with him; he was sentenced to seven years in Joliet State Prison for a robbery but was released early in 1900. He headed back to Omaha planning a "big fix," and maybe personal revenge as well.[15]

Although Pat Crowe seemed to be the only suspect in the Cudahy kidnapping, no one could find him. Anonymous sightings came in from all sorts of places in the early months of 1901: Crowe allegedly had been seen in St. Joseph, Missouri; in Chicago; on Nantucket; on an ocean liner headed to China; and on the steamer *Dudley* en route to Honduras. On January 30, 1901, Edward Cudahy received a disturbing letter, unsigned, that was never proven to have been sent by Crowe, although its wording was similar to the kidnapper's previous ransom demand. The writer demanded that Cudahy withdraw his reward offer for the kidnapper's arrest or else he would return to Omaha and "finish the job" by killing his son. "If any man, whether guilty or innocent, is ever arrested, a bullet will close the boy's mouth." Cudahy, undeterred, swore publicly that the reward offer would stand.[16]

In mid-February 1901, there was an apparent break in the case when James Callahan, Pat Crowe's former butcher-shop partner, was arrested and charged with being an accomplice in the kidnapping. Callahan was suspected primarily because of his known association with Crowe; he had been seen keeping company with Crowe shortly before the crime and was also seen spending quite a bit of gold currency shortly afterward. Also, Eddie Cudahy was able to identify Callahan by voice as the Irish-accented tough who had stood guard over him.[17]

But the state had a legal problem. It seemed that Nebraska did not have a statute applicable to the Cudahy fact pattern. Kidnapping was so rare that the legislature had never gotten around to modifying its definition of the crime, as the Pennsylvania legislature had in the aftermath of the Ross tragedy. As Nebraska law read in 1900, kidnapping was punishable by two to seven years' imprisonment, but only if the offender's intent was to transport the victim across a state line, which had not occurred here. There was also statute to prohibit "child stealing," but that applied only with a victim less than ten years old, and Eddie was fifteen. The only charges the state could allege against Callahan were false imprisonment, larceny, and robbery related to the extortion of the ransom.[18]

When prosecutors initiated the case, they probably were not optimistic they could make the charges stick. The jurors found Callahan not guilty in two separate trials: first for robbery and a second time for perjury, for lying during the first trial. Apparently, they were not convinced that he actively participated in "robbing" Edward Cudahy Sr. of money. But as the press speculated, there was also likely a political subtext to the verdict. The jury was drawn from all sectors of Omaha's population, including the masses of workingmen who despised Cudahy as a plutocrat who lived large off the non-unionized labor of his slave-wage employees.[19]

Pat Crowe was still at large, and so he would remain until 1905. There were rumors that he had journeyed to South Africa and joined the Boer army that was fighting the imperialist British invaders of the Transvaal, which depicted Crowe as he wanted to be seen, sticking up for the underdog against the powerful. The rumors were probably false. In the spring of 1905, Crowe returned to Omaha and told a reporter from the *World-Herald* that he was "weary of living as a fugitive and anxious to begin life anew." He was willing to turn himself in but would not admit legal culpability in the kidnapping. Nothing came of his overture, but in September 1905 Crowe and his brother-in-law, Frank Murphy, were involved in a street shootout with four plainclothes Omaha policemen. One of the officers was wounded, and Crowe escaped.[20]

When Crowe finally was captured in Butte, Montana, in October 1905, the press gave top billing to "the most famous outlaw in America." He received throngs of visitors in jail, many of them women who brought him gifts of fruit and flowers. He waived extradition to Nebraska, and when he departed the Butte train depot, fifteen thousand people turned out to see him off. Arriving in Omaha, he was met by another crowd at the station, many of them chanting, "Hooray for Pat Crowe."[21]

Separate trials awaited Crowe in December 1905 and February 1906. First, when he was tried for the September shootout with the policemen, the jury found Crowe not guilty, apparently believing he had fired in self-defense. Second, like James Callahan, he was tried for robbery in the Cudahy kidnapping. He had a jury of workingmen with occupations such as delivery clerk, cigar dealer, and packinghouse employee. Eddie Cudahy took the stand, where he recounted the principal kidnapper's threat to shoot his co-conspirator during the argument over the ransom. But due to the masks and blindfold, he could not positively identify Crowe. And Eddie was now a twenty-year-old more than six feet tall, and the jurors were less likely to view him as a sympathetic child victim.

The state's case also could not have been helped by the fact that, at the moment Crowe was on trial in Omaha, the Cudahy Packing Company was involved in antitrust litigation brought by Theodore Roosevelt's Justice Department in federal court in Chicago. One anonymous Omaha resident probably got it right when later asked to speculate about the jury's reasoning: "Cudahy, in their minds, is robbing the people in small amounts three times a day, and Pat Crowe got back a part of this money in one big chunk and didn't hurt anybody at all. There is no doubt but that the jury thought it no worse to steal one child than it is to starve many."[22]

Thus, for the second time in two months, Pat Crowe walked out of Omaha criminal court a free man. In a fit of pique, the presiding judge lambasted the jurors, telling them he hoped none of them ever served on a jury again. The police chief publicly lamented that there was no legal means to prosecute the jurors "for neglect of their duty and send them all to jail." And the *Washington Post*, reflecting the disgust shared by most of the East Coast press, observed caustically that "Omaha is apparently a happy hunting ground for savages and malefactors."[23]

In October 1906, eight months after his acquittal, Crowe became the published author of *Pat Crowe—His Story, Confession, and Reformation*, in which he admitted to kidnapping Eddie Cudahy and extorting the ransom and praised the jury for setting him free. He also became a popular speaker on the lecture circuit, criticizing the money-hungry trusts with all of his moral indignation.[24]

By the time Pat Crowe was released in February 1906, Kenneth Beasley had been missing for a full year, with no legal proceedings brought. But even before Kenneth stepped into the woods on February 13, 1905, the Cudahy affair was known half a continent away. From the kidnapping in 1900 through the legal proceedings in 1905 and early 1906, the story had been covered by the North Carolina and Virginia press.[25]

The entire history of ransom kidnapping in the United States up to the point of Kenneth's disappearance consisted of those two crimes: the kidnappings of Charley Ross and Eddie Cudahy. What guidance might those cases have provided to someone who either was contemplating a ransom kidnapping or was trying to retrieve the victim of such a crime?

Consider the second question first, and the sorrowful predicament faced by Sam Beasley. The senator was dealing not only with grief for his lost child but with the strain of caring for his other two children and his wife, who was, at least from press accounts, physically and mentally incapacitated to the point that she required hospitalization. From the beginning, when he posted his reward offers in the papers, he declared publicly that, above all, he wanted his boy back. He and his wife believed all along that Kenneth had been kidnapped, and they long held out hope of finding him, although as time passed they grew despondent and perplexed at not receiving any credible ransom demand.[26]

At least that was the public face the senator presented to the newspapers.

Curiously, even after a year had passed, the senator did not comment publicly on the well-circulated rumors that Joshua Harrison was the kidnapper. It is unknown what Beasley thought about those rumors, or if he acted upon them in private. One might expect the father of a missing child to do so. Beasley could have communicated with Harrison through some intermediary.

Edward Cudahy would have done just that. If his son's kidnappers had not made their ransom demand so quickly, he would have reached out to them on his own and paid them off. Cudahy had plenty of cash and had no political or ethical constraints. He already was unpopular around town and didn't particularly care what anyone thought. He just wanted to get his son back and had the means to do it.

Sam Beasley was in a far more sensitive position, more so than even Christian Ross. Perhaps money was a problem for him; little is known about his family finances, but he made his living by running a small farm and a business that must have been seasonal, depending as it did on fishing and hunting. At any rate, the dollar amounts that he put forth as reward for his son—five hundred, then a thousand—were tiny compared with those at stake in both the Ross and Cudahy cases. And even more significant, he was an elected official in a small community; he had to care what people thought. He must have considered the consequences were he to cut a backroom ransom deal with a despised character such as Harrison. Would anyone have been able to keep a secret like that? What would the neighbors have thought if such a deal had become known? And more importantly, would people have been afraid they would get murdered in their beds if they let the story slip?

Also, from the standpoint of a kidnapper, whether Joshua Harrison or someone else, there were obvious risks. The Beasleys were more sympathetic victims than the Cudahys, and the despicable nature of the crime could have provoked a lynch mob.

But the Cudahy case might also have offered encouragement to a would-be kidnapper. Here was a case of a successful ransom collection, made possible by the kidnappers' level-headedness and audacity, and of course by the parents' desperation to recover their son despite the cost. Both Crowe and Callahan had eventually walked away from the crime, due partly to weaknesses in the law. That might have appealed to Harrison. As much as he may have been perceived as a bastard and scalawag, Harrison had political connections. He also had a long, extraordinarily successful track record of beating the rap in criminal court.

And it is an amazing fact that, in 1905, kidnapping technically was not even a crime in North Carolina. The kidnapping laws of Pennsylvania and Nebraska may have been weak or inexplicit, but in North Carolina they were nonexistent. The state legislature had never seen fit to include mention of kidnapping in the state statutes, presumably because it had never happened before.[27] Assuming the crime was planned in advance, an abductor might well have believed he would be immune from prosecution.

Throughout most of 1906, there were no new developments in the case. It was a gnawing, torturous mystery that many people thought would never be resolved. But then in early September 1906, almost nineteen months after Kenneth Beasley disappeared, the case broke wide open.

The state's newspapers reported Kenneth Beasley's February 1905 disappearance, the ensuing search, and, a year and a half later, the arrest of a suspect—declared the actual "kidnapper" by one paper.

CHAPTER 7

DELAYED RECKONING

For anyone who lived outside the Currituck community and who knew of Kenneth's disappearance only from reading the papers, the news would have come as a surprise. It started with a routine hearing in civil court and developed into a major criminal-court drama—by local standards, at least, in a sleepy county seat where drama was rare and press attention rarer. The fall session of court began in September 1906. It was the event of the season in Currituck Courthouse, the name given to both a building and a community.

It is still located along the shore of the sound roughly twelve miles north of the landing at Poplar Branch. Back in 1722, the first settlers thought it was as good a place as any to build a wood-frame courthouse, and over time a few stores and houses grew up surrounding it. Like Poplar Branch, it was a good place for sailing vessels small enough to navigate the shallow Currituck Sound waters to unload their wares. But it never grew into anything more than that. Around the old historic courthouse, little has changed in years.

By 1906, there was at least a new building, this time a fine one constructed of brick. It bears some resemblance to the Georgian stylings of the James River plantations, which are not far away, after all. The county fathers gave it a major renovation in 1897, and its tidy red-brick exterior, white trim, and hip roof made it an impressive sight. On the inside, the spacious courtroom took up the full second floor. Offices for the clerk and the register of deeds were on the first.

And beside the courthouse, just a few dozen feet away, is another august symbol of government authority, this one far more stark and forbidding: the old county jail. Two stories tall, it has a solid cast-iron door and iron horizontal bars across the cell windows. It also has brick walls thirty-two inches thick. Built in 1857, it looks like either a dungeon built to keep human chattel chained within or an armory built to stop rebellious slaves storming from without.[1] It may well have been built with both purposes in mind. The infamous slave revolt led by Nat Turner in 1831, which saw at least sixty white people slaughtered with knives, pikes, and pickaxes, occurred just sixty miles away in Southampton County, Virginia.[2]

This was the place where Joshua Harrison came to court, along with numerous other folks from the surrounding farms and communities who had business before the Currituck County Superior Court in the first week of September 1906. The newspapers did not report the nature of the case that brought Harrison to court, except to note that it was a "civil suit." By at least one account, Harrison's case was heard and disposed of, and then he left to return home. But before he got far, "the Sheriff in company with a number of citizens went after him and over[took] him on the road, and arrested him and

Old Currituck Courthouse, left, and the 1857 Currituck County Jail.

carried him back to Currituck."³

The grand jury had just met and issued a true bill of indictment against Harrison for the abduction of Kenneth Beasley. At first, the prisoner was kept secure in one of the rooms in the courthouse, not in the jail just next door. He was brought back before Judge McNeill, who set a bond of twenty-two hundred dollars for his release. It was a significant amount, which he was not able to secure immediately. Pending Harrison's release, the judge took the unusual step of sending the defendant, escorted by deputies, to the more secure Pasquotank County Jail in Elizabeth City.⁴

Despite Harrison's prominence in the community as the brother-in-law of former governor Jarvis, one man present in court that day was heard to remark "that there was not one single expression favorable [to Harrison] heard during all day yesterday at the courthouse." Harrison's arrest came as "no surprise" after the rumors of the past eighteen months. And he was, after all, a man with a "checkered career" about whom many wild stories circulated. Plus, word was spreading that one of the witnesses had told the grand jurors Harrison had finally broken his silence and made a ransom demand: "When Mr. Beasley put up enough money, the child would be forthcoming."⁵

Also, for the first time, the papers were speculating about a motive on the part of Harrison. The *Daily Economist* noted that he had been, for several years, well known in the community as a "maker and dispenser of wines." Sam Beasley, since he was first elected to the State House in 1898, had been an advocate for "regulating the sale of spirituous liquors in Currituck County." The widespread belief was that Harrison saw his livelihood threatened by a political crackdown on liquor. Perhaps inspired by Pat Crowe in Nebraska, he wanted personal revenge against Beasley, and may also have seen an opportunity to extort money.⁶

Raleigh's *News & Observer*, well known as the journalistic mouthpiece of Beasley's Democratic Party, was even more pointed in its aspersions against Harrison. It praised Beasley for his courage in vigorously prosecuting the "blind tiger men"* who were violating the state's temperance laws: "Like the good citizen he is, Senator Beasley went actively to work to prevent the continued violations."

---
*   "Blind tiger" was a euphemism, well known at the time, for a backroom bar or a bootleg liquor operation.

The paper went on to reprint the full content of its article from February 1905, which first reported the vague rumors about Harrison's involvement in the disappearance and recalled his trial for the murder of his father years before. And now, after the indictment, the paper was confident enough to presume the defendant's guilt in its front-page headline: "Kidnapper Put Behind the Bars: Harrison in Pasquotank County Jail: Feeling Is Strong."[7]

Harrison, for his part, did not take it lying down. His family quickly retained the services of Edwin F. Aydlett, of Aydlett and Ehringhaus, a legal powerhouse in Elizabeth City.[8] In less than a week, he made his twenty-two-hundred-dollar bond. The money was pledged by two relatives, father and son, who lived near him on the outskirts of Jarvisburg. Walter S. Newbern Sr. and Jr. owned a small boat dock, known as Newbern's Landing, along the sound a couple of miles from the Harrison farm.[9] Walter Sr. was the brother of Worth Newbern, who was married to the newly indicted defendant's sister, Virginia Harrison Newbern. Walter and Worth, both in their late fifties by 1906, were two of the ten children fathered by John Newbern, who was born in Currituck in 1815 and died there in 1888. If he was not the same John Newbern who sat on the jury that acquitted Joshua Harrison of murdering his father in 1871, then he certainly was related to him.[10]

Nor did Harrison intend to remain silent. With the assistance of his attorney, Aydlett, he drafted a statement that was, as he must have intended, carried by the papers. It was a blanket denial. Harrison said flatly that he had no part in the disappearance of Kenneth Beasley. So far as he could remember, he had never met the boy and did not know him by sight. On the Monday that Kenneth went missing, he had been working on his farm. He had not heard of the disappearance until the following day, when a neighbor came over for dinner and spoke of it. He then described his comings and goings over the next few days; he had traveled to Coinjock on Wednesday and to Elizabeth City from Friday until Saturday, and he named witnesses to that effect. Like everyone else, he speculated about the boy's fate and thought most likely he had gotten lost in the woods and died from the cold.[11]

As for his rapport with Senator Beasley, Harrison said, "My relations with Mr. S. M. Beasley have always been of the most pleasant character so far as I know. I am a Republican and Mr. Beasley a Democrat, but our relations have been so pleasant I have voted for him each time he ran as a candidate to represent the county and when he ran for the Senate." Further, Harrison claimed the anti-liquor legislation that Beasley pushed through the North Carolina General Assembly had caused him "no damage whatsoever."[12]

Having secured his release through bond, Harrison intended to return home to his farm and prepare as best he could for his trial, set for March of the following year. But he must at least have felt apprehensive about his prospects, if the proceedings of his bond hearing are any indication.

There is no transcript of the bond hearing held before Judge McNeill on September 5, 1906, shortly after Harrison was arrested and brought back to the courthouse. What is known comes from affidavits filed by the parties in late February 1907, when the court was considering the defendant's motion for change of venue. Harrison, not surprisingly, wanted the trial moved out of Currituck County. He claimed the county was so filled with friends and supporters of Senator Beasley that he could not be assured of fairness or even safety. He alleged in his affidavit that the prosecutor, Solicitor Hallet S. Ward, had told the judge at the September hearing that he "gravely feared violence" if Harrison were even to be granted bond.[13]

Solicitor Ward and Senator Beasley each filed affidavits in response, arguing against any change of venue. Beasley pointed out that eighteen months had passed between his son's disappearance and Harrison's arrest, and no one had attempted to harm the accused. Nor had anyone done so in the five months since his arrest. And even when Harrison was first taken into custody, Beasley recalled, the sheriff had not taken the precaution of putting him into the heavily casemented jail next door to the courthouse. In other words, there was no prejudice on the part of the citizens of Currituck County that might lead them to "hasty action," as the senator delicately put it.[14]

Solicitor Ward also gave his recollection of Harrison's arrest and bond hearing. It is a curious account. As Ward told it, he did in fact urge Judge McNeill to set Harrison's bond as high as possible in September. He told the court that he thought "a larger bail would be effective to avoid public violence."

Whereupon the judge asked the solicitor, "Do you fear danger of violence to the Defendant? If you do, I will remove him at once to Pasquotank County."

At that point, Ward asked the court for a brief recess, which was granted. The solicitor then walked outside to see who was milling around in the hallways and outside the courthouse. Seeing a few men standing about, he asked them, "Gentlemen, have you heard anything of any proposed lynching of Harrison?" Ward returned to the courtroom and represented to the judge that, no, there apparently was not any talk of lynching, but he had heard "expressions of impatience" about the sheriff's "partiality" to the defendant. Some of the locals apparently were afraid the sheriff might let Harrison escape.

For that reason, and not for reasons of prejudice or fears of mob justice, Ward had asked the court to set a high bond and to order the sheriff to put Harrison in the jail rather than "pet and nurse" him around the courthouse.[15]

Granted, if the locals were concerned about any partiality toward the defendant on the part of the sheriff, they may have had reason stemming from the Harrison family connections. Specifically, they concerned Robert Lee Griggs, Joshua Harrison's nephew by marriage. He was the husband of Martha Newbern Griggs, the daughter of Worth and Virginia Harrison Newbern; he was also the nephew and cousin of the two Walter Newberns, father and son, who would eventually supply the bond for Harrison.[16]

Robert Lee Griggs was either the sheriff of Currituck County at the time or soon to take over the position. The question remains because the sources conflict. The newspaper articles covering Harrison's indictment and arrest refer to "Sheriff Barnard," who was presumably John E. Barnard. The best and most comprehensive source on Currituck genealogy, *The Heritage of Currituck County 1985*, states that Barnard served as sheriff from 1905 through 1910, succeeded by Griggs, who served until 1917. And yet the trial transcript in Harrison's case states that Griggs was the sheriff when the indictment was issued in 1906.[17]

Even if Griggs did not yet occupy the top post in 1906, it appears he was affiliated with the sheriff's office. Later, when the case came to trial, at least one witness would be asked whether he recalled making a statement to a "Deputy Griggs."[18] In all likelihood, that was Harrison's nephew.

Harrison's family tie with the sheriff might also explain the reluctance of witnesses to accuse Harrison publicly in the eighteen months after Kenneth Beasley went missing.

Whatever happened in that September 1906 bond hearing, it is known that Joshua Harrison was placed under a substantial bond and hastily spirited to a more secure location in the jail in Elizabeth City. The case also was attracting attention in the national press, including the *Washington Post*, which reported the proceedings under the front-page headline, "Lynching Party Foiled." As the *Post* told it, there were rumors that if the sheriff "had not brought the prisoner to this place last night, Harrison would have been the subject of a 'necktie party.'"[19]

THE WASHINGTON POST

Senator Beasley and the prosecution, at least for the record, and at least for the time being, seemed determined for the legal process to go forward without interruption. As public men, they wanted to uphold the appearance and solemnity of the law. Lynching, like any form of "hasty action," was an affront to the established political order, something to be discouraged.

Yet consider a statement Senator Beasley would make to the press a year later, after all the legal proceedings surrounding Joshua Harrison finally came to a close: "Had I wanted Harrison to die, I could have accomplished this by expressing the desire to my fellow countrymen in Currituck. They would have lynched him without hesitation if I had simply said the word. I waited for the law to take its course."[20]

That was a remarkable public comment from a state legislator. It reflects that mob justice, although nasty and distasteful, was not at all foreign to people in that time and place.

Defendants brought to Salisbury, N.C., for trial. The day this newspaper photograph appeared, three of them were hanged by a lynch mob, the second Salisbury lynching in four years.

CHAPTER 8

A CULTURE OF LYNCHING

One day in the early 1900s, a boy named Paul sat down to lunch and some interesting conversation with his family at their small farm near Buies Creek in the tobacco- and cotton-growing flatlands of central North Carolina.

Paul was born in 1894, which made him two years older than Kenneth Beasley. They both were farm boys, growing up in families who had a wealth of land, although far less of ready cash. Paul would remember his first school as a one-room log cabin, a setting with which Kenneth could have identified.[1]

To supplement their farm income, Paul's mother and father took boarders into their home. One of them was a roustabout named Moody, who had a job operating a sawmill nearby. On this particular day at lunch, Moody announced he was not planning to go in to work that afternoon. Paul asked him why not.

> He said that he had to go to Sanford and help lynch a nigger and so we didn't saw. . . . That night when he came back and we were eating supper, I kept looking at his hands. . . . He had nice long, sinewy hands . . . and after supper we went out on the porch and I kept wondering, I had to find out what happened. Finally I said, "Mr. Moody, what happened at Sanford?" He said, "Oh, goddammit, I got there too late. They had already lynched him, but I put three or four bullets through his damned head."[2]

Paul Eliot Green turned out to have sharp recollection and a talent for making stories into art. After working his way through the University of North Carolina, he became a versatile author, ranked with William Faulkner and Eugene O'Neill among the brightest talents of his generation, even if he did not match their fame or commercial success. It was as a playwright that he made his most profound mark. *The Lost Colony*, an outdoor drama depicting the original English settlement on Roanoke Island in the sixteenth century, has been performed since the 1930s and remains a North Carolina icon to this day. But he also wrote novels and collections of short stories, most of them drawing on memories of his rural childhood. And throughout his long life—he died in 1981—Paul Green was an outspoken voice for progressive causes and most of all against segregation and bigotry.

In fact, the work that brought Green his first major renown was rooted in the eastern North Carolina of the post-Reconstruction era, and in the soul-crushing racism that pervaded all aspects of life at the time. *In Abraham's Bosom* won the Pulitzer Prize for Drama in 1927 and was lauded as the first theatrical work to depict African-Americans as sympathetic, multi-faceted personalities, rather than blackface caricatures.

The play is set in the Carolina pinewoods over a twenty-year period beginning roughly in 1885. Its central character is an idealist whose modest ambitions are doomed from the start. Abe McCranie, the illegitimate half-black son of a plantation owner, wants to start a one-room schoolhouse for the local black children. Everyone scoffs, although Abe's determination eventually wins him the respect of his father, who provides him land and materials to build the school. Abe gives it his all, but most of his students drift away, compelled by threats or their own poverty to stay away from the school. He grows more and more embittered and in a moment of rage kills his white half-brother, who had mocked his aspirations from the beginning. Finally, Abe summons all of his courage and dignity and walks calmly out of his house to face the bullets of the inevitable lynch mob.

In Abraham's Bosom concludes around 1906, at just about the same time Moody regaled young Paul with the tale of the lynching in Sanford, twenty-five miles west of the Green farm. That was also the year Joshua Harrison was taken to jail, reportedly under threat of a hangman's noose.

The story of the Sanford lynching may have been apocryphal. Moody could have invented it over the dinner table, thinking the wide-eyed boy would be entertained. Or the whole thing might have been creative license by Paul Green. The history of lynching in the South is shadowy territory indeed. For example, one history published in 2009 compiled records of 99 lynchings in North Carolina between 1890 and 1930. None was known to have taken place in Sanford.[3] And in 2015, the Equal Justice Initiative of Montgomery, Alabama, released a report based on five years of study of lynchings in twelve Southern states between 1877 and 1950. It came up with the names of 3,959 victims; again, none of those lynchings occurred in Sanford, North Carolina, but at least 700 of those names had never been included on any previous list. New records and evidence come to light all the time, and even the new numbers are likely deficient. No one disputes that many lynchings went unreported and unrecorded.[4]

But even if no lynching ever occurred in Sanford, there were enough documented "necktie parties," as they were euphemistically called, in that corner of North Carolina to plant seeds in the fertile imagination of a young Paul Green. There was the case of Henry "Hen" Jones, an unlucky African-American who met his fate in the tiny community of Harpers Crossroads in Chatham County, just north of Sanford. One day in January 1898, the body of Nancy Welch, a fifty-seven-year-old white Confederate widow, was found stabbed to death in the woods. Predictably, and unprovably, she was also alleged to have been raped. A crowd of more than a hundred people gathered, including two deputy sheriffs, by some accounts. Suspicion fell upon Jones, who was lashed up, dragged nearly to death behind a horse-drawn buggy, and then hanged from a tree. Afterward, hundreds more people gathered to gawk at the mutilated corpse, to throw rocks, and to fire bullets into it.[5] There was also George Rittle, a black man known to history only as an alleged "informer," hanged by a mob in the Moore County seat of Carthage in March 1900.[6]

To be sure, the vast majority of these mob murders were inflicted upon black people by whites. It was part of the practice of enforcing social and legal inequality through fear. Yet some crimes were deemed offensive enough to white Southerners' sensibilities to turn the mob's anger toward one of its own. The kidnapping and possible murder of a white state senator's son would have been such a crime, as Joshua Harrison may have come close to discovering. The rape of a virtuous white schoolteacher was another, as Silas Martindale, a twenty-five-year-old white man, *did* discover in Carthage on March 10, 1901, just a year after the Rittle lynching. A mob of about fifty men broke into the Moore County Jail, removed Martindale, and marched him down Main Street to the most convenient tree, where they put the noose around his neck and lifted him off the ground several times, trying to extract a confession to the rape. Eventually, he strangled to death. Later, arrest warrants were issued for "several prominent local citizens" in connection with the lynching, but when each of them produced an alibi, the charges were dropped.[7]

The Martindale lynching was the first in North Carolina after Charles Aycock became governor in January 1901. For Aycock, who took office on a pledge to move his state forward from the poverty and stagnation that had marked its Reconstruction era, lynchings were a political embarrassment. To finance his vaunted school construction campaign, he needed capital, whether in the form of philanthropy from wealthy Northerners such as the Rockefeller family or from industrial development that would swell the tax base.[8] No one would want to invest in a place marked by lawlessness, and so the state had a tangible interest in keeping mob violence out of the papers.

The governor and all of the state's political establishment were playing a balancing act. They wanted to build North Carolina's reputation as a peaceful place friendly to business, with a hardworking population that could, through education, rise from its history of poverty. And yet the same political establishment was avowedly white supremacist. Its ideology was based upon keeping black men down so white men could lead, and inevitably that attitude manifested itself in physical intimidation.

Consequently, Aycock's first inclination, as stated in his inaugural address, was to urge North Carolina's black citizens to behave themselves, to "learn that crimes which lead to mob law must cease, and then mob law shall curse our State no more."[9] As Aycock had said ominously during his gubernatorial campaign, white people were going to be the masters of North Carolina, whatever happened: "There are three ways in which we may rule. We have ruled by force, we can rule by fraud, but we want to rule by law." Historians would describe this as a "double-edged sword of the Southern master class." Whites would profess paternalistic concern for the welfare of blacks, urging them to earn white people's respect through religion, education, and obedience to the law. But the concern was always blended with the threat of violence for those who stepped out of line.[10]

It was much like the sentiment expressed by Senator Beasley when he commented after Joshua Harrison's trial that he could have ordered Harrison to be lynched, but as an upstanding public man he thought it better to let the authorities deal with him. Better, but not essential. If a white man behaved badly enough, and especially if he managed to evade justice in the courtroom, the mob would come calling for him just as they would for a Negro.

Aycock's double-edged sword proved so ineffective in deterring lynch mobs that an organization based in Seattle, Washington, with the utopian-sounding name of the International Council of the World issued a five-hundred-dollar reward for the arrest of anyone participating in a lynching. The reward offer drew a rebuke from the governor, who denounced lynching as "a great blot on the State" but still maintained there was no need for "outside aid in securing law and order in North Carolina."[11]

Law and order would remain difficult to secure. On June 19, 1902, two black men, James and Harrison Gillespie, were locked in the Rowan County Jail in Salisbury, a railroad town in North Carolina's central Piedmont. They were accused of the murder and robbery of a white woman. Word reached Raleigh that a mob was forming, and Aycock ordered a company of National Guard to secure the jail. However, the mob proved quick and efficient; before the Guard could organize itself, the mob stormed the jail, seized the prisoners, and hanged them. Embarrassed, the governor offered a three-hundred-dollar reward for information leading to the arrest of any lynchers—essentially the same remedy he had spurned when it was proposed by meddlers from out of state.[12]

No one jumped at the reward offer. Even if most white people in Salisbury were not violent and would never have participated in a lynching, there would have been great public pressure to keep quiet and let the racial order prevail. And of course, no black person was going to risk the mob's wrath by implicating a white man.

In his 1903 biennial message to the General Assembly, the governor made a request that it enact a new anti-lynching statute, yet he did not specify any provisions he wanted or make any personal effort to get any such bill passed. The General Assembly basically ignored it.[13]

Robert B. Glenn, who succeeded Aycock as governor in January 1905, had little more success in suppressing mob violence, although he did make a more personal effort to do so. In May 1906, Anson County was the scene of an outrage when John V. Johnson became the last white man lynched in North Carolina. He was on trial for shooting his brother-in-law, but when the jury took too much time in deliberating, the mob grabbed and hanged him. Glenn made a trip to the county seat of Wadesboro and told the sheriff that he wanted indictments issued against the lynchers. Sixteen suspects were arrested and put in jail, and although the temporary imprisonment may have scared them a little, everyone clammed up, and nothing came of the charges.[14]

Two months later came the worst atrocity of all. In Rowan County, three black sharecroppers—one of them only fifteen, and two of them relatives of the Gillespie men lynched in 1902—were accused of the horrific ax murder of the Lyerly family, consisting of a local farmer, his wife, and two of his young children, who lived just outside Salisbury. In a brutal replay of the other lynching four years earlier, the mob barged into the same jail, marched the accused down the road beyond the city limit as they pleaded their innocence, then clumsily strung them up to the same tree limb.[15]

Governor Glenn had attempted to forestall the lynching by dispatching the state militia to Salisbury by train. But they arrived too late, which the governor suspected was due to the local court officials' intentionally delaying to notify him of the pending emergency. Furious, the governor made another special trip, and this time made certain that George Hall, one of the leaders of the lynch mob, was arrested and tried. The governor even testified at Hall's trial, an extraordinary gesture that led to an extraordinary result: Hall was found guilty of conspiracy to murder and sentenced to fifteen years' imprisonment. He was the first man in North Carolina, and surely one of the first anywhere, to be convicted of a lynching-related offense.

And yet Hall's prison sentence did not stand for long. He served less than four years before Governor William W. Kitchin, Glenn's successor, issued him a pardon.[16]

Leaders such as Aycock and Glenn expressed dismay that their white citizens could not refrain from violent acts. But even politicians themselves were not immune from being victims, or at least near-victims, as when Aycock's predecessor encountered public disturbances during the midterm elections of 1898. Governor Daniel L. Russell, a Republican, was traveling by train from Raleigh to his home in Wilmington to cast his vote. On his return trip, as the train stopped in the small towns of Hamlet and Maxton in the tobacco-growing southeastern part of the state, it was surrounded by troops of gun-toting ruffians on horseback. As they attempted to barge into the train, people in the mob shouted, "Lynch him! Lynch the fat son of a bitch!" The governor did not end up swinging from a tree, but only by chance.

As contemporary journalist Rob Christensen noted, "North Carolina avoided what would have been one of the ugliest moments in American history only because the governor was hidden in a baggage compartment." [17]

TOP ROW: Senator Jeter C. Pritchard. Senator Marion Butler, leader of the Fusion Politics movement.

MIDDLE: Congressman George H. White. Governor Daniel L. Russell.

BOTTOM: Senator Furnifold M. Simmons, leader of the White Supremacy Campaign. Josephus Daniels, editor of the Raleigh *News and Observer*.

CHAPTER 9

RACE AND POLITICS

North Carolina. The Southern state that, as dyed-in-the-wool Tar Heels like to claim, has always been more forward looking and less traditional than the others. The vale of humility lying betwixt the two mountains of conceit. The state that sent the most soldiers to fight and die on the front lines in the Confederate army, while the plantation aristocrats from Virginia and South Carolina—who actually started the war—got all the glory. The enlightened Southern state where yeoman small farmers had the foresight to build the nation's first state-supported university at Chapel Hill.

But looking back over the state's political and historical landscape, the only fair way to characterize North Carolina is as an inseparable part of the conservative South. It is a traditional state that remained mostly rural until the past few decades, where deep religious values have always held sway for many people, and where racial tensions have always influenced political life.[1]

So, when a wave of political upheaval and violence swept the South in the 1890s, it is not surprising that the wave was felt in North Carolina as elsewhere. Many people today are shocked to discover that the governor of North Carolina came within a hairsbreadth of being lynched by a mob in 1898, as it seems so contrary to the image of moderation the state has worn for so long. It is only in the past few years that historians have made it a point to study the uncomfortable truths about the South in those turbulent post-Reconstruction years.

Reconstruction, at least in the legal sense, ended in 1877. The disputed presidential election of 1876 was resolved in Congress with a back-room deal that federal troops would be withdrawn from the old Confederate states, where they had been overseeing elections, tamping down Ku Klux Klan violence, and generally maintaining order. When the troops left, white former Confederates, virtually all of them Democrats, quickly gained control of the election machinery around the South, and the state governments became Democratic. It is tempting to look at 1877 as the beginning of the Jim Crow era of racial discrimination and disenfranchisement, but actually that process took some time to develop. The 1870s and 1880s, although by no means a period of racial equality, were marked by black-white relations that were far more civil than in the following decades.

The 1880s were the days of New South boosterism through much of the old Confederacy. A new generation of Southern journalists and businessmen wanted to move beyond the bitterness surrounding the Civil War, which they believed was holding the South back from developing economically and socially. Henry Woodfin Grady, publisher of the *Atlanta Constitution*, was the best-known proponent of the new mantra. He traveled widely throughout the North giving speeches, telling his audiences that the South had changed and was deserving of investment if Yankee philanthropists and industrialists would give it a chance. For his inspiration, Grady gave credit to Benjamin H. Hill, a Georgia politician who served in the Confederate Senate despite having opposed secession at first. As early as 1871, Hill had given a speech to the University of

Georgia Alumni Association proclaiming that the system of slavery had been wrong all along. It was not only oppressive but regressive and inefficient, and the South should never have fought a war to preserve it. What the South now needed was education, as well as manufacturing and a body of free laborers, black and white.[2]

Certainly no one among the New South movement, least of all Grady, was yet advocating for racial equality. They did not deviate from the longstanding belief that the white race was intellectually and morally superior and was best fit to lead. But they recognized, even if many other Southern whites were reluctant to accept it, that racial antagonism was self-defeating, and that nothing would be gained by keeping blacks in ignorance and poverty through the sharecropping system. Grady proudly proclaimed that "in the South, there are Negro lawyers, teachers, editors, dentists, doctors, preachers, multiplying with the increasing ability of their race to support them." He was joined by many religious leaders, such as the Reverend Atticus G. Haygood, president of the Methodist Emory College in Oxford, Georgia, on the outskirts of Atlanta. Throughout the 1880s, Haygood exhorted his white students to give praise for the abolition of slavery and to work for "the elevation of our black brother" through education.[3]

One could hear similar sentiments from the African-American leadership as well. Back in North Carolina, Charlotte was home to a small but vibrant black middle class centered around Biddle Institute, known today as Johnson C. Smith University, a college for blacks founded by Northern philanthropists in 1867. The city had at least one black-owned newspaper, the *Charlotte Messenger,* edited by William C. Smith, who urged his fellow blacks to stay on white people's good side by embracing the right values: hard work, self-discipline, good manners. Black religious leaders such as A.M.E. Zion bishop Henry Clinton concurred with the admonition to "be quiet, gentlemanly, attentive to your own business, and you will find that you will get along much better than if you laugh loud, swagger, smoke cheap cigars and drink cheap whiskey."[4]

Most importantly, black people in North Carolina voted throughout the 1870s and 1880s. It is true that white registrars and other officials controlled most of the electoral machinery, and that there was voter fraud and probably intimidation in many places. But fifty-two African-Americans were elected to the North Carolina House of Representatives between 1876 and 1894, mostly from eastern North Carolina, where the black vote was most heavily concentrated.[5] The Second Congressional District in particular was a locus of black political strength. Centered around the Rocky Mount and Tarboro area, the "Black Second" was a gerrymander created in the early 1870s by Democrats intending to pack as many African-American Republicans as possible into one district. But once it was created, blacks ran it. Four different black U.S. congressmen were elected from the Second District in the late 1800s, along with many black county commissioners, justices of the peace, and magistrates. The congressmen also had influence over federal patronage, including the appointment of postmasters, most of whom in the Second District were black. Later, it would become a point of major controversy.[6]

In the early 1890s, the veneer of stability over race relations in the South began to crack. It started with economic hard times, which impacted blacks and whites alike. When people lose their jobs, it is natural to look for scapegoats, and for white Southerners, blacks were the most obvious target. But it is interesting to note that the racial recriminations did not set in immediately. They took awhile to take effect, and it happened only after a series of unusual political events.

It all began with the financial panic of 1893, which was a serious trauma nationwide. Sparked by crop failures and declining currency markets overseas, financial speculators in the United States started a run on gold currency. With the money supply depleted, many businesses went under, and millions lost their jobs.

North Carolina, especially the Piedmont region, where the textile industry had been growing rapidly, was hit hard. Cotton mill workers were left bitter and destitute. Many of them had moved to the towns and mill villages from the countryside due to falling prices for agricultural goods, hoping for a better life. Instead, they found long hours and minuscule wages. In Charlotte in 1890, skilled mill hands earned between $1.00 and $1.40 per day; for unskilled workers, it was more like 40 or 65 cents per day. These were jobs that required exhausting hours in non-air-conditioned brick factories, where it was not unusual for workers, many of them children, to suffer debilitating injuries when their hands or arms got caught in the machinery. And then, after the markets crashed, even many of those jobs disappeared, leaving people rootless and hungry. In 1896, the *Charlotte Democrat* lamented "the unusually large number of beggars and tramps investing this place."[7]

Poor Southern whites, after the effects of the financial panic set in, had cause to be angry with just about everyone. They could no longer make a living on the farm, and for that they blamed industrialists and railroads for overcharging them on shipping fees for crops, as well as banks for charging too much interest. Neither could they make a living in the towns. It caused them to question their allegiance to the Democratic Party, which they had long viewed as the upholder of the Confederate tradition. The party now seemed too closely bound to the industrialists and railroad barons.

Farmers led the exodus from the Democratic fold. North Carolina's Farmers Alliance, which had begun as an agricultural trade group, formally allied itself with the Populist Party in the 1894 elections. Joining the Populists' calls for lower tariffs and free (but inflationary) coinage of silver, which they believed would bring relief to debt-ridden farmers and workers, they broke with the Democrats and, amazingly enough, allied themselves with the Republican Party, which in North Carolina consisted overwhelmingly of blacks. This political alliance has gone down in history as the "Fusion" arrangement. Some have called it a political marriage of convenience, although it might just as well be called an act of desperation. By 1894, the price of cotton had slumped to five cents per pound, and many were asking just how much worse the rural economy could get. Joining with the Republicans seemed the best way to gain political leverage and survival.[8]

But as an alliance between blacks and poor Southern whites, created out of exceptional economic circumstances, the Fusion was a tenuous political arrangement. It would not last long and was probably doomed from the beginning.

At first, it had some remarkable successes. In 1894, the Fusionists—the Republicans and Populists combined—swept control of the General Assembly. They took the State Senate with thirty-seven seats to twelve for the Democrats and the House by seventy-nine to forty-one seats. They won six of North Carolina's nine seats in the U.S. House of Representatives, and with control of the General Assembly, which then had the power to elect U.S. senators, they also took both Senate seats.[9] Democratic senator Thomas J. Jarvis, originally of Currituck County, was replaced by Republican Jeter C. Pritchard, and Democrat Matt Ransom, a former Confederate brigadier general, was succeeded by Marion Butler, a Sampson County farmer and newspaper editor who had organized the Farmers Alliance and headed the Populist campaign.

With their hands firmly on the wheel, the Fusionists passed some notable reform measures in the General Assembly. They increased spending on education, raised corporate taxes, and enacted a 6 percent interest ceiling on loans. And most significantly, they adopted home-rule legislation that allowed county elections to be overseen by popularly elected local boards—which, in black majority areas like the Second District, meant black people supervised the votes. The results of the reforms were tangible. In the following election in 1896, some 85 percent of registered voters did in fact vote. For the time, it was an amazing display of biracial voting power.[10]

The Fusionists were able to follow up on their accomplishments of 1894. Even though legendary Populist orator William Jennings Bryan did not win the presidency in 1896, he carried the South, and North Carolina in particular.[11] The Fusionists picked up even more seats in the General Assembly and elected Republican Daniel L. Russell as governor. A former Confederate officer and the son of a wealthy Brunswick County plantation family, Russell was a curious figure. He believed in civil rights for blacks and in curtailing the political power of big corporations. For that, he would be hounded throughout his political career as a scalawag and a traitor to both his race and class.[12]

For the Democrats, it amounted to a shocking reversal of fortune. Since the 1870s, they had exerted a firm control over the state government. With financial backing from North Carolina industries such as the railroads and the textile and tobacco manufacturers, they had maintained a stable, fiscally conservative image for the state. And most importantly, they had kept a lid on simmering racial tensions. But now, they saw themselves thrown out of office by blacks and poor whites voting together. Of course, those accustomed to power and privilege never give them up easily and will fight to get them back.

The counter-revolution lost no time in gearing up for the 1898 midterm elections. It was inspired and directed by a man who never held elected office but probably had more political influence than anyone else in North Carolina at the time. Josephus Daniels was the publisher of the *News & Observer*, the largest newspaper in Raleigh, which also was distributed by mail throughout eastern North Carolina. Daniels knew the region well, as he had grown up in Wilson, a crossroads town in the coastal plain. He made it a point to cover stories from the eastern part of the state, as the *News & Observer*'s coverage of Kenneth Beasley's disappearance would later demonstrate.

Daniels quickly seized upon the political formula for winning back power for the Democrats. Almost all black voters were Republicans, and the Democrats had long held the loyalty of most whites. The way to un-fuse the Fusionists would be to drive a wedge between the poor white Populists and the blacks. Daniels suspected that white voters had been surprised by the Fusionist successes in 1894 and 1896, and that many of them were uncomfortable with how those successes had empowered black officeholders. Those Populists could be brought back into the Democratic fold by promising to restore the "dear treasure of [the Populist's] superiority as a white man," as the historian W. J. Cash described it.[13]

Also, Daniels probably foresaw that the Fusionists, exhilarated by their success, would overplay their hand with boastful rhetoric—especially dealing with race—that whites would find hard to swallow.

The Democratic campaign needed stump speakers who could travel the state and speak to the voters directly at town rallies. For his star attraction, Daniels seized upon Charles Aycock, a boyhood friend who had grown up with him near Wilson. An up-and-coming attorney and state legislator, Aycock was also known as a compelling orator who could entertain voters with tales of his older brothers who served in the Confederate army. Along with Lost Cause nostalgia, Aycock pushed the cause of education. He told crowds a story about how his parents grew up poor and his mother never learned to read; once, he recalled her having to sign a deed just by marking an X on the page. He did not want North Carolina's future generations to live with such shame.[14]

Along with Aycock, there were Robert B. Glenn of Winston-Salem and Locke Craig, who was born in eastern North Carolina but later moved to Asheville in the mountains. Both were accomplished speechmakers. As Daniels described them in his memoirs, the pugnacious Glenn would "use the meat axe" on the stump, while the more erudite Craig's "sentences were beautiful, his speeches ornate, and he had fire and oratory."[15] All three men would later be elected governor of North Carolina, Aycock in 1900, Glenn in 1904, Craig in 1912.

While the speechmakers crisscrossed the state, the campaign was coordinated by another Daniels confidant, attorney Furnifold Simmons of New Bern. Simmons was the son of a plantation family that owned more than a thousand acres and a hundred slaves before the war. Like Aycock, Glenn, and Craig, he was an attorney who ventured into politics. He came up in the Black Second and lost two legislative races to black candidates before finally winning election to Congress in 1886. In the process, he appealed openly to black voters. While in Congress, he secured funding for public works and post offices in black neighborhoods. But then in 1888, Simmons lost his re-election bid to a black Republican school principal.[16]

Hell hath no fury like a white patrician defeated by a black man in a fair fight. Simmons was never a strong public speaker like the others, but he was a master at back-room political horse trading, and he would direct the 1898 White Supremacy Campaign—as Daniels and others unashamedly called it—with single-minded tenacity. He intended to make it so that no black would ever exercise political power in North Carolina again. Simmons would later win election to the U.S. Senate in 1900 and hold the seat for thirty more years, in which time he never wavered from that commitment.

Daniels, with his editor's pencil, provided the politicians with much of the material for their speeches, so much so that Aycock later commented that "any man can make speeches if he would read the *News & Observer.*" All through 1898, the *N&O* carried salacious stories of malevolent blacks abusing white people. Some of them alleged violent crime, especially the well-worn theme of the rapist preying on white women. But the most affecting stories were probably those that told of black government officials lording their authority over whites. In New Bern, white women were supposedly being tried in misdemeanor court by a black magistrate, and black sheriff's deputies in Wake County were said to be serving subpoenas on white men. In Vanceboro, white ladies were required to visit a black clerk in order to list their taxes, while "young white women in Wilmington [were] pushed off the sidewalks by Negro policemen on their beats."[17]

Wilmington was a focal point of the rhetoric. At the time, it was the largest city in the state. It boasted a population that was 56 percent black and had a small but growing middle class of black merchants and tradesmen. After 1896, the mayor and six of the ten city aldermen were Fusionists, two of them black. A corresponding number of the police and other city officials were also black, and so Wilmington's city government made a tempting target for the white supremacists.[18] Local businessmen formed a White Government Union to solicit funds for the campaign. One of its leaders was John D. Bellamy, the Democratic candidate for Congress, who said in a September 1898 speech that the voters would decide whether North Carolina's political affairs would "be controlled by the vicious, or whether they shall be put in the hands of the intelligent people of the State—the white people."[19]

But the city also had a black-owned newspaper, the *Wilmington Daily Record*, edited by a light-skinned black journalist named Alexander Manly. The editor was reputed to be the mixed-race grandson of Charles Manly, a Wake County plantation baron who served a term as governor of North Carolina in the pre–Civil War years. Being familiar with the subject of miscegenation, Manly stepped up to answer the accusations about black men preying on white women.

In an editorial responding to a speech given by Rebecca L. Fulton of Georgia, in which she advocated the lynching of black rapists, the *Daily Record* asserted that not every black man who slept with a white woman was a rapist, that many black men were "sufficiently attractive for white girls of culture to fall in love with them." And even among poor whites, the editorial claimed that "the women of that race are not any more particular in the matter of clandestine meetings with colored men than the white men with colored women." And for good measure, Manly warned whites, "Don't think ever that your women will remain pure while you are debauching ours. You sow the seed—the harvest will come in due time."[20]

The words were so inflammatory that some have questioned who actually wrote them. At least one historian, Philip Gerard, has pointed out that the infamous editorial is not characteristic of Alex Manly. It does not fit his writing style, and prior to it he had not been so provocative. Most of his editorials dealt with mundane issues such as construction of city bicycle paths to help black mill workers save money on streetcar fare.[21]

But whoever wrote the words, the *Daily Record* editorial became the dominant campaign issue after it was recirculated by the indignant white press. It did nothing to help the Fusion campaign; poor whites did not appreciate the suggestion that they slept with blacks. And for the White Supremacy Campaign, it was a rhetorical godsend.

The Democrats brought in South Carolina senator Ben Tillman, a virulent racist, for a speaking tour. The theme was "redemption" of both white government and white womanhood. In Sanford, twenty-five hundred people attended a speech in which Tillman urged them to "rub the black pitch from the Tar Heel State." Thousands more turned out for speeches in Rockingham, Roxboro, Burlington, and Charlotte. As for Alex Manly, Tillman asked the crowd with mock incredulity, "Why didn't you kill that damn nigger editor who wrote that?"[22]

Everywhere Tillman and the other political celebrities gave their speeches, the threat of gunfire hung in the air. The Democrats had an unofficial partisan militia of troopers, known as the Red Shirt brigade, who accompanied their campaign. Mounted on horseback and carrying rifles, the Red Shirts stood watch over Democratic campaign rallies, lest any blacks cause a disturbance. Even Daniels, writing years later, commented that "I then understood why red-shirted men riding through the country, even if they said nothing and shot off no pistols, could carry terror to the Negroes in their quarters. . . . They usually rode horses and had weapons, and their appearance was the signal for the Negroes to get out of the way, so that when the Red Shirt brigade passed through the Negro end of town, it was as uninhabited as if it had been a graveyard."[23]

Election Day arrived on November 8, 1898—the election in which Fusionist governor Russell was nearly lynched from his train as he attempted to vote. It turned out to be a total victory for the Democrats, who picked up 5 congressional seats and won 134 of 170 seats in the General Assembly.[24] North Carolina's experiment in biracial Fusionist politics, barely more than four years after its birth, was dead, destroyed by a calculated campaign of racial hatred.

Just two days later, on November 10, Wilmington was the scene of a momentous and disgusting event. The city's municipal elections were not scheduled until the following year. But after their resounding victory in the state election, the city's white fathers were not going to let the Fusionist mayor and city council sit in office that long. Led by Alfred Moore Waddell,[25] a former congressman, they orchestrated what may have been the only governmental coup d'état in American history. Waddell gathered a mob of roughly five hundred armed men and began a march through town with city hall as the objective. Any black man on the street was an open target, and many were shot on sight in what turned into a running battle through the city. The mob hunted down and killed Daniel Wright, a well-known black politician. On arriving at city hall, the men demanded the resignations of Fusionist mayor Silas Wright and the city council, which were given. The following day, all of the deposed blacks and white scalawags were placed on a train heading out of town, and Waddell was sworn in as mayor in an impromptu—and thoroughly illegal—ceremony.[26]

Alex Manly's newspaper office was burned, the looters triumphantly posing for a photo in front of it. He and his family escaped, making their way to Washington, D.C., and then Philadelphia, where he remained until his death in 1944. He had to work as a house painter to support his wife and two young sons.[27] Such were the costs of allegedly overplaying one's hand.

No fewer than twenty-two blacks were killed and nine wounded in what became known as the Wilmington Insurrection, although some have estimated the death toll as high as sixty. Under the lingering threat of violence, at least two thousand others emigrated from the city in the coming months. Daniels's *News & Observer*, mindful of the narrative it was sworn to uphold, ran as its headline, "DAY OF BLOODSHED," followed by the sub-headline, "Negroes Precipitate Conflict by Firing on Whites." [28]

Wilmington was the scene of North Carolina's most egregious violence of 1898. But in towns across the state, both before and after the election, tensions were no less palpable. Elizabeth City, another port town with a mixed-race population, was a case in point. In late September 1898, the town's Democratic newspaper reported the formation of a White Men's Union, much like the one created in Wilmington, with the purpose of electing Democrats. The paper prophesied that "if the white people all over the state will become interested in these unions and do their duty, on the 8th of November the Republican Party will be hurled from the pinnacle of exultation into the slough of despond. Otherwise many fear there will be a hot time in North Carolina some day."[29]

On the same page in the same edition, the paper reported the recent indictment in Pasquotank County of one John Barrington for "slander of a woman" and perjury. Barrington was reputedly a "negro politician, high up in the councils of the negro party, . . . a whipper-in of colored voters," and a "connecting link between the negro and Anglo-Saxon races, a piggin-headed, bullet-faced negro of the bacon-colored type." Like Alex Manly, Barrington was said to be a mulatto and a dangerous Republican operative who had been rooted out by the quick action of law-abiding whites.[30]

And also on the very same page, the *Weekly Economist* reported it had received a visit from the Currituck County Democratic candidate for the State House. Of course, it was none other than Samuel M. Beasley of Poplar Branch, whom the paper praised as a selfless patriot who wanted only to serve his state with no promise of personal reward. Enthusiastically, the paper recommended him: "Let him go in with a whoop, endorsed by the white men of the county."[31]

Six weeks later, when Election Day came around, there was evidence of considerable "whooping" in Elizabeth City. It did not erupt into open bloodshed as in Wilmington, although it could have. Local business owners closed up shop and monitored the polls, many of them carrying guns, to cajole their employees into voting Democratic. As the editor of the *Weekly Economist* described it, "In being armed, they were not law-abiding, but an old classic proverb says that laws are silent amid arms." Elizabeth City Democrats warned Republicans and Populists that they would "pay the first blood" if they dared to vote in force, and that only the Democrats' effective voter intimidation tactics "saved [the city] from scenes that would have made humanity shudder."[32]

It is not clear whether the same intimidation tactics were used in Currituck County, just twenty miles from Elizabeth City. Sam Beasley won election to the State House by an overwhelming margin, winning 976 votes compared to a total of 420 for the Republican and Populist candidates. Two years earlier, in 1896, the Democratic candidate for the same seat had won a far closer race with 713 votes to 612 for the Republican.[33] Thus, the total number of votes actually increased in 1898.[34] Whatever intimidation may have been at work, it apparently did not keep people from the polls, although the possibility of ballot-box fraud cannot be discounted. But unless the boxes were completely stuffed, something motivated the voters to shift away from the Republicans after 1896, and the answer is certainly race. The proportion of men voting Democratic in 1898 was almost equivalent to the proportion of whites living in the county at the time.[35] It was the same basic pattern witnessed throughout North Carolina that year.

With the Democrats firmly in control of the General Assembly after 1898, they lost no time in doing the one thing that would assure their continued dominance: barring black voters from the polls. Simmons and Daniels, as the orchestrators of the campaign, came up with a devious legislative strategy that, while race-neutral on paper, effectively decimated the black vote in North Carolina. They planned to amend the North Carolina Constitution to require all voters to pay poll taxes and pass a literacy test, which would eliminate black voters who were poor and/or illiterate. Of course, plenty of whites also were poor and illiterate, so they added a grandfather clause that waived the literacy requirement for any man or his descendant who had been registered to vote prior to 1867—in effect, that meant white men only. The new General Assembly quickly adopted the measure, and Democrats were so confident of their newfound ability to manipulate the voters that they put it up for a public referendum during the 1900 election.[36]

In preparation for the vote, the Red Shirt campaign cranked up again. Aycock, Glenn, Craig, and other stump speakers crisscrossed the state, accompanied by their armed, horse-mounted troopers. By their own reckoning, they covered four thousand miles by train and a thousand by carriage, addressing crowds of up to seventy-five thousand people. In the end, on the same day Aycock won the governorship, the voter disenfranchisement amendment passed by a margin of 59 to 41 percent. Remarkably, in each of North Carolina's eighteen counties where blacks comprised a majority of the population, a majority of voters chose to deprive black men of the vote, a result that defies explanation unless one factors in intimidation, voter fraud, or both.[37]

The numbers tell the story. In 1896, there had been 126,000 black registered voters in North Carolina. By 1902, there were only 6,100.[38] White men were firmly in control of the political machinery, and even while the Aycock administration pursued its school construction program, the long, dark era of Jim Crow began. Almost immediately, new laws were passed to extend legalized segregation into every aspect of daily life—not just schools but also railroad cars, restaurants, drinking fountains, and cemeteries. So it would remain for the next sixty years.

As the twentieth century dawned in North Carolina, the white political consensus was clear. Negro corruption, criminality, and licentiousness had to be stamped out. The white establishment now had the political wherewithal to make it happen.

Disenfranchisement and segregation were the start but by no means the end of the story.

"The Sun Will Rise Tomorrow on a State Redeemed from the Whiskey Evil–Saloons and Dispensaries will be Hunting for a City of Refuge," Raleigh *News and Observer*, the day before North Carolina's 1908 Prohibition referendum.

CHAPTER 10

THE ANTI-LIQUOR CRUSADE

When the *News & Observer* printed the story of Joshua Harrison's indictment in the disappearance of Kenneth Beasley, under the blaring front-page headline that named him as the "Kidnapper," it made a point to emphasize his alleged dealings in "spirituous liquors" and his reputation as a "blind tiger man."[1] Alcohol and the public dangers associated with it were the themes of the day.

Any reader glancing across the same front page would have noticed another headline, perhaps even more shocking: "Bloody Revenge: Rastus Spurrer Refused Liquor to Negroes, They Knocked Him Senseless and Laid Him on the Track Before a Train, Which Finished the Ugly Work." The story came from Charlotte, where apparently a white man had been murdered by two African-Americans because he refused to give them a drink when they demanded it. Another white man apparently witnessed the crime, and after he identified the offending Negroes, they were apprehended. A coroner's jury was assembled, and within one day of the killing, the jury "returned a verdict that the Negroes were guilty of murder in the first degree."[2]

In that period of relative calm during the late 1870s and 1880s, when paternalistic white leaders were preaching the gospel of education and moral "uplift" for blacks, some of them sought common political cause with black leaders. One issue where common ground seemed possible was liquor prohibition.

Among those who sought to restrict alcohol consumption or even to ban it outright, black and white leaders each saw an advantage in working with the other. For white prohibitionists, the calculus was simple: they needed votes, and at least for the time being black Southerners were a viable voting bloc. As for blacks, they saw their participation in the anti-liquor movement as a way to gain acceptance and respectability from whites. The great Booker T. Washington, who always urged his fellow blacks to make themselves worthy of white people's respect, believed that abolition of alcohol would bring his people benefits "second only to the abolition of slavery."[3]

It seemed like political alliances between blacks and whites were feasible in North Carolina and elsewhere in the South. But it did not last for several reasons. The biggest factor was the crashing economy in the 1890s, which turned everything upside down and stoked the same white racial resentments that ultimately doomed the Fusionist political experiment in North Carolina. It also ruined whatever goodwill existed between black and white prohibition activists.

The first steps toward prohibition in the 1890s concerned the regulation of sales, not the banning of alcohol outright. The first method was a legal innovation known as the "dispensary." It was a sort of government-run liquor store, and a forerunner of the local Alcoholic Beverage Control (ABC) stores that even today are the only facilities where bottled liquor may be sold legally in North Carolina. In 1899, at least thirty towns petitioned the General Assembly to pass ordinances to ban private saloons and establish a dispensary within their town limits. In Fayetteville, for example, supporters of the dispensary submitted a petition signed by "more than 1,100 white men and 68 white women"—and, by implication, no blacks. They also testified before a legislative committee that a competing petition to oppose restrictions on liquor sales was signed by "200 Negroes and 150 drunkards."[4]

In Raleigh, Josephus Daniels was involved in a similar fight. Through his influence, the General Assembly placed a public referendum on a dispensary on the 1900 ballot. Daniels, a dedicated Methodist, viewed alcohol as a social evil. But he also saw this as an opportunity to flex the muscle of North Carolina's recently enacted voter disenfranchisement laws. In his memoirs, Daniels recalled the scene when blacks sought to vote in the precinct surrounding Raleigh's historically black Shaw University. He issued a formal legal challenge to each black voter in the precinct, except for a few he knew to be teachers, ministers, or other educated types. Due to the legal challenge, the registrar had no choice but to compel the black voters, while standing at the polling place with a crowd gathered, to read from a portion of the North Carolina Constitution, to define the term *ex post facto law*, or to pronounce correctly the words lieutenant governor. Wrote Daniels, "I justified my act by reflecting that these Negroes were being used by the liquor forces to their own undoing in the debauchery of their race.... But it was cruel.... After a dozen had made the attempt and failed, the other uneducated Negroes did not seek to vote."[5]

The outcome of the 1900 Raleigh referendum need come as no surprise. With the black vote effectively neutralized, Raleigh not only approved the dispensary but also passed an ordinance to prohibit alcohol production within the city limits.[6]

The Raleigh referendum illustrates the larger political trend that eventually led to complete prohibition of alcohol in North Carolina. After 1900, with blacks no longer a viable voting bloc, prohibitionists had free reign to shape whatever legislation they pleased. And they lost little time in doing so.

In his message to the General Assembly in 1903, Governor Aycock called for a statewide law to prohibit both the sale and manufacture of liquor, although not beer or wine, everywhere in North Carolina except in incorporated towns; the distinction between towns and the countryside was important, since towns already were able to enact local ordinances and had police departments to enforce them. U.S. senator Furnifold Simmons, Aycock's patron and the godfather of the White Supremacy Campaign, gave his enthusiastic support. In a public statement, Simmons proclaimed that small distilleries scattered throughout the countryside "debauched the morals and the politics within the radius of their influence. Besides, many of them have become recruiting stations for the Republican [read: black] party. . . . In a large measure, they are undoing the work of the schools and churches in these communities."[7]

As Simmons, Aycock, and their followers saw it, the problem was not just violent black men drinking too much cheap booze; it was the white liquor distillers who put the bottle into the Negroes' hands. Thornwell Jacobs, a white Presbyterian clergyman and later president of Oglethorpe University in Atlanta, put it succinctly in a 1906 book, "What is the Negro problem? Rakes and rum—white rakes, white rum." White liquor producers "make a brute and demon of the already brutish Negro, and cause him to commit outrages on our noble womanhood."[8]

The resulting North Carolina legislation, which effectively prohibited all liquor production in unincorporated areas, was named the Watts Law, after the Democratic leader of the House, Alston D. "Aus" Watts of Iredell County. It was introduced in January 1903, on the second day of the legislative session. It passed in February in a largely party-line vote and took effect on July 1, 1903.[9]

Meanwhile, the few Republican-leaning newspapers remaining in North Carolina called foul, claiming the legislation was motivated not by any legitimate concern over public safety or morality but by simple greed for political control. They charged that the Watts Law would eliminate five hundred small distilleries, owned primarily by Republicans in unincorporated areas, "because a few rich men who were members of the Democratic Party wished to drive out the small establishments in order that they might have a monopoly of the business in North Carolina."[10] And because those wealthy Democrats wanted to eliminate liquor as a Republican recruiting tool.

At the same time it was enacting the Watts Law, the General Assembly churned out a curious series of local ordinances—at least forty between January and March 1903—creating new municipal entities where none existed previously, some with the explicit purpose of banning certain types of liquor in certain neighborhoods. For example, "An Act to Incorporate Bethel Baptist Church in Orange County" forbade production of any alcoholic beverage—except grape wine, for some reason—within four miles of the church; "An Act to Incorporate Powellsville Methodist Episcopal Church South in Bertie County" prohibited all liquor production within three miles of the church.[11]

And then there was Chapter 276 of the Public Laws of 1903, entitled "An Act to Prohibit the Manufacture and Sale of Spirituous Liquors Within Certain Localities." To anyone accustomed to reading statutes, it seems a masterpiece of collaborative legislation. It prohibited sale and manufacture of liquor within one mile of eight specific sites, mostly churches and schoolhouses, in four different counties; within one and one-half miles of four such sites in three counties; within two miles of seventy sites in twenty-four counties; within two and one-half miles of three sites in three counties; within three miles of ninety-four sites in thirty counties; within three and one-half miles of one site in one county; within four miles of forty-two sites in nine counties; and within five miles of one site in one county.

In today's political parlance, one might call it "spot zoning": deliberately drawing legal boundaries to benefit or damage someone's personal interests. Otherwise, what could have been the purpose of such an elaborate patchwork? One suspects that the Democrats, having won control of the General Assembly, were determined to run roughshod over those who had opposed them while protecting the interests of their supporters.

Representative (later Senator) Sam Beasley of Currituck County was in on the act. He sponsored and won legislative approval for Chapter 378 of the Public Laws of 1903, "An Act to Prohibit the Manufacture and Sale of Liquors, Cider, or Medicated Bitters Near Certain Churches in Currituck County." Effective July 1, 1903, it was illegal to manufacture or sell any of those types of drink—but not wine, significantly—within three miles of six designated spots in the county. Five were churches, ranging from Asbury Methodist near Coinjock in the northern part of the county to Powells Point Missionary Baptist in the south. And then there was the sixth location: Odd Fellows Hall in Poplar Branch.

What exactly was going on in those shadowy, swampy woods behind the schoolhouse? If Joshua Harrison was running a bootleg operation, possibly with the aid of one or more accomplices, it would not have been out of character for that time and place. Although popular folklore, stoked by legends such the Hatfields and the McCoys, tends to associate moonshining with Appalachian mountaineers, it has a long, documented history in the northeastern North Carolina swamps as well. Frank Stephenson Jr., the son of a long-serving North Carolina Alcohol Law Enforcement agent, wrote about the bootlegging industry that flourished in the Prohibition era and continued into the 1990s. It was especially widespread in the nearly inaccessible region along the Roanoke and Chowan Rivers, where thick woods were interspersed with countless winding creeks. According to Stephenson, hundreds of stills operated in that area and were never detected.[12]

As Stephenson tells it, a moonshiner looked for three factors in choosing a location for his still. He needed isolation, a plentiful water supply, and a luxuriant canopy of trees to provide cover.[13] All of those things abounded in the Maple Swamp. Plus, Currituck County had another asset for bootleggers: by water, it was not far from Norfolk, a seaport city growing bigger and more notorious for its dives and speakeasies. In fact, the Norfolk market provided support throughout the Prohibition era for Buffalo City, a former logging community in the deep woods of Dare County, just across the Albemarle Sound from Currituck. Although the site of Buffalo City now lies abandoned in the swamp, in the early 1900s it had a population of three thousand people, nearly all of whom were involved in producing moonshine rye whiskey. Thus, it well earned its reputation as the moonshine capital of the United States. Buffalo City men transported their goods to Norfolk by dark of night "in rows of casks tied on trotlines towed behind boats. If the feds pursued a boat, the crew cut the lines and the kegs sank—to be retrieved later."[14]

Whatever was happening in the Maple Swamp woods, Sam Beasley soon found reason to amend the statute he had pushed through the General Assembly in 1903. On January 9, 1905, it passed a new ordinance, adding new restrictions to the 1903 statute. Now, wine production was prohibited, along with that of hard liquor and other alcoholic drinks. And in addition to the six localities mentioned in the 1903 statute, alcohol sale and manufacture was now prohibited within three-mile distances of two new spots: Hebron Methodist Church, located one mile from Joshua Harrison's farm in Jarvisburg; and Newbern's Landing, the dock on Currituck Sound owned by Harrison's relatives, who would later supply his bond money.[15]

When the time came to testify in court, Senator Beasley made no bones about why he had structured his legislation this way. He openly swore he did it for the purpose of putting Joshua Harrison out of business, because everyone in the county knew Harrison, despite his advantageous marriage years before, was a public menace. He was a purveyor of scuppernong wine, as well as a Republican, a scalawag, a terrorizer of the community, and an all-around brute.[16]

Although Harrison claimed in the press that Beasley's anti-liquor strategy had not caused him damage, there is evidence it had. The Currituck County court records, sparse as they are, show that the new ordinances at least caused him inconvenience, and probably financial trouble. And like Pat Crowe, who claimed his butcher shop had been squelched by the Cudahy business conglomerate out in Omaha, he may well have been angry about it.

In the September 7, 1904, session of Currituck County Criminal Superior Court, Harrison found himself charged with "selling vinous liquor without a license," apparently under the 1903 statute. As with his previous charges, the record of what happened in court is sparse: details of the factual allegations, where the alleged sales occurred, the identity of the jurors or the attorneys, how the trial was conducted. The Minute Docket says only that Harrison, as in most of his previous courtroom encounters, was able to contrive a verdict of not guilty. During the March 2, 1905, session, Harrison was again in court, charged under the revised 1905 statute, this time with the more general offense of "selling liquor without a license." And finally, in the September 1905 session, he was charged with "disposing of mortgaged property." It is not clear what that meant, but it suggests Harrison was having financial difficulty. In all three cases, the verdict was the same: not guilty.[17]

In the meantime, of course, Kenneth Beasley had disappeared into the woods behind the schoolhouse on February 13, 1905.

North Carolina's anti-liquor crusade continued. Some prohibition advocates, seeing how difficult it was to prosecute bootleggers such as Harrison under local ordinances, wanted to go farther and pass a statewide referendum prohibiting all forms of alcohol in all of North Carolina, whether incorporated or not. They put it on the ballot for a special election on May 26, 1908. In the run-up to the vote, the usual Democratic dignitaries made another statewide speaking blitz. They argued that statewide prohibition would prevent the Negro from regaining political influence,[18] as if the disenfranchisement amendment had not already accomplished that objective.

One prohibition advocate, in a message printed and distributed statewide prior to the referendum, called for North Carolinians, and especially public officials, to act with singular purpose in stamping out the bootleg menace:

> The effectiveness of prohibition, like all other prohibitory laws, depends upon the local authorities. If we have sheriffs and constables and police and magistrates who are in sympathy with blind tigers, the blind tigers will flourish. If these officers are in enmity with the blind tiger and in full sympathy with a rigid enforcement of the law, the blind tiger will soon seek other fields for his devilish operations. Hence the necessity for a great big majority for prohibition. Let us make it so large that the officers of the law will know that the people are earnest and that they mean to see the law enforced. Let us make it so big that the wretch who would engage in the illicit manufacture or sale of liquor will know that there is no hiding place for him in North Carolina, and that, if he would engage in this wicked business he must go beyond her borders.

Those words were composed by Thomas J. Jarvis, the wizened former governor and senator,[19] whose family allegedly included one such "wretch." Jarvis might have taught even Aus Watts, who later would resign in a prostitution scandal, a few things about political hypocrisy.[20] But before Jarvis wrote this soliloquy, he had some family business to dispose. In March 1907, he found himself in an Elizabeth City courtroom, acting as defense counsel for his black-sheep brother-in-law.

Part III

The Trial

Defense lawyer and former governor Thomas J. Jarvis, 71 years old at the time of trial.

CHAPTER 11

BATTLE LINES DRAWN

Governor Jarvis could not have relished the thought of representing Joshua Harrison at trial. Even if he thought his brother-in-law was being railroaded, the mere allegation of child kidnapping was despicable. The trial would inevitably bring out rumors of Harrison's bootlegging activities. Like Josephus Daniels, Jarvis was a devoted layman in the Methodist Church, and he must have known that none of it would sit well with his neighbors, let alone the press.

Jarvis was seventy-one years old by 1907. He had his legal practice in Greenville, which he had established after his return from Rio in 1889, but by the 1900s he was looking to wind things down. In 1904, John C. Kilgo, the president of Trinity College, had offered Jarvis the deanship of its new law faculty. The Methodist school, located in Durham, was growing rapidly thank to an infusion of tobacco money from the Duke family, for whom it would later be renamed. But Jarvis politely declined, believing he was too old to take on the responsibility.[1] He would rather spend his later years as a philanthropist and elder statesman, not as a hands-on administrator, and certainly not by trying vicious cases in the courtroom.

But if Jarvis's sister came to him to save her husband one more time, he hardly could have refused. He would sit at the counsel table, where hopefully his white-bearded, Confederate veteran[*] presence would make an impression on the jury. But the nuts and bolts of the defense would be left to younger colleagues.

Two of those colleagues would provide political balance to Harrison's defense. In a politically charged case, a defendant would need to keep his bases covered.

Edwin F. Aydlett, who had stepped into the case immediately after Harrison's indictment and represented him in the pre-trial motions, was more than just the head of Elizabeth City's largest law firm. He was known as the "Grand Wizard" of the Democratic Party in the First Congressional District. According to Keith Saunders, the son of W. O. Saunders, Elizabeth City's pioneering newspaper editor, "No political move was made, no public enterprise projected, no public improvements undertaken, no political candidacy announced without the sanction and approval of the Grand Wizard. From his law offices on Main Street he made and unmade politicians, and no business could prosper that thwarted his will."[2]

Aydlett's co-counsel was Isaac M. "Ike" Meekins. Thirty-two years old in 1907, Meekins was an up-and-comer among Elizabeth City's legal community. And unlike the majority of the town's white citizens, he was a Republican. In 1897, at an extremely young age, Meekins had served briefly as mayor of Elizabeth City. It was an experiment in Republican government that did not last long, due to the events of 1898.[3]

On the prosecution side, former senator Beasley went to the trouble of hiring special counsel to argue the case against Harrison. It was a routine practice, although it would seem questionable today

---

[*] As most courtroom observers were aware, Jarvis's right arm was paralyzed from a wound he received at the Battle of Drewry's Bluff in the futile defense of Richmond in May 1864.

for a crime victim's family to hire a prosecutor to try to send someone to prison. Any victim with deep pockets might, for example, hire an attorney who would then owe his paycheck to the victim, who might want nothing more than personal vengeance. The duty of a state prosecutor, by contrast, is to seek justice rather than vengeance, and to pursue a case only to the extent justified by the law and the facts. Private prosecutions are no longer permitted at all in federal criminal cases, and there are few instances, if any, where they are allowed at the state level.[4]

But in that era, state budgets were small, and the prosecutor's office consisted of only one man: Solicitor Hallet Sydney Ward, who had to balance his prosecutorial duties with his private practice. If Senator Beasley wanted to hire his own legal guns to assist in dealing with his child's kidnapper, who clearly had means to hire distinguished counsel of his own, the court was not about to stand in his way. So the senator brought in four such guns, all of them tough, experienced local attorneys: J. Haywood Sawyer and Walter L. Cohoon of Elizabeth City and William M. Bond and William D. Pruden of Edenton.

Not that the state's solicitor, Ward, lacked ability. At age thirty-six, he had been in practice, both civil and criminal, more than a dozen years. As the solicitor for the state's First Judicial District, which covered most of the northeastern quadrant of North Carolina, he traveled over rough roads from one county seat to the next. His secretary, Fred Kelly, recalled years later that Ward was not able to carry all of his Supreme Court Reports—published volumes of court decisions—with him on horseback, so he memorized all the case names and page numbers, which never failed to impress the judges. Ward also was known for his fiery, uninhibited courtroom oratory, so much so that he earned a nickname that played on his first and middle initials. People called him "Hot Shot" Ward or "Hot Stuff" Ward, depending on the source. In fact, when he was called upon to speak at events such as Fourth of July picnics, he rarely was introduced by his given name.[5]

Beasley and Ward shared a political kinship. They were both solid Democrats, and Ward had also served briefly in the General Assembly; he won a seat in the State Senate in 1898, the year of the landslide, when Beasley was first elected to the House. And when Ward was first appointed to the solicitor position in 1904, it of course came from their mutual ally, Governor Aycock.

It may well have surprised them, then, to see Charles B. Aycock riding into town, making his appearance on the opposing side of the courtroom. Aycock had, in fact, been retained as Harrison's lead defense counsel. The Republican scalawag, accused bootlegger, and child abductor would be defended by North Carolina's most acclaimed Democrat, the champion of its children, its women, and its morality.

Why in the world did Aycock agree to fight that battle? He had left the governorship in early 1905, as the state constitution at the time limited the governor to one term. But by 1907, he was still only forty-eight. Although he had not expressed interest publicly, he might well have contemplated another run for office, perhaps for the U.S. Senate. Aycock must have known Joshua Harrison's trial would make banner headlines across the state, and his defense of such a notorious character might tarnish him, especially if he failed to make a strong case for his client's innocence.

The simplest explanation may in the end be the correct one. The former governor needed to make a living. He was in a law partnership, based in Goldsboro, with Frank Daniels, one of his boyhood friends and the brother of editor Josephus. Like any attorney with an office to run, he needed business. Aycock, who was getting back into the hustle of private practice after several years of low-paid government service, also had to support a wife and seven children, all under the age of eighteen.

Aside from the money, Harrison's plight may have appealed to Aycock's sense of injustice. Whatever he thought of his client, Aycock had always viewed himself as an advocate for the underdog; those sentiments had, after all, motivated his rural education crusade. Looking at Harrison, he may have seen a friendless man who was in desperate need of an advocate and who might, for all Aycock knew in the early stages of the case, have been the victim of a political purge. Harrison had been charged with a crime more than eighteen months after the fact, based on eyewitness accounts that seemingly appeared out of the blue with no explanation. To any skilled defense attorney, that would have sounded suspicious, like a case in which jurors might have reasonable doubts.

For Aycock, it probably seemed like a case he could win, and at that stage in his life he definitely wanted a win. For all the success of the school-building campaign, his governorship had ended on some discouraging notes. It bothered him that he had not been able to curtail the lynchings, and he had concerns about side effects the vitriolic White Supremacy Campaign had brought to North Carolina, even if he would never dare to say so publicly.

School funding, for example, had turned out to be a more contentious issue than he expected. Underneath all the racist campaign rhetoric, Aycock was serious about educating black students as well as white. His methods were rooted in white paternalism, and his goal was to keep blacks content with their subservient role. But Aycock wanted blacks—or at least the most capable of them—to learn to read. As soon as he took office, that put him at odds with other Democrats, who would have been pleased for every Negro in North Carolina to remain an illiterate field hand. In 1901, those Democrats in the legislature proposed a new amendment to the North Carolina Constitution intended to divide school funding based upon the taxes paid by whites and blacks. Essentially, black schools would be funded only with taxes collected from blacks, most of whom were dirt poor. Aycock correctly saw that the measure would slash the already pitiful amount of money the state spent on black schools, and although as governor he did not have veto power, he was determined to prevent that action. Only a few months after leading his party to its groundbreaking 1900 victory, Aycock discreetly spread word in the General Assembly that he would resign the governorship if the amendment passed.[6]

The legislators withdrew the amendment in the face of Aycock's threat; it simply wouldn't do for the White Supremacy Campaign's most visible public spokesman to abandon it so abruptly. But the issue was raised again at the Democratic State Convention of 1904 in Greensboro. Just as Aycock was about to leave office, the most virulent white supremacists in the party introduced a resolution calling again for a division of school funding by race. It appeared to have broad support at first, and some urged Aycock not to speak against the resolution, for fear he would be shouted down. But he stood his ground and was able to sway the delegates to his side by appealing to their "statesmanship, and not passion or prejudice." Aycock's speech was seconded by former governor Jarvis, his ally and a "great friend of education."[7] Jarvis had done Aycock a big favor, which he no doubt remembered two years later.

Despite those victories, Aycock had to watch as his successor, Governor Glenn, backtracked on the effort to support black schools. Glenn had never concurred on the need to educate blacks, and over time the disparity between funding of white and black schools increased. Aycock viewed it as a betrayal of commitments he had made in his own campaign.[8] Also, as Glenn's term progressed, the lynchings continued.

In 1905 and 1906, as Aycock appeared in court in Raleigh and elsewhere, his fellow attorneys noticed an air of resentment about him. He hated losing a case, which was nothing unusual for a trial attorney. But Aycock also was sensitive to any criticism of his performance and would respond to it in vehement, personal terms, even toward judges. In one case, when he unsuccessfully appealed the embezzlement conviction of one Thomas Dewey, Aycock wrote a vituperative letter to Justice Henry Groves Connor of the North Carolina Supreme Court complaining that "our fathers once fought a fight against priest-craft. If things continue on as they are now it will be necessary for somebody to make a fight against judge-craft." Justice Connor saw that as a tactless blunder and rebuked him for it. But if Aycock was chastened by the criticism, he did not remain so for long. When he heard rumors that other attorneys were disappointed that he chose to represent another unpopular client, Aycock proclaimed in a courtroom speech, "I wish to say that if every man in this court were a devil and he were seeking my blood, I should say what I please." And so he did. In another case, after Aycock won an acquittal for his client by challenging some of the state's evidence, he could not resist a parting jab. With the judge, jury, and gallery all still assembled within earshot, he turned to his client and told him, "Well, you're clear now, and don't go stealing any more corn."⁹

It may be that the former governor, by the time Joshua Harrison's case came around, just was not as concerned about his political image as he once was. The opportunity to win a case, to strike a blow for the accused—and to make some money in the process—may have been more important to him than seeking office again.

Also, Aycock may have been encouraged that the presiding judge in Elizabeth City was to be a political ally and yet another of his best friends. Judge William R. Allen was a fellow Wayne County native who had known Aycock since childhood. Before taking his seat on the bench, Allen had served in the State House, having been elected in 1898 and 1900. He was one of the most loyal supporters of Aycock's agenda for the schools, prohibition, and everything else.¹⁰

And so by the time the trial commenced on March 14, 1907, anyone could see that it would be quite a show—a full-blown trial with nine attorneys, two of them former governors. It promised to be North Carolina's courtroom drama of the year.

The location had been determined well in advance. The court, sitting in Currituck County, had consented to the defense motion for change of venue. Currituck was just too small, and the parties too well known, for an impartial jury to be seated. The court selected Pasquotank County, only a short distance by road from Currituck, and the defense had argued for it to be moved even farther.¹¹ But Elizabeth City at least promised a convenient locale. It was a bustling riverside town of more than six thousand people in the 1900 census, a number that had nearly doubled since 1890.¹² The Norfolk Southern Railway, which had recently completed its link between Norfolk and Elizabeth City, had spurred much of that growth. New dockyards and warehouses were springing up along the Pasquotank River, plus hotels, bars, and at least two daily newspapers. And there was a beautiful brick Colonial courthouse, finished in 1882, finally replacing the wooden structure lost in the Civil War fire.

The courthouse remains in use today with some alterations. New wings have been added, but the central portion looks much the same inside and out. The Superior Courtroom had an immensely high ceiling bordered with a pressed-metal molding, and the cream-colored walls were lined with tall Italianate Victorian windows.[13] It was designed to evoke a sense of reverence and judicial majesty, as it probably did, even if the dramas played out there were often less than reverential or majestic.

Judge Allen called the trial to order at 9:45 on Monday morning, but on motion from the defense actual business did not start until 2:30 that afternoon. From the beginning, Harrison's attorneys probably noted some ominous signs. Between them, the state and the defense had subpoenaed more than one hundred people as potential witnesses. But upon arriving in town, the defense discovered that some of its witnesses—which ones are unknown—were refusing to confer with them because the state also had subpoenaed them.[14] Aycock asked the judge to order the witnesses to cooperate with the attorneys, which he did, giving them several hours to confer.[15] But for any attorney, it is disconcerting to go into a trial without a firm grasp of what his witnesses' testimony will be, and whether the witnesses are really on his side or not. Had Aycock more hair on his balding head, he might well have been tearing at it.

A look around the courtroom gallery also would not have offered encouragement. Everyone expected a large crowd; high-profile cases had a way of drawing people to the courthouse, especially in small towns without much else going on. But the first day of this case brought out an "immense audience who crammed every available foot of space" in the courtroom.[16] And in a bad sign for the defense, it looked like most of the crowd were Currituck residents who had taken the trouble of traveling the twenty-five-mile dirt road for the trial.[17] The defense had wanted to escape the local prejudices—and maybe the lynching risk—in Currituck County by changing venue, but it probably thought the trial had not been moved far enough.

The jury selection was a quick affair, lasting no more than an hour or so. The prospective jurors were asked variations on only three questions: (1) whether they were related to the Harrison or Beasley families, (2) whether they had heard anyone discussing the case, and if so, to what extent, and (3) whether they already had formed an opinion about the case. All twelve jurors were seated, the defense having excused just three people for cause and the state only one.[18]

As testimony in his trial began, Joshua Harrison had one advantage that many criminal defendants of that time and place did not. Every one of his twelve jurors was, like him, a white male. And most of them surely had voted for Charles Aycock for governor six years earlier. If an attorney's rhetorical skill could have any sway over the jury, then Harrison had reason to be hopeful.

Not surprisingly, the state called Sam Beasley as its first witness. Prosecutors often begin their cases with testimony from the victim's family, as it helps to introduce the jurors to the victim and to build sympathy for the family's loss.[19] By all accounts, the former state senator made a strong impression. Wearing his business suit and eyeglasses, and with the skill of a practiced public speaker, he testified authoritatively and with feeling, at times he seeming "visibly affected" when speaking about his young son.[20]

Although the press did not report that Beasley made any gestures or glances toward Harrison, it must have been a tense moment in the courtroom. The defendant was sitting with his attorneys at their table only feet away from the witness stand, wearing a thin-striped suit, turn-down collar, and black ribbon tie.[21] It was a typical outfit for a gentleman farmer of that time, which doubtless was how he wanted to be seen. But throughout the trial, as the prosecution witnesses spoke, "Harrison sat glaring, his gray-bearded jaw set like granite."[22]

Solicitor Ward began by asking Beasley about the last time he had seen Kenneth, just before bedtime on the Friday evening before the senator left for Raleigh over two years earlier. He said, "At that time, I had three children."[23] By placing Kenneth in the past tense, Beasley let the jury know that although Harrison was charged with kidnapping, not murder, he had no doubt about what really had befallen his son.

Patiently, Ward had Beasley recount how he was informed of his boy's disappearance, his hasty return home, and how he and the neighbors spent the next week searching the swamp behind the Odd Fellows Hall. Beasley brought with him an illustrated map showing the layout of the schoolhouse, the adjoining parcels of land, and the roads. The map was admitted into evidence as an exhibit,[24] which the jurors probably found helpful, as the confusing topography would have been hard to picture otherwise.

Beasley also revealed details of the search that had not yet been reported in the press. For a couple of months after most of the neighbors had given up looking for Kenneth, Beasley kept combing the woods with his older son, Moran, and a few friends. After the damp winter weather subsided, they went back to some parts of the swamp where the water had been too deep to search completely. They poked through every brush pile they could find, plumbed stagnant pools of water, and still found no remains.[25] By telling the jury this, Beasley wanted to show that he had not jumped to a conclusion that Harrison or anyone else had run off with his son.

He had not jumped to the conclusion despite having reason to be suspicious. At this point in Beasley's testimony, he went into Harrison's motives for wishing him harm. Yes, he had drafted the 1903 anti-liquor ordinances with Harrison in mind. And in October 1904, he had a chance encounter with Harrison when they passed each other somewhere on the road between Poplar Branch and Jarvisburg.

According to Beasley, Harrison had questioned him aggressively about the "wine legislation for Currituck County, and especially Poplar Branch Township." Harrison seemed angry because he had heard through others that "the legislation I [Beasley] had passed about wine in Poplar Branch was intended for him."[26]

To that, Beasley retorted that Harrison had indeed inspired the legislation because he was the only man in the township who was making a disturbance by selling wine, and the local "church people" had petitioned the legislature about "prohibiting its sale in the Township."[27]

Harrison, his temper flaring, shouted back, "If I cannot sell it on my own premises, I'll be goddamned if I don't sell it on Miss Anne's. If I cannot sell it in gallon quantities, I will sell it in barrels!"[28] According to Manly Wade Wellman's account, Beasley testified Harrison had then added, "When they stop me from selling it they'll be goddamned sorry for it!" The trial transcript does not reflect that statement.[29]

Battle Lines Drawn

There were no other witnesses to this roadside encounter, but one must say that Beasley's recollection of it carried a ring of truth. The 1903 legislation was in fact targeted to specific neighborhoods, including Poplar Branch. And just over two months after the encounter, in January 1905, Beasley had indeed sponsored the new legislation focused on Harrison's farm and family land. It is not clear what Harrison meant by "Miss Anne's," but it might have been any of his wife's family properties at Jarvisburg, which was named after the family. Beasley foresaw that Harrison would move his bootlegging activities away from Poplar Branch to evade the 1903 law. And the 1905 legislation made another notable change. Under the prior law, it was still legal for someone to produce wine and liquor on his own property in quantities of ten gallons or more—that is, in barrels. After the 1905 revision, that was no longer allowed.[30] It was as if Beasley had listened to Harrison make his threats, then drafted the new law expressly to preempt them.

Beasley and Harrison did not see each other again until late February 1905, the second Monday after Kenneth disappeared. Harrison and his teacher daughter, Miss Nina, made an unannounced call at the Beasley homeplace. Ostensibly, the teacher wanted to express her sympathy to Kenneth's mother, who by all press accounts was grief stricken and near collapse. But as Beasley recalled it on the stand, Harrison wanted to get down to personal brass tacks.

Harrison took him aside and asked if he had read the *News & Observer*'s February 24 article, the one that hinted about Harrison being seen riding away from Poplar Branch with a boy in his buggy. Harrison claimed to Beasley that the story was false, that he could prove his whereabouts on February 13 and afterward, and that he would appreciate it if Beasley would write to the newspaper's editors and denounce the story. Beasley quoted Harrison as saying, "It is perfectly absurd to entertain the kidnapping idea."[31]

Beasley responded that he was not going to make any public statement, and that no possibility seemed too absurd to consider, since he and the neighbors had searched the area and found no trace of the boy. Above all, he just wanted to get his son back. Harrison, as he was leaving, said, "If your son was kidnapped, some of your neighbors done it."³²

According to all recorded testimony, press coverage, and personal recollections, that was the last documented communication between Sam Beasley and Joshua Harrison. So far as anyone knows, they did not encounter each other again until the trial commenced two years later.

Finally, before Beasley left the stand, Ward asked about Kenneth's pocketknife. It was as if the ghost of Charley Ross had entered the courtroom, which may have been the solicitor's intent. Beasley said he had no idea where Kenneth could have gotten the knife, but Ward told the judge he intended to link the knife to the disappearance. The clear implication was that Harrison or someone connected with him had given the knife to Kenneth as bait to lure him into the woods, like the candy Mosher and Douglass had used to coax Charley into their wagon. Aycock, probably picking up on the allusion to the notorious case, objected to the speculation. Judge Allen said he would defer ruling on the objection until later, to see if Ward could prove what he promised.³³

Once Beasley was excused, it was clear he would not be asked about one item that had been reported in the papers. Neither side had brought up the attempted ransom drop in Rocky Mount in April 1905. For the state, there were obvious reasons for not broaching it. If the ransom demand was legitimate, and if it had been made by someone that far away, it would suggest someone other than Harrison was involved. For the defense, that might have been a helpful seed to plant in the jurors' minds, but it did not fit into its theory of the case. As the defense would later show, it wanted to convince the jurors there was no kidnapping at all, just an accidental, tragic disappearance.

The court was planning to adjourn for the evening at six-thirty, and the time was drawing near. Beasley was followed on the stand by Professor Jennings, the head teacher at Kenneth's school. He recounted how the boy had gone missing and how he had spread the word to the neighbors. And then the professor revealed a detail unreported in the press up to that time. He, like Miss Nina, was an itinerant teacher who boarded with a local family. At the time

Kenneth disappeared, he was residing in the home of Sam and Cassie Beasley.[34]

Toward the end of the day and continuing into the next morning, the jury heard from the neighbors: D. W. Woodhouse, who owned the store just down the road from Odd Fellows Hall; J. W. Poyner, the sheriff's deputy; W. A. Doxey; and E. B. Gallop. All of them had taken part in the nearly week-long search of the woods, the swamp, and the sound shoreline, and they all corroborated Beasley's account of it. They had assembled dozens of searchers and combed the area as exhaustively as they could, given the weather and the terrain.[35]

And then came the eyewitnesses. In any criminal case, these witnesses provide some of the most crucial testimony, and also the most troublesome. If the state has credible eyewitnesses to place the accused near the victim and crime scene, then it is a problem for the accused. But people's eyesight, memories, and even truthfulness can all be faulty, and the defense will naturally jump upon any flaw in the testimony. This case would be no exception.

Ward presented four witnesses in quick succession: Millard Morrisette, J. L. Turner, John Berry, and Lemuel Sivells.[36] All of them lived in northern Currituck, at various points along the main road running up the spine of the peninsula and on toward Norfolk. Morrisette and Turner lived near Coinjock, Berry and Sivells near Currituck Courthouse. Each told a similar story, although it varied in some specifics. Basically, it was the same story related in the "letter" described in the *News & Observer* article of February 24, 1905.[37] It told of a strange man with a boy in a buggy drawn by a dark-skinned mule, traveling north on that bitter, rainy afternoon of February 13.[38]

Morrisette testified that the odd travelers passed at around four in the afternoon. By that time, word of Kenneth's disappearance had not spread to that part of the county; none of the witnesses was aware of it yet. The boy was wearing a blue cap and appeared to have light hair and complexion, although Morrisette did not take particular notice of the driver and could not say for certain it was Harrison. Turner, testifying next, had known Harrison for twenty-five years and was sure he was the driver. As they passed, he saw Harrison throw a blanket over himself and the boy, as if to conceal them; underneath the blanket, the boy was wearing brown stockings, although that would seem difficult to spot with the passengers seated in the buggy. Turner also claimed to have spoken to Harrison but received no reply. Berry testified to the buggy and dark-skinned mule and said the boy was covered with a "storm apron" or some other material. The driver was speaking to the boy in a reassuring manner, something to the effect of "There, there." But although Berry knew Harrison, and the voice sounded like him, he could not positively identify Harrison as the driver. Sivells also testified to the same buggy and mule and saw the boy wrapped in a blanket—except for his head, curiously, which was still covered by the blue cap. But like Berry, Sivells had known Harrison for years and could not say for certain he was the driver.[39]

Aycock and Aydlett took turns with cross-examination of these witnesses, which the press described as "severe."[40] This is where one sees a flaw in the court's written transcript of the trial. It does not record every question and answer verbatim; in many places, it shows only the substance of the testimony, in summary. But it is not hard to guess the questions any competent defense attorney would have asked. An attorney would have hammered the witnesses for their vagueness and the uncertainty in their identifications. And the most obvious question of all: If they saw this strange man and boy ride past you, and shortly afterward they heard news that a boy had gone missing from school, why did they not report what they saw to any authorities until eighteen months later?

Why not, indeed? Of course, these men lived on isolated farms, where they worked hard all day and kept to themselves. They probably did not even have telephones. But still, it seems like discretion carried to an extreme. Was the sixty-six-year-old Harrison really so powerful and dangerous that he had these men afraid for their lives if they talked?

The records do not reflect how the witnesses responded to those queries, except for Turner. Even though he also had known Senator Beasley for years, he said nothing about it to him until September or October 1906 because "I did not think it was any of my business." Yet both the *News & Observer* and the *Charlotte Observer* described

Turner's testimony, and that of the other eyewitnesses, as "unshaken" by the cross-examinations.[41]

Perhaps what was so unshaken about this testimony was not the facts stated but the emotions they evoked. Imagine what the jurors and the crowd in the gallery must have felt as Millard Morrisette described, in his spare words, how the travelers drove by him in the rain. "The boy turned his head, put it out of the buggy, and looked at me for some time."[42]

KENNETH BEASLEY KIDNAPPING CASE

Harrison on Trial Charged With the Crime.

HAD UTTERED THREATS

Had Been Hard Feelings Between the Father and Defendant on Acconut of liquor Legislation, and Harrison Had Declared that Some One Should Suffer.

Elizabeth City, N. C., March 14.—

THE FARMER AND MECHANIC, RALEIGH

CHAPTER 12

REVENGE ON HIM OR HIS FAMILY, ONE

Around midmorning on the second day of the trial, the jury heard from another witness, one of several who claimed to have seen Kenneth in the aftermath of his disappearance. But he was perhaps the only one who was not mysteriously closed mouthed about it.

It was J. J. Pierce, who saw a boy he thought was Kenneth riding a streetcar in Norfolk roughly three weeks after he went missing. About one week after that, Pierce heard the story about Kenneth's going missing, whereupon he immediately contacted the senator, although the testimony does not indicate *how* they communicated. Pierce said he recognized Kenneth from having seen him on two prior occasions, one as long ago as 1902, when the boy would have been only five years old.[1] Pierce's testimony, like the others, is shrouded in uncertainty, but it does coincide with what the other eyewitnesses claimed to have seen. If it really was Kenneth in the buggy that rainy afternoon, then he was being driven north, toward Norfolk.

And Pierce, for whatever it was worth, had four character witnesses who testified briefly after him. They all attested that his reputation for honesty was good.[2]

Then came several more witnesses who recalled hearing Joshua Harrison speak with resentful, even violent, anger toward Sam Beasley for the damage he was causing to Harrison's livelihood. They all testified in quick succession, and the newspaper reports barely mention them. In fact, only their last names are in the trial transcript. But the theme of their testimony is clear. Mr. Ballance, a local steamboat captain, recalled purchasing some wine from Harrison in 1904. Harrison had commented to him that Beasley was attempting to pass a law against selling wine and said "God damn him, I will get revenge on him or his family, one." Mr. Dudley, at about the same time in 1904, heard Harrison voice the same sentiment, and that Beasley ought to be tarred and feathered, and "I [Harrison] would like to stir up the sticks." Mr. Levin testified Harrison had commented that Beasley was a political hack who "could be bought for fifty dollars," and that if he had the nerve to prohibit wine selling, "he would be damned sorry for him and his family."[3]

This type of testimony called for a healthy dose of skepticism. These witnesses claimed, more than two years after the fact, that they heard the defendant threaten, in advance, to do the very thing he was now accused of doing. The jurors might well have had doubts in their minds.

The same was true of the next witnesses, Mr. A. B. Parker and a Mr. Bunch. Parker claimed he had seen Harrison in Elizabeth City five days after Kenneth went missing, and Harrison told him that the boy was not lost, and he could put his hands on him at any time. Like the eyewitnesses along the Norfolk road, Parker did not relate this information to Senator Beasley until September 1906 because, in precisely the same words given by J. L. Turner, he thought it "none of his business."[4]

Bunch recalled a conversation with Harrison in December 1905, when Kenneth had been missing for ten months. Bunch had speculated to Harrison that the boy had died, lost in the woods. But Harrison said he knew better, that the boy was not lost and that although not enough money had yet been offered for his release, the boy would "come in" as soon as Harrison was paid off.[5] Bunch's testimony was vague and, like the others', late in coming. But here was the first testimony alluding to a ransom motive for the kidnapping.

And then, just after the lunch recess on Tuesday, the prosecution brought forth Thomas L. Baum to testify. Baum, like Millard Morrisette and John Berry, was one of the original grand jury witnesses against Harrison.* His testimony reads like a replay of what the jury had heard earlier that morning. Like Ballance, Baum claimed Harrison had made an offhand remark to him—in 1902, not 1904—that Beasley was trying to interfere with his wine business and would be "damned sorry for it." Also like Ballance, Baum went to Harrison to buy some wine—not in 1904, but on August 20, 1906, shortly before the grand jury met—and on that occasion Harrison blurted out his guilt but boasted that he felt safe because "it's catching before hanging."[6] Harrison told Baum, "By

---

* The Record on Appeal spells his name T. S. Bauman. Such misspellings were common throughout this case, in news articles as well as court documents. A.B. Parker, for instance, became A.B. Baker in some reporting.

BEASLEY'S SON TRACED

Witnesses Say They Saw Missing Boy with Harrison.

ALLEGED THAT HE CONFESSED

In Elizabeth City Kidnapping and Murder Case, Damaging Testimony Is Introduced Against Defendant — Witnesses Say He Told Them He Could Produce the Boy at Any Time.

Special to The Washington Post.

Elizabeth City, N. C., Mar. 15.—In the trial to-day of Joshua Harrison, charged with kidnapping and murdering Kenneth Beasley, the nine-year-old son of State Senator S. H. Beasley, of Currituck County, several witnesses testified to seeing Harrison on the day of the alleged kidnapping driving along a country road with a young companion who answered in many details the description of the missing lad, even to the color of the cap and stockings the boy is known to have worn the day of his disappearance.

Threw Blanket Over Boy.

One witness testified that upon his approach to the buggy Harrison threw a blanket over the boy, apparently to conceal him, and another witness testified to hearing Harrison trying to calm and soothe some one concealed under a blanket. A witness for the State testified that about the same time indicated by the other witnesses he saw Harrison driving rapidly in his buggy, holding between his knees a boy that answered the description of Kenneth Cross-examination failed to shake the testimony of these witnesses in any particular.

In the attempt to further establish a motive for the alleged kidnapping, the State introduced R Leven, who said he heard Harrison declare that Beasley ought to be tarred, feathered, and tied to a stake, and that he would like to apply the torch. T L Baum testified that Harrison told him before the kidnapping that Beasley would be sorry he ever introduced the liquor bill in the legislature.

Said Boy Was Not Lost.

A B Baker related to the jury a conversation with Harrison after the kidnapping in which Harrison said that the boy was not lost, and that he could lay his hands on him any time

T. C Woodhouse testified that Harrison said to him after the boy disappeared that Beasley had not offered enough money for the lad's return Harrison asked the witness to see Beasley and tell him so, remarking that it was expensive to keep the boy in the way he was being kept Woodhouse testified that Harrison told him he could produce the boy at any time.

The defense opened late in the afternoon with the testimony of two sons of Harrison who testified that their father was at home the day of the boy's disappearance

THE WASHINGTON POST,

god, they shall never see [the boy]," but it was "damned expensive" to keep him in the way he was being held, whereupon Baum cautioned him against making such "rash statements."[7]

But Baum, unlike the previous witnesses who supposedly had heard Harrison make rash statements, named two other people who were present with him on that August 1906 date. When he went to purchase the wine from Harrison, he was accompanied by J. W. Fisher and a black man identified variously in the record as Charlie Harris or Charlie Harrison.[8] And now the defense, aware of how the racial politics of liquor would play against their client, saw a welcome opening for some race-baiting.

For those who had seen Charles Aycock speak on the campaign trail, rather than in court, he was about to turn over a different leaf. In all the speeches he delivered in his political career, it is hard to find one in which he used the word *nigger*. Or at least when he did use it, he did so with irony or humor. All during the White Supremacy Campaign and afterward, Aycock pontificated at length about Negro political domination, Negro corruption, and Negro immorality. But he did not like the vulgarism now cautiously referred to as the "n-word." On the campaign trail, he wanted to be seen as folksy, yet gentlemanly and peace promoting, a spokesman of the people. *Nigger* was just such a low, degrading term—degrading to those who used it as well as to those it insulted. People who heard him speak often commented that Aycock's rhetorical style was that of "an evangelical preacher or great revivalist who wanted to arouse feelings of sin, guilt, and repentance" in his listeners. He wanted them to see their fault in allowing the Fusionists to take office in the first place, and then seek salvation by returning the Democrats to their rightful place of power.[9]

In 1898, a witness to one of Aycock's stump speeches recalled it like this: "After graphic narration of harrowing conditions in the state, he paused and said he was *not* yelling, 'Nigger! Nigger! Nigger!' And then, striding forward to the front of the stage with a stalking gesture, in the voice of a father speaking in reproachful shame to an offending child, he cried out loudly, 'White man! White man! White man!' " The audience erupted in a "frenzy of repentance" and resolved immediately to go out and vote against the Fusionists.[10]

That was back when Aycock was looking ahead to running for governor. Now, in the courtroom, he had a single purpose in mind. He had a professional duty to give his client a vigorous defense, and in those days of classic courtroom oratory and theatrics, that meant seizing an opportunity to ham it up in front of the jury and gallery.

As soon as the state finished its direct examination of Baum, Aycock lit into him on cross-exam with a "storm of raillery and satire" about how Baum had gone out to purchase wine with an African-American.[11]

"Did you give the nigger a drink?" asked Aycock. When Baum appeared confused, or maybe flustered, by the question, Aycock kept badgering him. He insinuated that Baum had met with Harrison to try and dupe him into confessing to the kidnapping, that Baum was trying to collect the thousand-dollar reward Sam Beasley had put forward, and that he had brought along a black man to corroborate the story, maybe promising to split the money with him.[12]

Then Aycock seemed to challenge Baum's Caucasian bona fides, demanding to know why he was socializing with a black man. "What was the nigger with you for? Did you take him because you thought he [Harrison] wouldn't tell [confess to] a white man, but would tell you and a nigger?" At some point, Hot Shot Ward must have objected, and there followed "considerable satirical merriment on the part of opposing counsel." Reports do not reflect exactly what Ward said, but after Aycock asked several more questions about "a man with his nigger," Ward probably thought he should refute any suggestion that he would rely on the credibility of a black to convict a white man. Of course he, as the elected solicitor, would never do anything like that; nor, as the good Pasquotank County jurymen knew, did he ever get any votes from black people. Whereupon Aycock shot back that everyone knew damn well he had never gotten any more black votes than Ward had.[13]

All along, the gallery was yukking it up. As the *Tar Heel* reporter noted, there was "laughter in court, suppressed by the Sheriff," who was probably standing in a corner behind the bench, shouting everyone to order.[14] And there was Judge Allen presiding over this show, with two attorneys—both of them his political allies—essentially trying to out-"nigger" each other in front of the jury.

Eventually, Baum was excused, and two character witnesses came forward to say that he was generally honest. But then the atmosphere in court went from the comical to the strange. Before the next witness took the stand, the judge instructed all ladies to exit the courtroom. The record does not reflect which side made that request, but presumably it was the state, since it knew the substance of its next witness's testimony. It was Thomas Clingman Woodhouse, named for one of North Carolina's legendary former U.S. senators and Confederate generals, and the brother of D. W. Woodhouse, the Poplar Branch storekeeper.

Woodhouse said he had known Joshua Harrison all his life and that, not long after Kenneth vanished, he and Harrison had encountered each other by chance. Harrison remarked that "Beasley's making a damned sight of fuss about one little boy. Give us two women and we can make us two nicer boys in a few minutes." Apparently, the court determined that comment was too smutty for female ears, and even the press concurred. Although the trial transcript contains the full statement, the *Tar Heel* account redacts it after the words, "Give us two women."[15]

And then Woodhouse recalled meeting Harrison at an auction on September 1, 1906, only days before the grand jury, where Woodhouse testified, issued its indictment on September 5. Harrison told Woodhouse he wanted to have a "heart-to-heart," but that they should meet in a less public place. The following day, they happened to meet on the road near Harrison's farm, and Harrison told Woodhouse the same thing he had said to Bunch and Baum: that Kenneth wasn't lost, that he could locate the boy at any time, that Senator Beasley had never offered enough reward, and that Harrison was tired of the expense of holding the boy hostage. Harrison then asked Woodhouse to convey this message to Beasley, which Woodhouse did the next day when he encountered Beasley at Currituck Courthouse.[16]

After hearing Woodhouse's story, Beasley asked him to return to Harrison with a promise that he would pay any amount of ransom for Kenneth's release, whereupon Woodhouse somehow arranged to meet with Harrison at Woodhouse's "room," location unknown. While the two men were in the room alone together, Woodhouse locked the door, ostensibly to prevent Harrison from sneaking away and to get Harrison "to own what he had owned before [to admit to the kidnapping]." At that point, Harrison refused to discuss the matter with Woodhouse. Apparently overcome with fear or shame, Harrison sat down and cried, though "no tears flowed."[17] Woodhouse claimed he then returned to Beasley to report he had failed to work out the ransom deal, and Beasley then resolved to take the case to court.

According to the state's version of the case, this was the culminating event that led to the indictment of Joshua Harrison. The alleged kidnapper, a grizzled, profane, sixty-eight-year-old farmer who had won not-guilty verdicts in trials for two previous murders and several other crimes over a forty-year period, broke down and cried when confronted about his previous admission of guilt in the kidnapping of Kenneth Beasley.

Just after Woodhouse finished his testimony, Sam Beasley was recalled to the stand. He confirmed Woodhouse's version of the events, as well as the stories told to him by Turner, Parker, Levin, and Pierce. He also added that before he asked Woodhouse to return to Harrison with his offer to pay the ransom, Beasley had consulted with his legal counsel. But he did not identify the attorney. Nor did he elaborate on *how* all of this pre-telephonic, horse-and-buggy communication came together over a five-day period, from the first conversation between Harrison and Woodhouse, to the gathering of Morrisett, Berry, Baum, and Woodhouse as witnesses, to the seating of the grand jury and its indictment.[18]

With that, it was the end of the day, and the state rested its case. Hot Shot Ward apparently felt confident about what he had put forth, although he did reserve the right to call rebuttal witnesses after the defense presented its case. Later, he would find that opportunity useful.

The defense strategy, to highlight weaknesses in the prosecution case, highlighted some of its own.

CHAPTER 13

Laying Out the Alibis

The defense began its case first thing the following morning, and it turned out to be a brisk affair. It called at least fifteen witnesses and was able to squeeze them all into one day of court. Aycock performed most of the direct questioning, with Ward, Sawyer, and Bond taking turns with the cross-examinations. Naturally, the magic words for any criminal defense are reasonable doubt, and it did not take long to see how Harrison's attorneys intended to get the jurors into that bent of mind. They would establish doubt as to whether there had been a kidnapping at all, and even if so, whether it was physically possible for Harrison to have been the culprit.

There had been plenty of weaknesses in the state's case, and the defense did all it could to highlight them. But in the end, if Aycock and his colleagues could have spoken candidly, they would have acknowledged that their own case did not go well. Too many of their witnesses had credibility problems that at times seemed to mirror the flaws in the prosecution testimony.

As with the prosecution, the defense had witnesses situated along the road to Norfolk north of Poplar Branch on the afternoon Kenneth disappeared. They also told of the man driving the buggy drawn by the dark-skinned mule, accompanied by a boy. Whereas the state's four eyewitnesses thought the driver was Harrison, the defense's three thought it was not. A Mr. Mercer testified he was traveling down the road in the opposite direction and did not recognize the man in the buggy but was sure it was not the defendant. Mathias Dudley also happened to cross paths with the buggy, coming within eight feet of it. Although he knew Joshua Harrison well, he did not think he was the man driving; that man appeared considerably younger than the defendant, maybe forty or so years old. But on cross, Dudley had to admit that "his eyes were not very good."[1]

Those two were followed by E. G. Swain, who lived near Coinjock and recalled seeing the man and boy in the buggy. He was certain the man driving was not Harrison, and he emphasized he could see the driver clearly because even though it was a "top buggy"—one with a retractable cloth awning that could be spread over the passengers to shield them from rain or sun—the awning was not in place at the time.

Swain's observation drew a pointed inquiry on cross-exam. Hadn't it been raining, and possibly snowing, on that cold afternoon, and wouldn't it be unusual to be out driving with the top down in such weather? Swain stood by his story but confirmed it had indeed been snowing and also "hailing." He may have been thinking of sleet instead, as any wise farmer knows that no storm ever produces snow and hail at the same time. Swain's story was greeted with "loud laughter" from the gallery.[2] The spectators were not impressed, nor likely were the jurors.

What, then, did the jurors think when the defense called a black man to the stand? It was a calculated risk, especially after Aycock had loudly ridiculed blacks during his cross-exam of Thomas Baum the day before. But somehow, somewhere, the defense had located a black witness who was willing not only to take the stand but to question the integrity of a white man.

First, Aycock laid the foundation by calling W. T. Nixon, a local businessman who apparently had some connection with Baum, although he did not elaborate on its nature. According to Nixon, Baum had come by his place of business in late August 1906, talking about his curious conversation with Joshua Harrison.

"Relate to the Court a conversation that you had with Baum concerning his making a thousand dollars," instructed Aycock on direct examination.

Nixon replied, "Yes, Baum told me he was going to make a thousand dollars and that he was going to give that nigger [Charlie Harris/Harrison] half of it if he would stick with him"—i.e., corroborate Baum's story about Harrison's admitting to holding Kenneth hostage.[3]

The African-American who followed Nixon to the stand apparently was one of his employees and was working in Nixon's shop when he overheard the alleged conversation. The trial transcript identifies him as Norris Walston, although the papers referred to him only by his first name, while describing white witnesses, without exception, as Mr. or Mrs. On taking the stand, he reiterated his employer's testimony of how Baum had bragged about collecting the reward by implicating Harrison.[4]

And Walston went farther. He claimed that Baum, the prosecution witness, had sought him out the previous evening in Elizabeth City and tried to threaten him into silence. As the papers recounted it, "Norris [Walston] created a sensation in court by testifying that Baum went to the negro skating rink in this city last night, called him out and told him that if he repeated the conversation in court today it would not be good for him." Yet Walston apparently was not deterred. According to the same print sources, "The negro stated on the stand that he was going to tell the truth if he died for it."[5]

It is hard to know what to make of this testimony, whether it was influenced by extortion or bribery, and from which side it may have been coming. While it may sound farfetched for a white man to venture to a black neighborhood to communicate a threat in that way, anything was possible in that time and place.[6] Any black man sitting on the witness stand in that courtroom, surrounded by white men, might well have feared for his life.

Afterward, the defense made a brief attempt to return to the scene of the disappearance. It called W. A. Sanders, John Parker, and Dan Harrison, the latter acknowledging himself to be the defendant's nephew. All three had taken part in searching for Kenneth on the afternoon and night of February 13, 1905, and they disputed the state's claim that the woods and swamp were searched thoroughly. Dan Harrison claimed that, in fact, only about a quarter of the woods were searched. In particular, there was a patch of especially thick underbrush—"gallbushes," he called them—just three hundred yards from the schoolhouse that was too tangled to enter without chopping the underbrush down, which no one did.

All three men also recalled seeing a footprint that looked like it was made by a child's shoe, pointing down a path headed into the woods from the schoolhouse.[7] But it is hard to see the probative value in that, even if it were true. The print may have come from Kenneth's shoes, or just as easily from one of the other boys. There was no dispute that they all had been playing around the edge of the woods where the print allegedly was seen.

Parker and Harrison also claimed to have heard a haunting sound emanating from the woods, something like a "child's voice in distress."[8] Here again, it is not clear exactly what the defendant's attorneys sought to establish with that. True, one can imagine some scenarios that could have helped the defense. Kenneth might have gotten lost, or perhaps he injured himself, maybe by stepping in a hole and spraining his ankle, and was crying for help. Or maybe someone other than Harrison had grabbed the boy and, instead of taking to the road in his buggy, was holding him hostage, possibly in the lumberman's cabin inhabited by the mysterious "Yankee." But if the searchers heard the child crying, why did they not follow the sound to locate him?

Eventually, it became apparent that if the defense was going to win the day, Harrison needed a solid alibi. It had plenty of witnesses to testify that he was nowhere near Poplar Branch on the Monday afternoon Kenneth disappeared. Most of them, however, turned out to be members of Harrison's immediate or extended family. For the jurors, being local people who understood the strength of blood ties, the appearance of contrived testimony would have been obvious.

And even the alibi witnesses who were not Harrison family members had issues.

Lee Thomas, for example, said he had passed the Harrison farm in Jarvisburg while on his way to the post office on the afternoon in question. Thomas had known Joshua Harrison since childhood and had seen Harrison in his field with a mule and a cart, apparently hard at work.[9]

But Thomas was a reputed chicken thief, and on cross he "became confused under a rain of sarcasm" from William Bond.

"Great man for seeing things. You saw a man's chickens, and he saw you. Saw you closer, as it were?" asked Bond. "And didn't you get filled with shot a little while before?" continued the attorney, evoking laughter from the gallery.

The witness finally replied that, no, he had not stolen anyone's chickens. And while he had in fact been marked with buckshot previously, the shotgun blast had come from a man who had gotten into an altercation with Thomas's son-in-law, who ducked, and Thomas had just been unlucky enough to receive "the load." Indeed, Thomas claimed he had been to court only once in his life, for a civil suit in magistrate's court, which he won.[10]

Thomas was followed on the stand by another Harrison neighbor, J. W. Fisher, who recalled seeing Harrison on the Wednesday after Kenneth's disappearance. Fisher had been traveling home from Norfolk by train, and one of the other passengers was Harrison's middle son, Marvin Hoge, called Hoge. They both had gotten off the train at Snowden station, then continued to the drawbridge that crossed the Albemarle-Chesapeake Canal at Coinjock, where Fisher saw the elder Harrison meet his son. And on the following Friday, Fisher had seen Joshua Harrison again on his way to Elizabeth City.[11]

By having Fisher describe Harrison's whereabouts on Wednesday and Friday, the defense was trying to dispel the idea that Harrison had snatched Kenneth on Monday, disappeared with him to parts unknown, and not returned for the rest of the week. That had been the accusation first leveled against Harrison in the mysterious *News & Observer* letter just days after the boy disappeared.

Fisher, incidentally, was probably one of the witnesses subpoenaed by both sides. He was the same Fisher who, according to Thomas Baum, had been drinking with him and Harrison the past August when the defendant had bragged about abducting Kenneth. When asked about that on cross, Fisher acknowledged being present and admitted having taken a drink with the others. But did he remember Harrison and Baum discussing the Beasley boy? Remarkably, the print sources do not show how he answered that question. He may have been too inebriated to remember, or simply was reluctant to do so.

Then, when Fisher was questioned on cross about his whereabouts on the Monday of the disappearance, he revealed something not helpful at all to the defense. On that morning, he was at his home, situated about four and a half miles from the Poplar Branch schoolhouse on the road between it and the Harrison farm. "Amid breathless silence" from the gallery, leaning forward in their seats to hear every word, Fisher testified that around ten that morning, before Kenneth went missing, he looked out his window and saw a "top buggy" pass by, headed *toward* Poplar Branch. He could not see who was driving, or whether it was pulled by a horse or a mule, but it was definitely a top buggy, like Harrison's.[12]

The defense, at that point, must have regretted calling Fisher to the stand.

As for the Harrison clan, they took their turns on the stand and maintained their stories consistently. But on cross-exam, the state found something unique about each of them to challenge their credibility and, in a few instances, to make them seem malicious as well as deceptive.

Harrison's oldest and youngest sons, Joe and Thomas, ages forty and nineteen, respectively, each testified that they were with their father all day on Monday. They spent the day at various tasks on the Jarvisburg farm, such as "hauling straw." The next day at about 1:30 P.M., Joe took one of their mules on a trip to Fisher's store, about a half-mile away. While there, he first heard news that Kenneth had disappeared. When he returned home at about 4:00, he found that his father's cousin Julia Forbes had come to visit. She also had brought news of the missing boy.[13] The day after that, Wednesday, Joe had gotten up early and, with his father's consent, headed to Poplar Branch to join the search party. Joshua, meanwhile, made his own trip to the store. When he arrived there, he received a phone message left by his middle son, Hoge, asking his father to pick him up at Coinjock, which he did. They all met up back at the farm Wednesday evening. On Thursday, everyone spent the day at home, and on Friday Joshua went to Elizabeth City on unspecified business, returning Sunday.[14]

That might all have been well and good except for the weather. Attorney Sawyer, when given the chance to question both sons, reminded them of the intermittent rain and snow on Monday, which seemed like odd conditions for hauling straw. And when Joe acknowledged that the weather had turned even colder and wetter on Wednesday, Sawyer asked him why he had taken part in the search that day but not on Tuesday. The young man said only, "I don't know."[15]

Then Joe was posed an odd question out of the blue. Sawyer asked if he recalled an incident during the following summer of 1905 when he had ridden on his horse past the Beasleys' home and sung out to them, in a loud and taunting voice, "Good bye, my honey, I'm gone."

"No sir, I did not."

Or another occasion around the same time, when Joe again passed the residence and saw Cassie Beasley in the front yard, had he waved his hand at her and sung, "Where is my wandering boy tonight"?

"I did not."[16]

What on earth did the prosecution expect the jurors to make of this? Ward and Sawyer must have presumed that at least some of them were music fans, and maybe owned the new phonographs that played tunes recorded on cylinders. Each of those alleged quotes was the title of a popular song of the day.

"Good-Bye, My Honey, I'm Gone," was a minstrel tune written for piano by M. H. Rosenfeld, whose body of work included songs such as "Hush Little Baby, Don't You Cry," "I'se Gwine to Weep No Mo'," and "Ring Dat Golden Bell." The ballad tells the story of a lovers' quarrel precipitated by infidelity. A portion of the lyrics, to give a taste of the whole, goes as follows:

> *I had a girl, and her name was Isabella,*
> *She ran away with another colored fella,*
> *And my load was all de stronger,*
> *And I couldn't stay no longer,*
> *Good-bye, my honey, I'm gone.*[17]

The second tune, "Where Is My Wandering Boy Tonight?" was much more poignant. It was written in 1877 by Robert Lowry, a charismatic Baptist minister from New Jersey. He wrote some religious compositions that are more familiar today, such as "Marching to Zion" and "How Can I Keep From Singing?" This particular tune was not a hymn but a sentimental weeper, its lyrics spoken by a mother searching for her wayward—and probably drunken—son:

> *Go for my wandering boy tonight;*
> *Go search for him where you will;*
> *But bring him to me with all his blight,*
> *And tell him I love him still.*

Whether the Reverend Lowry intended it or not, the song was adopted by the anti-liquor movement as one of its rallying themes. It was included in *Silver Tones*, a songbook issued by the Women's Christian Temperance Union,[18] and it was sung at many rallies, both religious and political.[19]

Was Joe Harrison, the alleged bootlegger's son, actually cruel enough to taunt the parents of a missing child in that way? Even if not, the accusation would have aroused indignation from anyone on the jury who was ill disposed toward black people or liquor.

Following Joe and Thomas, their brother Hoge, age twenty-nine, testified about his journey to Currituck from Norfolk on Wednesday, and how Joshua met him at the bridge. As for the rest of the week, he recalled his father's whereabouts just as his brothers had. On cross, Ward asked if he had ever traveled to the western part of the country, possibly to Oklahoma or Arkansas, to which Hoge replied he had not.[20] Ward did not pursue the subject further, and just let the idea hang in the jurors' minds until later.

After the Harrison boys finished, the defense brought forth the lady it probably viewed as its indispensable alibi witness: Ann Jarvis Harrison. The defendant's wife stuck to the same chronology as her sons and was emphatic that her husband was home all day Monday and at various places with their sons the following days, but not near Poplar Branch.

However, Mrs. Harrison also testified that she herself had made a trip over that way on the Saturday after the disappearance. She made a call at the Beasley home to check on the health of Mrs. Beasley and to sympathize with her as a mother. It takes some speculation to imagine how that would have occurred, since by all accounts Cassie Beasley was a nervous wreck on the verge of physical collapse after Kenneth went missing. Also, the senator was home by that time, presumably watching over his wife's delicate health, and in his testimony he made no mention of a visit by Mrs. Harrison, although he did recall the visit by Joshua and Miss Nina later in February.

According to Mrs. Harrison, she spoke with Cassie and expressed her regrets on Saturday. But then Ward asked if she also had apologized for not coming over sooner because her husband "was away all week, with only the three boys at home." Absolutely not, she said. She had not made that statement, which of course would have compromised her husband's alibi.[21]

Mrs. Harrison might well have gained some sympathy for her husband by playing the part of the dutiful wife. But then came her daughter Margaret Gallop, the widowed mother of three young boys, who lived and operated the boardinghouse in Norfolk, and who could have won an award for drama queen.

She took the stand apparently intending to tamp down suspicions that her father had brought Kenneth to her house after snatching him. In the Wellman account, Gallop was described by one trial observer as relishing the attention focused upon her. She was "gaudily dressed, haughty in her bearing, and simply full of unbecoming and unnatural display."[22] From her flippant responses to the questions, as shown in the trial transcript, there may be some basis for that characterization, chauvinistic though it is.

On direct questioning, Aycock asked Gallop what she remembered about the week of February 13, 1905, and how she had heard of Kenneth's disappearance. Was it from the newspapers, perhaps?

"I have not the slightest recollection of the day or week," she said with a flourish. "I am free, white, twenty-one[*] [actually, thirty-four], and a woman capable of taking care of myself. I have something to do besides read the newspapers."

"Do you know anything at all about this boy?"

"I don't know anything at all, except I suppose he has a family resemblance. I would know a Beasley if I saw him . . . for they all look alike."

When asked of her background and the untimely death of her husband in 1902, Gallop said, "Those things, Governor Aycock, are very tender to me." But she emphasized that her husband and

---

[*] "Free, white, and twenty-one," a then-common and now archaic catchphrase, was used by and about whites, to indicate they were beholden to no one.

Sam Beasley had been "very fond of each other" and that then-Representative Beasley had visited her husband during his illness and assisted them with their business affairs.[23]

The transcript does not include the content of Gallop's cross-examination. But according to Wellman, she felt satisfied with her performance and believed she had stood up well to Solicitor Ward's attempts to poke holes in her story. In the end, she looked beguilingly at Ward and said, "Now, sir, is there anything else you want to know about it? I have come a long ways to tell you, and I am ready to tell you whatever you want to know."

With "a fine show of gallantry," Hot Shot Ward smiled at her and said, "Only one thing, my dear madam, only one thing. Where is little Kenneth Beasley?"[24]

Maggie Gallop's second boardinghouse in Norfolk, an 1840 Greek Revival-style home known as the Glisson House, still stands.

CHAPTER 14

WAS THE ANSWER IN NORFOLK?

If Maggie Gallop knew where Kenneth could be found, it was a secret she would never share with any jury, whether under oath or not. But Hot Shot Ward knew quite well the direction in which he was leading the jury. All the state's evidence, however weak it might be, indicated that Harrison had absconded with the boy, then headed toward Norfolk. If he needed a secure place to stash the boy, then his daughter's house was the logical spot.

All accounts agree that Maggie Gallop was running a boardinghouse in the city at the time. She testified to it herself, and written documents show that she was. And yet there is doubt as to which house she was keeping in February 1905. If Kenneth Beasley's kidnapper did in fact have a Norfolk safe house, there are two known possibilities.

At least for a time, Maggie lived in a small house at 203 Granby Street, just yards south of the intersection with Freemason Street.[1]

Today, after several street renumberings, the location is 330 Granby,[2] and it looks nothing like it did in 1905. That part of downtown lying just north of the Elizabeth River has been repurposed many times since then. The enormous naval base did not yet exist as it does today, and over the years some of the harbor has been filled in with gravel, to build new streets and city blocks that did not appear on maps of the early 1900s.

The 300 block of Granby Street is now a modern cityscape lined with commercial buildings of varying ages. A couple of the foundations date to the 1920s, although most are newer construction, spawned by the development of the MacArthur Center shopping mall just a block east and the sleek urban campus of Tidewater Community College. Most of the buildings are now restaurants or college classrooms. Those who walk down the street on a typical afternoon are likely to see plenty of students carrying iPads and tablets, as well as a uniformed sailor or two.

Although it looked different in 1905, the area was no less bustling. Norfolk historians often refer to the early 1900s as the glory days of downtown, when everyone did their shopping there, as well as partaking of much of their business and entertainment. Granby Street—the intersection of Granby and Freemason in particular—was well known as the center of the neighborhood. Sometime around 1890 or 1900, someone stood there and was quoted to say, "By God, this is education, salvation, damnation, and starvation corner!" The four corners of that intersection were marked, respectively, by the Leache-Wood Seminary, a girls' school; Granby Street Methodist Church; the Merrimack Club, an upscale social spot; and a "middling boardinghouse."[3]

The boardinghouse at 203 Granby was not directly on the corner. The structure is long gone, and no photos are to be found. Property records indicate that it had no more than twenty-three feet of street frontage.[4] It might have been a narrow wooden townhouse of the sort common to the area at the time. At any rate, it was not a particularly large house and could not have accommodated many boarders.

Margaret Gallop never had legal title to the property. The owners were Sidney and Caroline Woodward, who purchased it in

February 1903 and kept it until at least 1911, when they took out a second mortgage on it.[5] But it is clear that Maggie resided there for a time, since the city directories for 1904 and 1905 listed her as the sole occupant. That would not have been surprising. If she was the manager/proprietress of the boardinghouse, the directories probably would have named only her, without listing any boarders who might have been staying only for months or weeks.

What is less clear is how long she stayed on Granby Street. Maggie testified at her father's trial that she lived in that house only until September 1903, moving out well before the alleged kidnapping.[6] That may or may not have been truthful. Although she made a bad impression on the jury and spectators with her vivacious manner, that does not mean she was deceptive about every factual detail. And although the city directories indicate she stayed on Granby Street longer than she claimed, that could have been an error on the part of the publishers. It might simply have taken some time for them to update their records.

To find Maggie Gallop's next residence, one need only walk two blocks west on Freemason and a few yards north. And this one is still standing, in all its stately eminence.

The West Freemason Street neighborhood is a remarkable example of historic preservation; in fact, it is one of the few areas of Norfolk that have retained their eighteenth- and nineteenth-century architecture through all the waves of military and commercial industrialization that have washed over the city. Before the Civil War, this was where wealthy merchants and shipping executives built their homes, a surprising number of which remain.

A few blocks' exploration of the district's cobblestone streets reveals an eclectic mix of styles. There are plenty of townhouses, many of them built of brick, although some are brownstone, designed in the Romanesque Revival style. There also are French Second Empire houses with their signature mansard roofs. And one can find all sorts of brick homes, ranging in style from Federal to Queen Anne to Greek Revival. One of the oldest, dating to 1791, is on the southeast corner of Freemason and Duke Streets. Known as the Taylor-Whittle House, it is today the offices of the Norfolk Historical Society, although in years past it went through a succession of private owners, most of them seamen. One of them was William C. Whittle Jr., the first officer of the CSS *Shenandoah*, the famous Confederate commerce raider that destroyed thirty-two Yankee ships during the war.[7]

Diagonally across the street is Maggie Gallop's second boardinghouse. And it is not hard to see that it must have been a major step up from the small house on Granby. This one can legitimately be called a mansion.

It is best known as the Glisson House, named for its builder and original owner, who, like his neighbors across the street, was a career sailor. However, he remained loyal to the Union. Oliver Glisson was an Ohio native who went to sea early in life, spent almost all his career in the U.S. Navy, and eventually rose to the rank of rear admiral. His career took him all over the world, including Japan, where he sailed as part of the 1855 expedition led by Matthew C. Perry, which first opened the country to Western diplomacy and trade. But he married a Norfolk lady, and they considered the city their primary home, at least until the Civil War.

They finished the house in 1840, and it remains a marvel of the Greek Revival style. More than six thousand square feet, it is an imposing structure of white-painted brick, three stories tall, three windows wide, and at least six windows deep, with two tall chimneys and a square cupola on top.[8] Just beside the house, between it and Freemason Street, is an attractive garden space with three magnolia trees. In years past, it was filled by a weeping willow that Commodore Glisson planted himself, from a cutting he brought back from one of his round-the-world voyages; the parent tree supposedly grew over the original grave of Napoleon Bonaparte on the island of St. Helena in the middle of the South Atlantic.[9]

The Glisson family held on to the house until 1860. The commodore probably sensed the war was coming, and that he needed to remove his family to friendlier territory. Mrs. Glisson and the children moved to Philadelphia, and the house was sold to Kader Biggs,[10] a gentleman whose Southern bona fides would never be questioned by anyone.

Biggs, like many drawn to Norfolk to make their fortunes, had North Carolina roots. He grew up in Williamston, a town on the

Roanoke River southwest of Elizabeth City. His brother, Asa Biggs, was an attorney who served as a congressman, then briefly as a U.S. senator from North Carolina in the mid-1850s, before resigning to accept appointment as a federal judge.

Before long, Kader Biggs found success in the Norfolk business community. In 1857, he was named one of the first directors of the Norfolk Corn Exchange. Three years later, in addition to purchasing his large house, he was vice president of the Merchants and Mechanics Exchange. In 1867, he was on the board of the Norfolk Hotel Company. Around that time, his brother Asa also moved to Norfolk and went into business with Kader.[11] Apparently, the judge had grown tired of Reconstruction-era politics in North Carolina and wanted to focus on making money.

Kader Biggs passed away in 1884, leaving his widow, Lucy, with title to the Glisson House. She continued to live there, but by the early 1900s Mrs. Biggs was in her seventies. She had a big house to take care of and perhaps was in need of an income stream.[12] It would have made sense to open the house to boarders. If Mrs. Biggs was not physically up to managing it herself, she could have brought in someone else to do it. And that is in fact how Maggie Gallop came to live there.

It is not clear how Maggie made the acquaintance of Mrs. Biggs. There is a good chance that Maggie's uncle, former governor Jarvis, had known the Biggses; they shared a similar political heritage, after all. If his niece and her three young children needed a place to live in Norfolk, Jarvis might well have introduced her to Mrs. Biggs. This is speculation, of course, but it is known that Maggie Gallop moved into the Glisson House as the boardinghouse keeper. The only question is when. Maggie testified that she made the move in 1903, although the Norfolk city directories do not show her residing at 192 Duke Street until their 1906 and 1907 editions.[13]

Incidentally, those directories list three people residing in the house in 1906 and 1907: L. A. (Lucy) Biggs, M. M. (Maggie) Gallop, and N. P. (Nina Pocahontas) Harrison, Maggie's sister. Apparently, Miss Nina did not continue teaching school for long after Kenneth disappeared. Nor did she remain in Poplar Branch, or in Currituck at all. She moved to Norfolk to stay with her sister.

Why did Maggie testify that she moved from Granby Street to Duke Street in 1903, if she did not do so until mid- to late 1905 or 1906? Perhaps to dissuade anyone from looking for incriminating evidence in the 203 Granby house—something buried in the basement, maybe. Or was she in fact living in the Duke Street house in February 1905, when her father may or may not have paid a visit to the city, bringing something he wanted to keep hidden? That huge brick boardinghouse could have made an excellent hiding place.

Either of those houses might also have been a good place to deal in liquor or sweet Currituck scuppernong wine, if that was more to the taste of whoever was boarding there. If Joshua Harrison wanted a market for his illegal brew, he hardly could have found a better distribution point than a boardinghouse in downtown Norfolk.

Since the devastation of the Civil War, Norfolk had grown so much that the place would have been unrecognizable to many. New railroad lines had been built since the 1870s: the Norfolk Southern extending to Elizabeth City and beyond, plus the Norfolk and Western, which ran to Danville, Memphis, and the West Virginia coal fields. They helped to build Norfolk into one of the world's biggest shipping ports—for coal and cotton most of all, but also for tar, turpentine, lumber, peanuts, and every other farm product imaginable.[14]

With all that industrial capacity came a new demand for itinerant labor, especially dockworkers and sailors, navy as well as civilian. The city's population doubled between 1890 and 1910. With massive new numbers of human beings, of course, came massive amounts of the human vices found in busy seaports, such as liquor and prostitution. So much so that, at one point in the 1890s, New York's *Town Topics* newspaper designated Norfolk as "the wickedest city in the United States."[15]

Much of that illicit activity was centered in a portion of downtown named by another condescending New York publication as "Hell's Half-Acre." This red-light zone actually stretched over more than two hundred acres, bounded on the north by Washington Street, on the east by Church Street, on the south by Water Street, and on the west by Bank Street. Within that rectangle were found most of the city's 240-odd retail liquor establishments, including bars, saloons, gambling parlors, and brothels.[16] The stench of prostitution in particular caused some newspapers to call the area by another name: the Tenderloin District.

Granby and Duke Streets were not situated within the Tenderloin, but they were only six or seven blocks—a ten-minute walk—from it. And Maggie Gallop's establishment at 192 Duke Street was just one of fifty-one boardinghouses in Norfolk, plus another fifteen across the river in Portsmouth, as listed in a 1907 directory of area accommodations.[17]

From the 1890s through the first decade of the 1900s, Norfolk saw a prohibition movement similar to that in North Carolina. The city government made an attempt to clean up its police department—long a hotbed of corruption—and enforce restrictions on liquor. In 1896, the police made 7,115 arrests for drunkenness and 209 for illegal sale of liquor; those were increases of 90 percent since 1894. However, the enforcement had the effect of driving many bars and saloons underground and having some of them renamed as "social clubs" that served only dues-paying "members."[18]

It is fair to contemplate how many of those "boardinghouses" were in fact brothels or bordellos in all but name. Or to use another term, blind tigers.

One fellow who knew the city well in those days was a brash young reporter named W. O. Saunders. In 1908, he founded the *Independent* newspaper in Elizabeth City, where he would make a name for himself as a journalistic bomb thrower, constantly highlighting local graft and corruption and advocating civil rights long before other newspapers did. But in 1906, Saunders was a struggling Norfolk gumshoe reporter who found some of his best stories by hanging out in the city's barrooms, most of which offered free lunches. Saunders's son, Keith, recalled later that his father got by in Norfolk by spending twenty-five cents per night for a cheap boardinghouse bed and had "two dollars left over for a visit to a brothel every fourth Saturday night."[19]

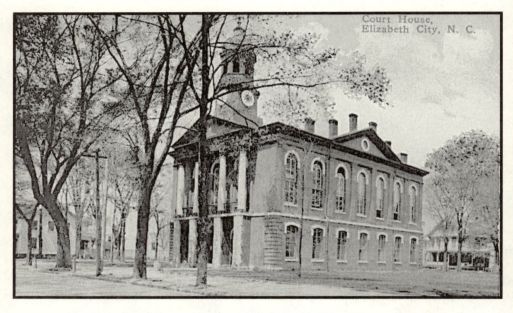

Period postcard shows the Pasquotank County Courthouse, in Elizabeth City, site of Joshua Harrison's highly publicized trial and the hearings that followed. Spectators and reporters scurried every day for seats.

CHAPTER 15

ONE LADY MUST BE LYING

Once the defense rested its case, the court allowed an additional day for each side to call several other witnesses. Some had been unable to attend court earlier in the week, due to illness or difficulties getting to Elizabeth City. But several were termed rebuttal witnesses because they offered testimony that refuted, or at least claimed to refute, the stories presented earlier.

Immediately, it was clear that the prosecution was focusing on Norfolk, especially that infamous district named after a certain cut of meat, and the goings-on for which it was notorious.

Up to the stand strode J. J. Woodhouse, yet another Currituck native who bore that common surname. After so many years, it is hard to know exactly how he was related to brothers D. W. Woodhouse, the storekeeper, and T. C. Woodhouse, who claimed to have carried the ransom communications.[1] It is also impossible to know how well J. J. may have known the brothers, if at all. But just like T. C., J. J. Woodhouse testified he had known Joshua Harrison since they were boys. And like T. C., J. J. told of a chance meeting with Harrison that had serious implications.

It happened in the early-morning hours of Tuesday, February 14, 1905, just after Kenneth went missing. And it happened on the streets of Norfolk, where Woodhouse now lived, and where Harrison obviously could not have been if the testimonies of his family and neighbors were to be believed. As Woodhouse told his story, "spectators craned their necks in breathless silence to hear every word that fell from this important witness's lips."[2]

Woodhouse remembered the day clearly. The day before, he had quit his job as a signalman for the Norfolk Railway and Light Company. Now, on Tuesday, he woke early and headed toward the switchyard to turn in his badge and key. But even though it was between six and seven in the morning, Woodhouse did not think it too early to stop by one of the local bars.

He went in the Onyx Saloon, located at 411 East Main Street, well within the Tenderloin and just blocks from either Granby Street or Duke Street. Woodhouse said he was planning to have a quick drink and to say hello to a friend, John White, who tended the bar. But once inside, Woodhouse was surprised to see his old acquaintance Joshua Harrison. They didn't talk much except to say hello. Then Harrison bought a quart of corn whiskey and headed out.[3]

At the time, Woodhouse had heard nothing of Kenneth Beasley. And later, even after hearing of the boy's disappearance, he had no reason to associate it with Harrison, his daughter, or her nearby boardinghouse. It was not until much later, after Harrison had been charged, that Woodhouse told the story to anyone. He mentioned it in passing to a neighbor, John Aydlett, who took the stand after Woodhouse. Aydlett confirmed that Woodhouse had told him about seeing Harrison in the bar, but that Woodhouse had not seemed eager to use the information to get anything for himself, such as a cash reward.[4]

Yet there was a witness who questioned Woodhouse's credibility, and seemed to have documentation to back himself up. J. J. Coogan was called by the defense to testify that, on both February 13 and 14, Woodhouse was not working at the Norfolk Railway and Light Company but actually as Coogan's employee at the Norfolk and Southern Traction Company. On February 14, in fact, Woodhouse had worked as a "car dispatcher" from 10:00 A.M. to 1:00 P.M. and also from 6:30 to 11:00 P.M., and Coogan brought written payroll records with him to show it.[5]

However incriminating Woodhouse's story may or may not have been, the testimony of the next witness went farther. It may even have been a little salacious, or at least as salacious as the court would allow.

Dennis F. Burfoot was yet another son of Currituck County who said he had grown up knowing Joshua Harrison, although he now resided in Princess Anne County, Virginia.[6] On that same night and early morning of February 13-14, 1905, he had been working as a "substitute policeman" on the streets of Norfolk, in an area he called "the block."

Burfoot did not describe the exact parameters of "the block," but they are not difficult to guess. The area must have included the intersection of Washington and Cumberland Streets, a spot right in the center of the Tenderloin District. The witness claimed that, at that street corner at about 2:30 A.M., he happened to run into Harrison. They were surprised to see each other and ended up talking for about twenty minutes.

When Burfoot asked Harrison what he was doing on the streets so late, Harrison allegedly lied that he had come to the city to bring his son to school, and that his wife had passed away two years previously. Of course, by this stage of the trial, the jurors knew that none of the Harrison boys had attended school in Norfolk at the time, and that Mrs. Harrison was very much alive. According to Burfoot, Harrison then asked him about "certain places in the neighborhood." Upon hearing that, Judge Allen saw where the testimony was going. He broke in and instructed the witness to be careful with what he recollected. The judge cautioned Burfoot to "omit certain statements" the defendant might have made, due to irrelevancy and also the "presence in court of a number of ladies."

Point well taken. Burfoot did not describe further statements, if any, that Harrison had made to him. He did, however, testify that, as a substitute policeman, his purpose for being on patrol was "to keep a certain kind of woman off the street."[7] It was as close as he came to a specific mention of prostitution, and was certainly enough to get the point across.

When Aycock got his turn to cross-examine Burfoot, the witness acknowledged that his testimony had been arranged on the spur of the moment. Only the day before, Sam Beasley himself had approached Burfoot in Norfolk and asked him to make the hurried rail journey to Elizabeth City to take the stand. Was that due to nervousness on the part of the prosecution, and concerns that it had not yet clinched the case? Was it just making things up, trying to put the final nail in Harrison's coffin? And could the sixty-six-year-old Harrison really have traveled fifty miles from Poplar Branch to Norfolk by buggy in just over twelve hours, through rain or snow, and then felt fit to cruise the streets in the wee hours? Maybe not, but the general impression in the press was that Burfoot's testimony remained "unshaken" by the defense's attempts to impeach him.[8]

Whatever doubts the jurors may have had about Burfoot or J. J. Woodhouse, the state's next witness carried a good bit more authority. E. W. Ansell was the elected clerk of court for Currituck County, just as he had been two years earlier when he was named in the mysterious *News & Observer* letter as one of the eyewitnesses to the abduction. He said he had not testified earlier, during the state's case-in-chief, because he was ill. But he was here now, and his story echoed what the jury heard on the first day of the trial.

At about four on the now-familiar Monday afternoon, Ansell had seen the buggy pass his house on the main road near Currituck Courthouse, headed towards Norfolk at a quick gait, drawn by the dark-skinned mule. He did not get a good look at the boy, who appeared to be crouched on the floor of the buggy, concealed by some sort of cloth. Nor did he see the driver's face. But he heard the boy, who was whimpering or crying, and he also heard the driver speak to the boy in a soothing manner, saying, "There, there," the very same words recalled earlier by John Berry. Ansell was fairly certain the voice was that of Joshua Harrison, whom he had known

One Lady Must Be Lying

for a dozen years or more.⁹

It was also around this time that Kenneth's young friends Benny Walker and Irving Gallop testified about his final day at school and, in Benny's case, about Kenneth's parting words before he slipped down the wooded path.¹⁰ Two years after the event, they were a little more mature but still just fifth-graders trying to make their young voices heard above the murmuring crowd, with all those adults watching them so intently, including the gray-bearded, hard-featured defendant, seated just feet in front of them. It could not have been easy for them.

The state also brought in T. N. Davenport, who said he had stopped by the Harrison farm around four in the afternoon on Monday, February 13. As he recalled, the defendant was not working in his field. A woman came into the yard and said Harrison was not home just then, although Davenport added that he did not recognize the lady, nor could he tell whether she was white or colored.

And why had Davenport paid the visit to the Harrison home? "For some of that good wine," he said, to laughter from the gallery.¹¹

In response, the defense brought in a couple of more alibi witnesses, although neither must have sounded terribly convincing. Grover Cleveland "Cleve" Newbern said he had passed the Harrison farm about four-thirty on the same Monday afternoon and saw two men working in the field. He thought one of them was the defendant but wasn't certain. One might have expected the witness to be more definitive, especially since he was another of the extended Harrison clan, his uncle having married Joshua Harrison's sister. Stephen Gordon testified he had also passed the farm in the middle of the day and had seen Harrison out raking straw, just as his wife and sons claimed. But Gordon had two problems. First, he was an African-American. Second, he revealed on cross that he once had been indicted for stealing hogs, although, remarkably for a Negro of that time and place, he was found not guilty.¹²

After Gordon finished, T. C. Woodhouse took the stand again for the state to attest that Gordon's character was "not good." But on cross, Woodhouse finally was confronted about his own character, and this time Judge Allen instructed all the ladies in court to excuse themselves to the lobby. Yes, Woodhouse admitted, he had a fondness for tenderloin and had once been charged with "seduction." Whether he was convicted is not clear; according to Woodhouse, he had "compromised the matter." He took no pride in the incident, nor did he appear to carry much guilt. To his recollection, "The woman was a young girl who worked for her living, and I courted her for what I could get out of her."[13]

At the end of the day, one of the newspapers summed it up in this way: "The Defense has rested solely on an alibi, which the Prosecution has vigorously attacked with the testimony of witnesses of irreproachable character."[14] It is hard to imagine the writer meant to include T. C. Woodhouse in that category. But he might have been thinking of someone else who testified in that concluding phase of the trial.

Toward the end of the afternoon, everyone in the courtroom must have ceased their whispers, drawn in their breath, and focused their eyes intently toward the front. Kenneth Beasley's mother was about to take the stand.

Many must have been surprised to see Cassie Beasley appear at all. When her husband was on the stand, he emphasized how delicate her health continued to be and said he did not want her to have to travel from Norfolk to endure the strain of the trial. Reporters were happy to abide by the senator's narrative. As she took her place in the witness box, she was "dressed in mourning, with a thin black veil over her face, a thin edge of white lace showing above her collar, and appeared weak and grief-stricken."[15]

Whatever the true state of Mrs. Beasley's health, the press's depiction of her need come as no surprise. Thirty years earlier, it had described Sarah Ross, Charley's mother, in virtually the same idealized terms. In all the years Charley's story was in the news, the press almost never interviewed her or quoted her directly. Her husband spoke for her, as Senator Beasley later did for his wife. And whenever Mrs. Ross was mentioned, she came across as little more than a cliché: she was "the poor mother," or "the stricken lady." Her grief was a badge of feminine honor, described by the *New York Herald* as "something so noble, so hopeful, so womanly."[16]

As it was in the Victorian 1870s, so it was in the Edwardian 1900s, and especially in the chivalrous South. Ladies lived on an exalted plane, untroubled by the right to vote, unsullied by the mundane hand of crime or political strife. Or at least proper white ladies, and that is certainly how the prosecution intended for Cassie Beasley to appear to the jury, amid the day's other testimony about hog theft, saloons, "working girls," and the like.

Charles Aycock, sitting at the defense table, surely recognized the game as he saw it unfolding. Countless times, he had said it himself in his standard stump speech in 1898, 1900, and afterward: "The goddess of North Carolina Democracy is the white womanhood of the state." Some years later, the idiosyncratic historian W. J. Cash would describe white Southerners' reverence for the feminine ideal as "gyneolatry."[17]

And yet it is curious that the state did not use Mrs. Beasley as a witness to the extent it might have. If she felt well enough to journey to Elizabeth City so late in the trial, surely she could have done so earlier in the week, to appear in the state's case-in-chief. She might have testified about Kenneth's final day at home, about his departure for school, and about what a wonderful child he was. No doubt, it would have been tearfully effective.

She also could have mentioned something about the puppies.

But she was not asked about any of that. Solicitor Ward put Mrs. Beasley on the stand only as a rebuttal witness, to refute the testimony of Ann Harrison. Yes, according to Cassie Beasley, the defendant's wife had dropped by to visit her at home on the Saturday after Kenneth disappeared. And yes, although Mrs. Harrison denied it under oath, she had told Mrs. Beasley that Joshua had been away from home all week.[18]

There is just no way around it. One of those two upstanding Southern ladies was either badly mistaken in her recollection or deliberately not telling the truth. It was a contentious issue that sparked arguments among the attorneys about whether the hearsay was even admissible. According to the *Tar Heel* writer, Solicitor Ward was "fervent, impassioned, and eloquent," while Aycock was "strong, technical, and masterful." Judge Allen did not rule immediately on whether the jury would be allowed to consider Mrs. Beasley's testimony, and the sources do not state what he decided. Since the trial transcript makes no mention of Cassie Beasley's testimony, the judge likely instructed the jury to disregard it.[19] Still, if the jury members heard Mrs. Beasley's words, it would have been hard to erase them from their minds.

Finally, after the parade of witnesses over nearly five days, it came time for the attorneys' closing arguments. Given the legendary assemblage, everyone knew the jury was going to hear quite a display of oratory. The crowd in the gallery, which had been increasing with each day of the trial, now filled it to capacity. "Every person who secured a seat, from the street urchin to the most cultured lady, held to it with a death-like tenacity."[20]

Arguments began the morning of March 19, with former governor Jarvis leading off for the defense. It is a shame that the official trial transcript does not include the closing arguments, although it is not standard practice. Closing arguments are not considered evidence; they are just the attorneys' interpretation of the evidence. It is necessary to rely on the recollections of the reporters, who left only summaries and blurbs. The *News & Observer* definitely was not in sympathy with Harrison but showed respect for his Democratic brother-in-law. It described Jarvis's argument as "a speech of great power," delivered by a man of "venerable appearance."[21]

Jarvis did, however, raise some controversy by spinning the testimony of his younger sister, the defendant's wife. Because he knew his sister so well, and she would never tell a lie under oath, Jarvis told the jury he was convinced Harrison was innocent. Further, he implied that he knew there had been no kidnapping, and that Kenneth Beasley's bones were still resting wherever he had gotten lost in the Maple Swamp. Not surprisingly, that drew an objection from Solicitor Ward.[22]

After Jarvis finished, the other counsels alternated back and forth between state and defense. William Pruden led off for the state, followed by Ike Meekins for the defendant. Meekins, the "Silver-Tongued Orator of the East," as the *News & Observer* flattered him, spoke for nearly two hours, followed by Walter Cohoon for the state. The day concluded with the speech by former governor Aycock, who gave "one of the most brilliant legal efforts ever heard in this courthouse." High praise indeed, which makes it curious that the

One Lady Must Be Lying

N&O did not describe the content of Aycock's speech in more detail.[23] In a nutshell, each attorney hammered the opposing side's witnesses without mercy, highlighting every doubt and inconsistency.

The next morning, it was Hot Shot Ward's turn. And it is clear he crossed the line. In fact, he came perilously close to violating legal norms and putting his case in jeopardy. But in the end, he made all the right moves to get his desired result.

For one thing, Ward lambasted Harrison for cowardice in not taking the stand in his own defense. Yet everyone knows a defendant cannot be compelled to testify, and Judge Allen stepped in to rebuke Ward for the comment.[24] But then the solicitor struck a surprising new note that brought the spectators to their feet cheering, although it may have left the jurors scratching their heads.

Ward told the jury that he had a letter in his pocket. The letter had never been mentioned during the evidentiary phase of the trial, and Ward said he could not divulge the full details now. He did not say where the letter came from, or what exactly it said. But based upon it, he said he was certain that Kenneth was alive and well and would be "returned to his mother's arms within six months."[25]

The papers did not report what the defense counsels said in reply, but one can picture all four leaping to their feet and demanding a mistrial. Not only had Ward attempted to sneak in evidence that had not been admitted through properly sworn testimony, he was hinting, without any factual basis, and despite Senator and Mrs. Beasley's apparent resignation that their son was dead, that Harrison or some co-conspirators were still hiding the boy.

Essentially, Ward was urging the jurors to find the defendant guilty, coerce him into releasing the child, and spare the Beasleys from the lifelong heartbreak that befell Charley Ross's parents. If they were to let Harrison walk free instead, the mystery would never be resolved.

There must have followed some quick repartee among the attorneys because the press reported that Ward made some remark that the folks in the gallery liked. They broke out into sustained applause that lasted over two minutes and caused Judge Allen to hold at least one spectator in contempt of court.[26]

After order was restored, the judge spent about an hour and

a quarter in delivering his instructions to the jury members. He explained to them the concept of reasonable doubt, and that the assumption of innocence rested with the defendant unless it was overcome by the state. He told them not to be influenced by the applause, by the attitudes of the spectators, or by the defendant's decision not to testify. The judge emphasized that they were not to consider anything except the sworn evidence, and should not be swayed by "the station or influence in life of anyone." In the end, they must decide the case in such a way that they could go home to their wives and children and say, "I've done my duty."[27]

The jury members began deliberating at about one-thirty in the afternoon. To their credit, they did not rush to judgment. They kept going through the afternoon, and then the judge instructed them to make use of the evening hours as well. It was not until ten that night that they returned a verdict.

Guilty.[28]

Apparently, most of the spectators decided to hang around for the results because the courtroom again rang with applause when

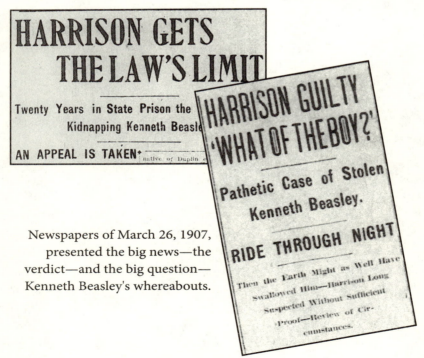

Newspapers of March 26, 1907, presented the big news—the verdict—and the big question—Kenneth Beasley's whereabouts.

the verdict was announced. The defendant had tears in his eyes as he was escorted to the Pasquotank County Jail, to be returned in the morning for sentencing.

The *News & Observer* claimed that, somehow, it got a direct quote from the sheriff's deputy who accompanied Harrison that night. According to him, the old man was distraught by the shame visited upon his family, but he still maintained his innocence.

"My God, isn't this awful? I do not know anything about that boy. If they were to take each member of my family, as dearly as I love them, and chowder them before my eyes, I could not tell them any more than I have already told."[29]

KIDNAPPER AND MURDERER.

Slayer of a Nine-Year-Old Boy Convicted in North Carolina.

ELIZABETH CITY, N. C., March 20.—The jury, in the case of Joshua Harrison, charged with the kidnapping and murder of Kenneth Beasley, the 9-year-old son of ex-State Senator Beasley, rendered a verdict of guilty to-night.

The trial, which has been held in the Pasquotank County Court, with day and night sessions, has attracted a great deal of attention throughout this section.

Joshua Harrison's conviction was national news. Readers of *The New York Times* saw the story on Page 1, although the article erroneously stated Harrison had been convicted of both kidnapping and murder, and that the victim had been nine years old, instead of eight.

CHAPTER 16

Eloquent Machinations

The trial was technically over, but the courtroom drama was not. The next morning, March 22, Harrison was brought back into court for post-trial motions, in which his attorneys would try to convince Judge Allen to set aside the jury's verdict. And if they failed to do so, the court would impose sentence. Although the precise terminology has changed over the years, these motions are familiar to any defense attorney. They are almost always denied, but the defendant has to go through them in order to preserve the issues for review in the appellate courts.

According to the clerk of court's notes, there were three motions. The first was a Motion for Arrest of Judgment for Defects in Bill of Indictment, and the defense was not entirely off base in raising that issue. When the grand jury indicted Harrison for kidnapping, it was in fact alleging a crime that had no legal definition in North Carolina. The grand jury, and now the trial court, had essentially made it up as it went along. It was clear that the North Carolina Supreme Court would have to render its opinion on what constituted a "kidnap."

The other two motions were of the same piece: a Motion to Set Aside Verdict and for New Trial in Exercise of Discretion, and a Motion to Set Aside Verdict and for New Trial for Errors Committed in Trial.[1] Today, these would fall under the title of a Motion for Appropriate Relief, in which the defendant alleges some defect in the trial process, such that his basic rights to due process were violated. The defense made, essentially, a two-pronged argument—first, that the public atmosphere in the courtroom was so hostile to Harrison that the jury was coerced, or at least intimidated, into finding him guilty; and second, that Hot Shot Ward had overstepped his bounds so severely that the entire trial process was tainted beyond salvage.

The defense counsels knew it was a long shot, and they would have to muster all their rhetorical talents to have a chance. Not surprisingly, Charles Aycock was chosen to present the argument. He was their best speechmaker and had the closest political relationship with Judge Allen.

Once again, it is a shame that the full content of the attorneys' arguments have not been preserved, and that snippets must provide a taste of the whole. Several years later, after Aycock's death, one of his opponents lamented that fact. William Pruden, one of Beasley's specially retained prosecutors, wrote a letter to Judge Allen, who by that time had been elevated to a seat on the North Carolina Supreme Court. Pruden asked Justice Allen if the text of Aycock's speeches in the Harrison trial could be arranged and published. In particular, he thought Aycock's argument on the post-trial motions was "superior" and should be preserved. Justice Allen wrote back to say that, to his knowledge, the speech had not been recorded. But Allen agreed it was "one of the most eloquent I have ever listened to."[2]

Aycock began by highlighting the "deplorable applause" from the gallery during Ward's closing argument. It showed that the solicitor had deliberately inflamed the passions of the spectators, especially with his surprise declaration that Kenneth Beasley was still alive.[3]

"The wail of a child in the night," Aycock exclaimed, "thrills and fills the hearts of men with such a passion that reason is blinded and someone must perhaps unjustly suffer. We fled from the passion of Currituck to get a fair trial here, and we find that Currituck has followed us and packed the courtroom."[4]

Aycock was thinking, first and foremost, of his client. But was he also thinking back to other recent cases when heinous crimes had aroused passions that led to lynch mobs, extra-judicial killings he may have regretted his failure to prevent? Very possibly so.

Next, Aycock spoke of his colleague, former governor Jarvis, who unfortunately had to depart the trial and head home to Greenville shortly before the jury deliberations, upon news that his wife was ill. "Who," he asked, "will tell my loyal friend Jarvis of the jury's verdict, and that his sister has perjured herself? The verdict has brought humiliation to the wife, disgrace to the children, and hopelessness to the grandchildren of Harrison. I want time in which the truth can be discovered, free from passion and prejudice. Women who are the pink of the city have broken into applause here—the feeling of the people broke into the jury box and influenced them. No action of Your Honor can take that influence out—come to the rescue of the law and set aside the verdict."[5]

Once again, an appeal to exalted womanhood. Not that Hot Shot Ward was going to concede that ground. While he could be fiery one moment, he could be smooth and chivalrous the next, as he showed when it came his turn to address the court. No, he insisted, he had not accused Ann Jarvis Harrison of perjury. She may have told a lie, but only a little white one.

"Perjury," Ward intoned, "catches its inspiration from a low, debased source, but loyalty and love that prompt a wife to swear for her husband catches its inspiration from the heavens. When her statement was placed upon the Great Book above, the recording angel dropped a tear and blotted it out."[6]

Only days before, these same attorneys had been tossing the n-word around the courtroom like sailors in a dockside saloon. Courtroom drama could range from the abysmal to the sublime, from vulgar racism to Shakespearean artistry. It was a different time, when the rules of courtroom procedure were less strict and judges gave attorneys more discretion to flex their personalities. If one finds a certain charm in classic judicial theater, something definitely has been lost with time.

After hearing from both sides, Judge Allen denied the defense motions and let the verdict stand. But although he did not have to do so, he expressed doubts about some of the state's evidence, particularly what he called the "Norfolk witnesses." Presumably, he meant J. J. Woodhouse and Dennis Burfoot, who claimed to have seen Harrison on the city streets late on the night of the disappearance. The judge thought their stories sounded shaky, especially when the state had brought them to Elizabeth City so hastily at the end of the trial.[7]

"There are a number of questions concerning which I would have had some doubts," said the judge, "but those questions were for the jury to determine, and they found him guilty. The Court is satisfied that the evidence was to them sufficient to convict him."[8]

With that, the judge sentenced Harrison to twenty years in the state penitentiary. It is not clear how he decided upon that term. It did not come from the state statutes, as the statutes did not mention kidnapping, let alone prescribe the punishment for it. Chances are that Judge Allen just figured twenty years was an adequate penalty for the near-septuagenarian Harrison.

On the spot, the defense gave notice of its intent to appeal the verdict. If anything, it may have felt encouraged by the judge's words. It was notable for a judge to voice public skepticism, however mild, about a jury's verdict. Aycock and his colleagues probably figured that word of the judge's doubts would get back to the justices on the North Carolina Supreme Court and make them more inclined to overturn the conviction.

Further, the judge was lenient enough to allow Harrison to post an appeal bond so he could remain out of custody while the case was pending in Raleigh. According to the press, there was "much debate" over whether bond was appropriate, and if so, how much. The state had concerns about Harrison's possibly planning to skip the state or the country. Eventually, the judge decided on three thousand dollars, which the defendant promptly paid.[9]

Harrison went home. Interestingly, Sam Beasley did not. The former senator had stayed in Elizabeth City for the verdict, but on the very evening after the motions were heard, Beasley jumped on a train to Arkansas.

A story had emerged that there was a boy in Arkansas who looked much like Kenneth and claimed to be him. The good folks of Elizabeth City collected a love offering of one hundred dollars to help the senator finance the trip to look into it.[10] Of course, Christian and Sarah Ross had gone through this drama many times years before, chasing down rumors that turned out to be baseless. So Beasley set off, probably feeling more resigned than optimistic, hoping against hope that his boy was waiting for him nearly half a continent away.

And yet something about this rumor must have sounded credible enough to invest the time and money in the long rail journey. Did it have something to do with the mysterious letter Ward mentioned in his closing argument? Some speculated that since Harrison had been found guilty and had nothing left to lose, he had finally come around and revealed where Kenneth was being held captive.

And was it only coincidental that Ward had asked Hoge Harrison, while on the stand, if he had made any trips west to Arkansas or Oklahoma?

As with so many points in this narrative, it is impossible to know with certainty. But in those days, it was nothing unusual for children to be uprooted and escorted by train to new adoptive homes in the Midwest.

The Orphan Train Movement is an often-neglected phenomenon of the late nineteenth and early twentieth centuries. In that era of economic growth and industrialization, the country's population was booming, especially in the cities, where shiploads of immigrants arrived regularly and overcrowded slums were getting worse every year. In places including New York, Philadelphia, and Boston, churchmen and social workers had an epidemic of children whose parents could not care for them. Organizations such as the Children's Aid Society of New York were created to get homeless children off the streets, and the best method they devised was to place them for adoption with families in rural areas. The children were gathered and placed on trains headed west, their arrival announced in advance in the newspapers of Midwestern towns. Anyone interested in adopting a child, or simply in taking on a new young farmhand, could place an application.

Between 1854 and 1930, an estimated 150,000 children were shipped west in this manner. Most came from Northern cities, and most were sent to states including Illinois, Missouri, Indiana, and Ohio.[11] However, some went to Arkansas. In Logan County in the Ozark country just east of Fort Smith was a Benedictine monastery and school known as Subiaco Abbey, founded by German seminarians. They had a relationship with Catholic charities in New York, who sent them at least some children to be adopted out.[12]

The Children's Aid Society, an organization with Protestant roots, also sent a number of children to Arkansas. One young boy who provides a fairly typical example was George Nelson. He was born October 13, 1901, at Sloane's Maternity Hospital in New York and lived at New York Foundling Hospital until January 1904. At just over two years old, he was placed for adoption with the Heim family of Morrison Bluff, Arkansas, a hamlet just a few miles from Subiaco. A letter of documentation from the hospital indicates he was "sent west on a train."[13]

Imagine if one lived in Virginia or North Carolina in 1905 and suddenly came into custody of an unwanted child one wished to disappear. A possible solution would be to send him west for adoption. And in the days before DNA or Social Security numbers, when even fingerprinting barely existed as a science, a child easily could have been tossed into the shuffle.

Still, deliberately trying to "lose" such a child carried risks. An eight-year-old such as Kenneth, for example, might be mature enough to identify himself and tell the names of his parents and where he lived.

Senator Beasley's trip came to nothing. It is unknown exactly where he traveled in Arkansas, or to whom he spoke. But after a few weeks, the press reported that Beasley had returned home empty handed. He had met with the boy who was thought to be Kenneth and who "resembled him in a marked degree," but it turned out not to be him.[14]

Back in Raleigh, the counsels were preparing their appellate briefs for the North Carolina Supreme Court. Aycock and Aydlett did the writing for Harrison, while the state's case would be argued by Hayden Clement, a new attorney from Salisbury who, at age twenty-eight, had just taken the job of assistant attorney general a few months earlier.

Harrison's defenders knew the burden of persuasion lay upon them. They probably also suspected people were whispering that their client had sent Sam Beasley on a cruel wild goose chase, and so their burden would be even heavier.

As with any appeal, they needed to cast a wide net. They raised a total of eighteen "exceptions," or points of law on which they claimed the court had made errors. Some of them, not surprisingly, were long shots. For example, they questioned whether it was proper for Senator Beasley to testify with the aid of a hand-drawn map of the Poplar Branch area.

More fundamentally, they questioned the court's decision to move the trial only the short distance from Currituck to Pasquotank County, which Aycock said had not been sufficient to shield the defendant from local publicity and anger. The defense still contended that Dare County, across the sound, would have been better. The state countered that when the trial court heard the defense motion to change venue, the judge had asked which counties it thought were unacceptable to its client, and the defense answered only Currituck and Camden Counties.[15] The judge then had asked the prosecutor which county he would prefer, and he named Pasquotank. And since the defense did not "except," or object, to Pasquotank at the time, it had waived the right to object now.[16]

There was also the lingering question of Kenneth's pocketknife. When he first brought it up at trial, Ward told the court he intended to introduce evidence later to show how the knife was relevant to the disappearance. For whatever reason, Ward never got around to it, and so Judge Allen instructed the jurors not to consider any mention of the knife in their deliberations. But of course, no one then or now has discovered a way to eliminate memories from jurors' minds. Aycock now argued that Ward had deliberately planted the red herring, and the misconduct entitled the defendant to a new trial.[17]

But above all, the defense maintained it had been placed in an untenable position as soon as the trial began. That was the primary theme of Aycock's oral argument before the North Carolina Supreme Court, which he presented on August 27, 1907. Everyone in the Pasquotank courthouse, including the jury and the spectators, was so absorbed with hatred toward Harrison that he could never have gotten a fair hearing. It was so pervasive, in fact, that Ward could play all the evidentiary tricks he wanted, and the defense was hamstrung by its fear of objecting too strongly.

"They say we didn't except!" exclaimed Aycock before the court. "We had got in a position where we were afraid to except— not afraid of being mobbed, but afraid of its effect on the jury." The most obvious example came during Ward's closing argument, when the gallery broke into sustained applause. Judge Allen had restored order, identified the main instigator of the disturbance and held him in contempt, and instructed the jury not to be swayed by the shenanigans. But although Aycock hated to criticize his old friend, he said it had not been enough. "The Judge did all he could to correct it, but he could not correct the fact. The fact was that the public was demanding a conviction. In the courtroom sat the wives and daughters of the jurymen. They were getting orders from headquarters, if you dare acquit, you will be held up to execration. They swept the jury off their feet."[18]

To further the point, the defense cited a precedent case that was less political but no less emotional, and in fact had been tried only five years earlier in the very same Elizabeth City courtroom. The trial of Jim Wilcox centered on the mysterious death of his enchanting young lover, Ella Maud "Beautiful Nell" Cropsey. Known more than a century later as the Albemarle region's most intriguing true-crime mystery, it has far eclipsed the Beasley-Harrison case in fame and notoriety.[19]

Nineteen-year-old Nell was known as the prettiest young lady in town. She lived with her parents, sister, and brothers in a lovely white house on the waterfront, and on a chilly day in November 1901 she spent the evening socializing in the family parlor with her sister, some friends, and her suitor, Jim Wilcox, age twenty-five, the son of a former sheriff of the county.

As the night wore on, the guests departed and Nell's sister went to bed, leaving Jim and Nell on the front porch. When daybreak came, Nell was nowhere to be found. Her worried father went to the Wilcox home and found Jim, apparently awakened from a deep sleep. He said he did not know where Nell was, as he had left her on the porch at about 11:15 the previous night.[20]

The neighbors immediately started a search along the riverbanks. They dragged the river bottom with hooks and fired cannons over the water, hoping the reverberations would bring the body to the surface. Wilcox was charged with criminal abduction and placed in the Pasquotank jail, but it was not until thirty-seven days later that the charges were upgraded to murder. That was when Nell's body floated into view and was recovered in a remarkable state of preservation for supposedly having been in the water so long.[21]

Quickly, a lynch mob formed outside the jail, but it backed down after the Cropsey family urged the crowd to desist and the governor dispatched the "naval reserves," a division of the State Guard, to secure the jail. Wilcox survived to go to trial, but it did not go well for him. The courtroom atmosphere was so toxic toward him that, during the defense counsel's closing argument, "about 100 people left the courtroom in a body and rang a fire bell with the fixed intention to destroy the force of the remarks of the defendant's counsel and distracting the attention of the jury."[22] Although Wilcox was found guilty and sentenced to hang, that breach of courtroom order was just too much for the North Carolina Supreme Court, which overturned the verdict and ordered a new trial.

Harrison's attorneys had some hope of a similar decision here.[23] And they were as familiar as anyone with the particulars of the Nell Cropsey case. Wilcox's lead counsel, the man whose argument had been interrupted, was Edwin Aydlett. And the governor who called out the reserves was Charles Aycock.

Mustering all his eloquence, Aycock pleaded with the court to undo what was essentially a legalized necktie party. Harrison had been "lynched under the studious form of law." Echoing some of his private correspondence, in which he worried about public emotion intruding into the legal process and "judge-craft" turning into "priest-craft," Aycock asked rhetorically, "Are the courts to become political conventions?"[24]

Anyone thinking back to 1898 and the White Supremacy Campaign might have felt Aycock was about ten years too late to be concerned about the integrity of the system. Had he tried as hard to ensure the safety of black defendants as he had that of Jim Wilcox? Maybe not. And had he not used political drama of his own in defending Harrison, his current white client? Of course he had, though he was well within his ethical boundaries to do so.

For the state, Attorney Clement responded that the trial had proceeded in as orderly a manner as possible. Judge Allen had acted properly to tamp down any disturbances of proceedings. And after all, if a defense team of four attorneys, including two former governors, could not secure a fair trial for its client, then how could anyone ever claim the system was fair?

The justices of the North Carolina Supreme Court took the case under advisement and would issue their decision in a few weeks, as was typical. But whether or not anyone in Raleigh knew it, new proceedings were brewing back in Elizabeth City.

On the state's motion, Joshua Harrison was brought back to court to address his bond. The state wanted to increase it, as it had

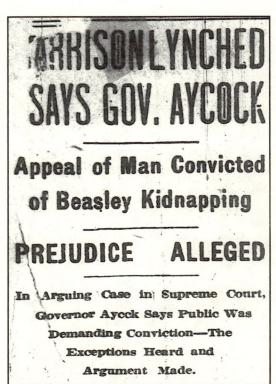

RALEIGH *NEWS AND OBSERVER*

reason to allege that "the Defendant has been continuously absent from the State, for the purpose of avoiding judgment in case it is affirmed by the Supreme Court." The court held a hearing on September 17, 1907, and the record reflects that Harrison was present for it. The court decided to increase his bond from three thousand to five thousand dollars, all of it to be secured in cash. In doing so, the superior-court judge found that Harrison had "absented himself from the State."[25] He perhaps had traveled up the road to Norfolk, either to visit family or to plan an escape.

Harrison was returned to jail briefly, although the record shows his relatives came up with the extra two thousand dollars almost immediately, at which time he was released. But that turned out to be a matter of regret. The Pasquotank County Courthouse probably was equipped with a telephone by that time, and if so, it was a shame no one in Raleigh placed a call to relay the North Carolina Supreme Court's decision, which was issued that same day, September 17.

The unanimous five-member court, in an opinion by Associate Justice George H. Brown, upheld Harrison's conviction and ordered that he serve the sentence imposed. The court considered each point raised by the defense but in the end dismissed them all, concluding that the court had not committed any error so significant that a new trial was warranted. The court took no definitive position on Harrison's guilt or innocence, as appellate courts are not called upon to do so. But in conclusion, it noted that "the State relies upon a chain of circumstances proven by different witnesses, no one of which, standing alone, would be sufficient to convict; but, when taken together, the State contends they point strongly to the Defendant's guilt. It must be admitted that the circumstances in evidence point to the guilt of the Defendant, and that there is not a circumstance which points to any other person."[26]

Therefore, Joshua Harrison would have to wear prison stripes. But now, someone would have to find him and bring him in.

Part IV

Resolutions

North Carolina's state penitentiary, built 1870 to 1884, for $1.25 million.

CHAPTER 17

AT HIS OWN HANDS

Twenty years in the state penitentiary. It would have seemed a harsh reckoning for anyone, especially a man pushing seventy who had spent most of his life as a big fish in a small rural pond, and who had used his money and family connections to evade so many legal predicaments over the years.

Joshua Harrison must have realized that if he submitted and let himself be taken through the prison gates, he was likely to end his days there. And whatever years remained to him were sure not to pass pleasantly. Any prison has a pecking order. Inmates who harm children are despised by their fellows. And even apart from that, an old man such as Harrison would have stuck out like a sore thumb.

The setting in itself could have intimidated even the most brazen young tough. The penitentiary was a massive, forbidding structure built on what was then the outskirts of Raleigh. The central building was designed to appear as a castle, a sort of conglomerate of medieval and Victorian styles. The frontispiece was four stories tall, surmounted with cupolas and spires on both ends. To the rear was the prison yard, a space of more than twenty acres surrounded by a wall of massive stone blocks twenty feet high and seventeen feet thick at the base.[1]

The construction was a massive undertaking, starting in 1870 and ending in 1884. When it was finally completed, Governor Thomas J. Jarvis would remember it as one of the proudest accomplishments of his administration, especially in light of the debacle that preceded it.

The Raleigh site was North Carolina's second attempt to build a state prison. In 1868, the Reconstruction government of Governor William W. Holden had spent a hundred thousand dollars on an eight-thousand-acre tract in eastern Chatham County, intending to build it there. Not until later did it realize it had been duped. The land was nearly worthless. The only access to it was by a single spur track owned by a railroad whose bonds were held primarily by Milton S. Littlefield, a New York financier and the same man who had sold the property to the state. When these facts came to light, the state was forced to sell the property at a huge loss. The incident came to symbolize "one of the worst stereotypes of carpetbagger misrule." [2]

Governor Holden, although a native North Carolinian, was widely denounced as a white-race traitor and a tool of the Northern military establishment that had put him in office. In 1871, in fact, the state legislature succeeded in impeaching and removing him from the governorship. The primary allegations were that he had exceeded his constitutional authority in trying to tamp down Ku Klux Klan violence, although the murmurs about financial impropriety could not have helped. When the Democrats were able to wrest control back from the Reconstructionists, one of their first major projects was to build the prison. They viewed it as a monument to their strength and purpose.

The cost of construction came to $1.25 million, a large sum for the time, but the state satisfied itself that the costs would have been higher if it could not have used convict labor. That was, in fact, the entire point of a state penitentiary. By statute, it was required to be financially self-sustaining. Inmates were to be put to profitable work, or at least to produce goods for sale.[3]

And so it was from the beginning. As soon as work on the prison began, inmates were brought to the site and housed in temporary shelters as they cleared the land and hauled stone. The work was hard and the conditions severe. For example, as of August 1875, the state had 794 inmates in its custody. By the end of 1876, some 106 of those inmates died, many of them in an epidemic of typhoid dysentery that swept through the camp in Raleigh.[4]

The statistics also show a severe racial imbalance in the numbers of men sentenced to prison. As throughout the South, black men made up a large majority of those serving prison time in North Carolina. In 1874, of the 214 men sentenced to prison in North Carolina, 190 were black.

The treatment a convict could expect to receive was determined at least in part by race. The times called for segregation by race, so the relatively few whites were more likely to be housed at the Raleigh penitentiary. Black inmates had a tougher time, for while a few of them were incarcerated in Raleigh, most were parceled out to work off-site. Some of them labored on road and bridge construction on the infamous "chain gangs." North Carolina continued using chain gangs longer than any other state, not eliminating the practice until 1972.[5]

Most black inmates, however, performed work that seemed transplanted directly from the plantation. In 1894, some 80 percent of North Carolina's prisoners worked on farms. Some of those farms belonged to private landowners, who paid pennies by the day for inmate labor. Yet the state owned quite a bit of agricultural land itself, for the express purpose of inmate cultivation. By 1920, it owned more than thirteen thousand acres worked by convicts.[6]

For white inmates at the penitentiary, conditions were less brutal but still strict and tedious. The cell blocks were operated according to the Auburn System, a governing plan that originated at the famous prison in Upstate New York in the 1820s and was centered around penitence, silence, and—most importantly—hard labor. Although inmates ate their meals together in the mess hall, no talking was allowed at any time, not even when they were at work, which was a large portion of the time. Inmates were expected to work for their keep, and the penitentiary had several options on the premises. Between 1898 and 1900, it opened a shirt-making and laundry business, a mattress factory, and a machine shop that produced and repaired wagon parts.[7]

Joshua Harrison could not have been looking forward to any of that, which was probably why he chose to "absent" himself from the state, as the prosecutors had feared.

After he left the Elizabeth City jail following the bond hearing on September 17, he lost no time getting out of town. Whether he knew for certain when the North Carolina Supreme Court decision would be issued is unclear, but he likely knew it was coming.

Harrison went immediately to Norfolk. He did not go to his daughter's boardinghouse, which would have been the first place to look for him. Instead, he checked into the Gladstone Hotel, a fine multistory stone building downtown, known for some of the city's best lodgings. Located at the corner of Main and Nebraska Streets, it had rooms starting at two dollars per night, with meals extra according to either the American or the European plan, depending on how many meals one wanted to purchase in advance.[8]

Around five in the afternoon on September 18, the Norfolk police received a telegram from Solicitor Ward. He had gotten a tip that Harrison was in Norfolk. After informing the Norfolk officers of the court's decision, he asked them to carry out the order for Harrison's arrest. Apparently, they had information about where he could be found, because the police immediately dispatched two officers, Detectives Wright and Dozier, to the Gladstone. Ward cautioned them to be wary and to disarm Harrison, as he had threatened to commit suicide.[9]

The detectives arrived about fifteen minutes after Harrison checked in. They sent a bellboy to his room to ask him to come down to the lobby to answer a phone call. The young man found Harrison in his room, but he was in no mood to talk. He was astute enough to know the jig was up, and that whatever foreign-bound vessel he may have hoped to jump aboard, it was now too late. He slammed the door in the bellboy's face. Before the young man could reach the top of the stairs to report back, a gunshot rang out.[10]

The detectives burst into the room and found Harrison lying full length on the bed, half dressed, as if he had been sleeping. He had an ugly bullet wound in the side of his forehead, "while his brains were oozing out onto the bed-clothing." By his side lay a .38 caliber pistol.

It was clear there would be no last-minute revelation from his lips, as there had been with Joseph Douglass after the Long Island shootout years before. The detectives rushed Harrison to St. Vincent's Hospital in their horse-drawn "patrol wagon," but the medical technology of the day offered no hope for a gunshot of that type. He was clinically dead the moment the bullet struck him, and after lingering into the early-morning hours, he was declared legally so.[11]

The only message he left was scrawled on hotel stationery, which the detectives later found in his coat pocket at the hospital:

> September 18, 1907. This day I have been notified of an unjust sentence of twenty years in the penitentiary. I am an innocent man. God knows it. My family knows it. I am about to end my life at my own hands. No one is in any way responsible save the cruel ones who imposed the awful sentence. May God bless my precious family. I believe the world will be charitable to them all. To the whole world I say good-by. Whoever finds my body, notify my daughter, Mrs. Gallop, 192 Duke Street, Norfolk.
>
> Joshua Harrison
>
> I leave in my pockets 55 cents. I want my effects returned to Mrs. Maggie Gallop, 192 Duke Street.[12]

An innocent man? Or maybe a guilty man who had finally gone too far, who had grown accustomed to skirting the law but in the end had tangled with the wrong people and committed a crime too despicable to get away with? Whichever it was, the truth still lay in the shadows, and Harrison's suicide note did little to change anyone's mind.

His wife and daughter, in their grief, stood by their man as they escorted Harrison's body home to Jarvisburg for burial. "My husband was innocent. God knows he was," said Ann Jarvis Harrison. Her daughter Maggie added, "My father was not guilty of the crime of kidnapping Kenneth Beasley. He was asleep at his home the night the boy disappeared."[13]

Sam Beasley, at home in Norfolk with his wife, spoke for both of them when contacted by the press. Harrison's plea of innocence left him cold. "I don't believe it. I am convinced that he was guilty, and ninety-nine out of every hundred persons in Currituck, where Harrison was known, are of the same opinion." As he turned his head away to wipe a teardrop from his eye, Beasley said, "[Harrison] has been tried for murder before, and he should have been tried for murder in connection with the disappearance of my little son, for as sure as I stand here I believe he murdered my boy. The character of the man and the threat he made against me leaves no room for doubt about this in my mind."[14]

The Beasleys and the Harrisons had no doubts. They knew what their hearts believed, as they would continue to do for years afterward. But for others, and especially the press, the case was fertile ground for speculation.

Any candid observer at the trial had to admit the evidence presented by each side was ambiguous at best. Upon Harrison's death, most now agreed that if he had in fact been guilty of abducting Kenneth, then the boy must now be dead, whether by accident, neglect, or murder. Surely, Harrison, to save himself from prison, would have given the boy up if he were still alive. But the question of guilt or innocence still hung in the air.

The Raleigh newspapers may have summed it up best:

> What went on in the room of Harrison, summoned by the officers of the law; what policies nerved his hand; what despair sat at his elbow; what desperation of guilt or cowardice of innocence pulled the trigger of his pistol; will never be known. Perhaps, after all, he figured upon the doubt—the haunting doubt—that he has raised. If so it was a cruel resource, not only to the father and mother of the kidnapped boy, but to the jury that convicted and the

courts that sought to execute their sentence as well! And now that it has ended, there is the cruelty of the doubt that will not be put to rest; there remains the mystery of Kenneth Beasley to excite hope and to baffle it.[15]

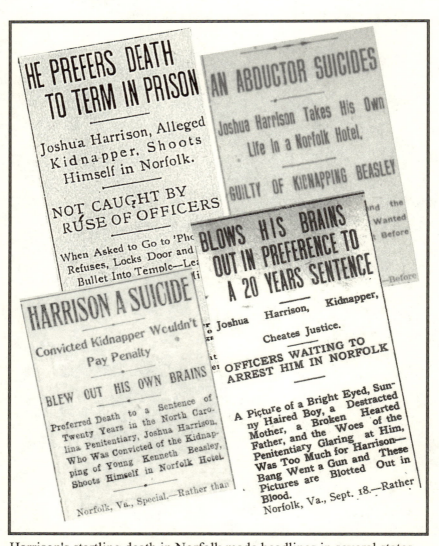

Harrison's startling death in Norfolk made headlines in several states—
and would forever leave a mystery.

CHAPTER 18

THEORIES OF LOST BOY CASES

Even after Harrison's death, no one came forward to return Kenneth Beasley to his family or to reveal what happened. The lost boy was never found, and more than a century later next to nothing is known of what became of him.

In fairness, it does not seem that many people have invested time in thinking about it. If most people in the Currituck region believed Harrison was guilty, then his suicide only confirmed their belief. And if the boy was now dead, as even his parents seemed to accept, there was no point in speculating on how the crime went down. Case closed, at least to most people's satisfaction. There has been no investigative reporting on the case since, unless one counts *Dead and Gone*.

Have any new theories arisen since 1907? For that question, it is logical to turn to the folks everyone in Currituck County seems to regard as the best authorities on local history.

In addition to teaching social studies in the Currituck schools for thirty years, Barbara Snowden has served as president of the Currituck Historical Society for at least twenty. In that role, she has written biographical accounts of several communities in the county, including Poplar Branch. Snowden has also taken the lead in identifying historically significant buildings for preservation; in fact, the old Currituck Courthouse and Jail might not still be standing today but for her interventions. For her efforts, she has been rewarded with a seat on the North Carolina Historical Commission, as well as the prestigious Order of the Long Leaf Pine from the governor.[1]

Another authority was the late Travis Morris, a born-and-bred Currituck native who founded one of the first real estate companies in the area. His father, the Honorable Chester R. Morris, served as a superior-court judge in the county. In addition to his real estate career, Travis Morris wrote eleven books about the history and folklore of the area, including *Stories of the Old Currituck Outer Banks* and *Duck Hunting on Currituck Sound*.

When asked whether anyone has come up with new insights into Joshua Harrison's guilt or innocence, Snowden, Morris, and others in Currituck County today answered a clear no. Harrison had his defenders, mostly within his own extended family, and they maintained that their kinsman would never have murdered a child. But since the mid-1900s, those who remembered the case personally have passed on or moved away. And even while they were still around, they never offered any plausible new explanation for what happened to Kenneth. All they could come up with was the same assumption that Harrison gave to the reporters prior to his trial—that the boy simply got lost.[2]

Basically, that leaves the same set of possibilities presented to the jury in 1907. Either Kenneth got disoriented in the Maple Swamp and died from exposure or from falling into a creek, and his body was never found; or he wandered over to the Currituck Sound shoreline, stumbled into the water, and drowned without trace; or someone snatched him.

Three theories, then. And even after more than a century, none of them is particularly strong.

THEORIES OF LOST BOY CASES

Before concluding there was a criminal act on anyone's part, it makes sense to weigh the likelihood of an accidental disappearance. On the afternoon Kenneth wandered off, Professor Jennings and the neighbors assumed at first he had gotten lost. The assumption was reasonable, as was their initial response: gathering as many searchers as possible and sifting through the woods. They did the best they could, although far more is now known about how children get lost, how they behave when they are panicked or disoriented, how far and how quickly they can move on foot, and how to organize a search for them.

One of the seminal studies on the behavior of lost persons was written in 1977 by William G. Syrotuck, a researcher with many years of experience in the field. In his study, Syrotuck analyzed 229 missing person incidents, including people of all ages and all walks of life, in a variety of settings ranging from wilderness areas to suburban neighborhoods, mostly in the states of New York and Washington. In doing so, he was able to recognize patterns in how people react when they become lost or disoriented. Some of those patterns are quite predictable according to the subject's age and maturity.[3]

Consider, for example, children between the ages of seven and twelve, as Kenneth was. Children in that group are growing more mature and self-assured, more willing to venture away from home to play with friends, and sometimes by themselves. But they also tend to overestimate their sense of direction and their ability to navigate between two known places. For example, a child may know where he lives and may be familiar with a playground several blocks away, but when he tries to walk back home by himself the first time, he may get confused about landmarks and intersections. He might attempt a short-cut down an unfamiliar street and lose himself in the process.[4]

Once a child of that age gets disoriented, he tends to become confused and upset, often acting in ways that seem irrational. He might feel embarrassed for getting lost and afraid his parents will discipline him, especially if he gets lost while doing something he shouldn't, such as playing hooky from school, as Kenneth might have. Some children have been known to hide from searchers and refuse to answer when they hear someone calling their names. Or they might panic and set off walking down the most obvious nearby route, such as a street or a wooded pathway, a behavior searchers call "trail-running."[5]

When that type of panic sets in, a child might travel a surprising distance in a short time. Today, search-and-rescue personnel estimate that a child between ages six and twelve can move an average of a mile to a mile and a half per hour on foot. Of course, it depends on the setting.[6] A child lost in a residential neighborhood would be able to move more quickly than one in a swampy woodland thick with trees.

A wilderness area, even a relatively small, circumscribed one like the Maple Swamp, makes the worst possible place to try to locate a child. That was the conclusion of Kenneth A. Hill, a search-and-rescue expert who studied Syrotuck's research and followed it up with his own published analyses in the 1990s. Hill investigated nine cases of children between ages seven and twelve who disappeared in wooded areas. Eight of them were recovered safely, but only as a result of diligent searching by rescue teams. *None* of those nine children was able to find his or her way out of the woods unassisted.[7]

By way of example, consider a tragic case in which Kenneth Hill was involved, and which inspired him to spend much of his career studying search-and-rescue strategy. It involved a boy close in age to Kenneth Beasley, and a setting that was fairly similar, although far to the north.

Andrew Warburton was a nine-year-old from suburban Hamilton, Ontario. In July 1986, he was on vacation with his parents and older brother near Beaverbank, Nova Scotia, about eighteen miles outside Halifax. They were staying in the home of Andrew's aunt in a deeply wooded area not far from Tucker Lake. On a warm day, Andrew set out from the house to meet his brother to go swimming at the lake, wearing trunks, a tank top, and sneakers. The trail to the lake ran through the woods for roughly half a mile. Although Andrew had walked the route previously when accompanied by others, this was his first time by himself.

Somewhere along the trail, he made a wrong turn. When Andrew failed to appear at the lake, the distress call went out and searchers gathered to tramp through the woods and poke through the undergrowth, calling his name. Eventually, five thousand people ranging from experts like Kenneth Hill to untrained volunteers took part in the search. Not until eight days later was Andrew found, dead of hypothermia, about two miles from where he was last seen. It was theorized that, after losing his bearings, he wandered in circles for four or five days. Although the summer days were bright and sunny, the Canadian nights were too cold for the lightly dressed boy to survive.[8]

Here, it seems, was a case of a child who simply was not as familiar with his surroundings as he thought. Once he found himself lost, he panicked and forgot the conventional wisdom of staying put and waiting to be found. As unlikely as it might seem considering the masses of people searching for him, he slipped through the dragnet.

Another such case occurred closer to home, in the Great Smoky Mountains National Park in June 1969, on Father's Day weekend. This time, the lost boy was Dennis Martin, not quite seven, the son of a Knoxville, Tennessee, architect.[9] Dennis was on a camping trip with his father, older brother, grandfather, uncle, and two cousins of similar age at Spence Field, a popular camping spot on a ridge just on the western side of the Tennessee–North Carolina line.

Around three in the afternoon, after the group set up camp, the four boys sneaked away into the dense woods, contriving a bit of harmless fun. They were going to circle back, jump out of the woods, and startle the grownups, who had noticed the boys whispering and were anticipating the prank. A few minutes later, three of the boys jumped out, and everyone laughed for a moment. But Dennis did not reappear. Within minutes, his father and grandfather were calling his name. Failing to find him, they hiked down the ridge to the nearest ranger station. The emergency call was sounded, and within hours masses of searchers gathered.[10]

The masses grew to as many as fourteen hundred, including teams of Green Berets recently returned from tours in Vietnam. They spent more than a week combing the ridges and picking through every conceivable type of underbrush. Unfortunately, a major thunderstorm moved into the area the night Dennis disappeared, dumping five inches of rain onto the mountain over the next three days. No doubt, the rain washed away many small signs, such as scent and footprints, that Dennis might have left behind.

Some clues were found but not investigated, due either to lack of communication or failure to recognize their significance. One searcher found a footprint made by a child's Oxford-style shoe, much like those Dennis was wearing, in a hollow about three miles downhill from where he disappeared. Yet the discovery was written off because searchers had already been in the area, leaving a mass of footprints, with no way to know who made them. Another man, at a point in the woods about nine miles from Spence Field, heard a startling sound that seemed like a child screaming, then looked up and saw "a rough-looking man moving stealthily in the woods." That sighting also was given short shrift by the searchers, who did not think Dennis could have traveled that distance in the time available, although studies since then suggest it was possible.[11]

Dennis Martin was never found. Sadly, the case is remembered today as a cautionary tale of how not to organize a search. One might say the same for the Warburton case. When too many volunteers gather too quickly and plunge into the search area with little organization, they are likely to overlook or trample critical clues that skilled trackers need to pick up someone's trail. It is much better to cordon off the search zone and give access only to experienced trackers who know what to look for.

Thinking back to Poplar Branch in 1905, it is not hard to see how a boy could have lost his way in the woods and slipped through the searchers' fingers. The Maple Swamp was at least as thick and shadowy as forests of Tennessee or Nova Scotia, and it had numerous dark paths winding through it. Certainly, a child might get disoriented, panic, start off trail-running, and get himself more lost. When the neighbors ventured into the woods in the snowy afternoon twilight, poking sticks into the underbrush and pools of water, there was no real organization to it. Who knows what they might have missed? Witnesses at the trial attempted to identify footprints near the schoolhouse as Kenneth's. But with so many children and adults tramping over the area, it was impossible to conclude any such thing.

Therefore, yes, there is a chance Kenneth Beasley got lost in the swamp and died there cold, frightened, and alone.

THEORIES OF LOST BOY CASES

Yet another factor makes the lost-in-the-woods theory less than probable. It boils down to a child's familiarity with his surroundings. While it is possible to lose a boy in the woods, it is much harder to lose him in *his own* woods.

Andrew Warburton and Dennis Martin were kids from the suburbs who got lost on vacation, in forests that were new to them. But Kenneth was born and raised in the country village where he disappeared. His daily routine was to walk the half-mile to the schoolhouse and back home. He and his buddies knew the area behind the schoolhouse as their playground. When Kenneth was not in school or doing chores at home, he and the other boys likely were roaming the woods and fields, playing one game or another. Chances are they had explored those woods behind the schoolhouse any number of times prior to February 13, 1905.

And if it is unlikely that Kenneth died in the swamp, it seems even less probable that he died in the sound. If he had gotten lost, he would have had to wander more than half a mile east to reach the shoreline.[12] To get there, he would have crossed the main Poplar Branch road. Although only a dirt wagon lane at the time, it was an obvious landmark that would have helped him regain his bearings. Even if he had crossed the road and kept wandering all the way to

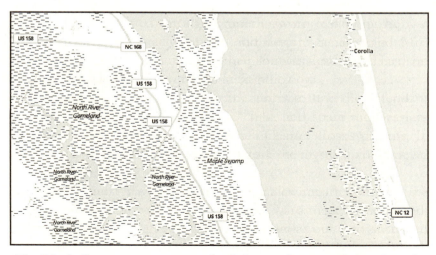

The Maple Swamp consumes much of the area between the modern-day U.S. Highway 158 and the Currituck Sound. Farther east are the Outer Banks and the Atlantic Ocean.

the shore, he would have reached it close to Poplar Branch Landing and the shops surrounding it. That was his father's place of business, a location he certainly knew. Surely, he could not have remained disoriented when crossing so much familiar territory.

If Kenneth for some unknown reason walked all the way to the shoreline, he might have fallen in the water and drowned. But his body was never recovered, and every scientific indicator suggests it would have been.

First, consider the hydrology and tidal patterns of Currituck Sound. Unlike the ocean, which is separated from it by the sand barrier of the Outer Banks, there is not much current in the sound. It is virtually an inland lake of 153 square miles. Roughly six miles wide at Poplar Branch, it stays approximately the same width as it extends south about sixteen miles until it opens into the broader Albemarle Sound. From there, the nearest outlet to the sea is through Oregon Inlet, some thirty miles beyond. What little current exists tends to flow in that direction, from north to south. But unless a significant wind is blowing, there is virtually no current that might carry a body away.[13]

Nor is there much chance for a body to sink out of sight in Currituck Sound. When someone drowns, the body tends to sink briefly, then resurface as the flesh decays and gases build up inside, increasing its buoyancy, although cold air and water temperature might slow the decomposition. A young child, being smaller and lighter, might not sink at all. And even if a child did, he would not have far to sink and would need little time to refloat. The average depth of Currituck Sound is only five feet, and nowhere is it more than thirteen feet deep.[14]

Statistics are available starting in 1913, when North Carolina began to require recording of death certificates, even in cases where the body could not be located. Between 1913 and 1930, one can find eighteen Currituck County certificates that note drowning as the cause of death—approximately one per year. This suggests that drowning deaths were not common, even though that era was the heyday for commercial fishing and duck hunting on Currituck Sound. Granted, many other certificates in the same period listed no cause of death, so only so much can be concluded from these records. But the fact remains that of those eighteen people who were confirmed drowning deaths, all except one were recovered and properly buried.[15] With so many hunting and fishing boats plying the sound, there just was not much chance of a corpse floating away undiscovered.

So if the body of Kenneth Beasley did not sink into the waters of Currituck Sound or the mud of the Maple Swamp, then where did it come to rest?

Prosecutor Hallet Sydney "Hot Shot" Ward, in his later years.

CHAPTER 19

ALL MISGIVINGS RELIEVED

Observers may be left with the best of the three lousy theories: that Kenneth was abducted and murdered. If so, two big questions still lurk in the shadowy morass of this tale: the who and the how.

As for who did it, the North Carolina Supreme Court was correct in its summary. The jury heard evidence pointing to Joshua Harrison's guilt and none pointing to any other suspect. The prosecution at least had a sound theory of the case, that Harrison had means, motive, and opportunity to commit the crime, and it also had witnesses to support the theory.

Harrison's defense never tried to identify an alternative perpetrator. Ultimately, it thought the safest strategy was to argue there was no crime, and therefore no criminal. It asked the jury to accept that the boy got lost while Harrison was at home or traveling with his family members. His attorneys must have known his alibi would depend on testimony from his own relatives, which would be open to skepticism. And yet they still thought that approach was better than suggesting that someone else lurking in the woods behind the school might have snatched Kenneth.

This despite the hints that there *were* alternative suspects. The papers, in the first few days after Kenneth disappeared, focused on the mysterious drunk in the log cabin behind the school. If it was true that the searchers made their way to that cabin—possibly because the bloodhounds had followed Kenneth's scent there—and found an inebriated "hermit" or "Yankee" inside, then that would have been an obvious fact for the defense to emphasize at trial.

One can imagine several scenarios. Maybe Kenneth, while roaming the woods, happened upon a whiskey still run by someone other than Harrison, and that person had to eliminate the witness to the illicit doings. Or, to go farther afield, maybe the person who gave Kenneth his pocketknife was not Harrison but some pervert who wanted to lure him into the woods for some twisted purpose.

But if anyone at Harrison's trial mentioned the drunk in the log cabin, it is not reflected in the transcript or the press reports. Some people, including Solicitor Ward, suspected that the defense did not bring it up because the "Yankee," whatever his name, was an acquaintance or business associate of Harrison's.[1] It would do no good for the defense to mention him because that would deflect suspicion back on to Harrison.

There is no way to know for certain who other than Harrison might have been creeping about the woods that cold February day. But if one takes the position that Harrison was innocent, then a lot of people were prepared to go to court to swear false witness against him. Some of the state's witnesses gave testimony that sounded fishy, as even Judge Allen noted in open court. But was Harrison such a despised character that they *all* were willing to lie to send him to prison?

The people who testified against Harrison may have been acquaintances or political supporters of Sam Beasley, but they had no obvious reason to go out of their way to perjure themselves. The same cannot be said for Harrison's wife, children, and other family members. On balance, when the credibility of all the witnesses who testified for the state is compared to that of all who testified for

Harrison, the state's case appears more credible.

That is not to dispute that the trial was a messy affair. Even if observers conclude Harrison probably did commit the crime, it is still fair to say that the jury, after seeing the attorneys' shenanigans and hearing the contradictory testimony, really *should* have concluded reasonable doubt and found him not guilty. There is no intellectual dishonesty in that; it's just that there is a distinction between factual culpability and legal guilt.

If Harrison did abduct the boy, how did he go about it, and what was the motivation? Was it a ransom kidnapping, or was Harrison vicious enough that he wanted to kill an eight-year-old child out of spite against the father for damaging his wine business?

When he testified, Sam Beasley seemed to downplay the ransom motive, focusing instead on Harrison's violent temper. According to Beasley, there was never any credible mention of ransom by anyone until more than a year and a half later, when Harrison supposedly asked T. C. Woodhouse to contact Beasley at the courthouse.[2] And by Beasley's telling, the ransom demand came as a complete surprise to him. If Harrison really wanted money, surely he would have made some effort to collect it sooner.

But if Harrison only wanted revenge against Beasley, not money, kidnapping would not have been necessary. When Harrison met Kenneth in the woods, he could have pulled out a pistol and shot the boy between his eyes, as he allegedly had done to Caleb Owens years before. He could have hidden Kenneth's body in the swamp or just left it there in the woods, where buzzards would soon begin to circle and lead searchers to it. Either way, it would have satisfied Harrison's thirst for revenge and left no witnesses. Why risk taking the boy into his buggy on a long ride north, where they might be spotted, if he intended only to kill him?

Generally speaking, murder is a simpler crime than kidnapping and tends to leave fewer clues. A kidnapper has no reason to abduct the victim, stash him in a secure place, and then release him with the risk he may identify the kidnapper—that is, unless he has a motive that goes beyond harming the victim. He also wants to extort something.

Consider an interesting conversation that involved America's most infamous kidnapper of all time. In February 1936, Bruno Richard Hauptmann was sitting on New Jersey's death row after being convicted of abducting and killing the infant son of Charles Lindbergh, the famed aviator. At trial, the state had minimized the chance that anyone other than Hauptmann was involved; he had been caught with a large portion of the ransom money hidden in his garage, and the ransom letters appeared to match his handwriting, among other things. But many doubted that one man could have pulled off the logistics of traveling from New York City to the Lindbergh estate in the countryside, sneaking into the child's second-story bedroom by climbing a ladder, and disappearing into the night after dumping the body in nearby woods. Also, two sets of footprints were found at the crime scene.

Sam Leibowitz, one of the best criminal defense attorneys of the 1930s, met with Hauptmann, trying to get him to name his accomplices in exchange for a commutation of his death sentence. But even with the electric chair just days away, Hauptmann denied any role in the crime. So Leibowitz went at him indirectly, playing to Hauptmann's expertise, and maybe his vanity. Rather than asking how he did it, Leibowitz asked Hauptmann to speculate about how the crime might have gone down.

When asked how the child might have been killed, Hauptmann said, "By accident." The kidnappers wanted money, and they would not have risked their chance of collecting it by murdering their collateral so soon. Instead, they likely slipped and dropped the child when descending the ladder, fracturing his skull. The financial motive was important, Hauptmann thought, because if the perpetrators only had some personal grudge against Charles Lindbergh, they would have smothered the baby in his crib.

"And if they did, they'd have left the body right there in the house," suggested Leibowitz.

"That's right," said Hauptmann.[3]

Yet if Joshua Harrison abducted Kenneth for the purpose of extorting money, why wait eighteen months? And frankly, the state's version of the events leading to the ransom demand in early September 1906 is strange enough to raise the eyebrows of any skeptic.

So many witnesses, from T. C. Woodhouse to Thomas Baum

to E. W. Ansell and Millard Morrisette, either saw Harrison driving away with the boy or heard him boast of the deed shortly afterward. And yet they supposedly kept their mouths shut until September 1, 1906, when Harrison first made his overture to Woodhouse. And then Sam Beasley somehow was able to gather all these witnesses in time for the grand jury meeting on September 5? And that is to say nothing of Woodhouse's tale of how he confronted Harrison in his room, causing Harrison to break down from either fear or remorse. It is all too impractical—and melodramatic—to accept at face value.

Ponder this: Suppose Sam Beasley knew Harrison was guilty long before he sought the indictment because he had heard from these witnesses privately. And suppose further that Beasley kept quiet about it because he wanted to work out a ransom deal in secret, partly to save face politically but mostly to get his child back safely and not arouse a mob who might lynch Harrison, ruining any chance of his son's being found. Perhaps ransom negotiations did take place, and maybe money was paid, and then Harrison reneged on the deal.

Perhaps Harrison refused to release Kenneth either because he was just that malicious or because the boy was already dead, whereupon Sam Beasley gathered the witnesses and resolved to convict the bastard any way he could. He would do it under the proper guise of the law, of course. But if he knew Harrison was guilty, and that he would not risk testifying in his own defense, and that he probably would have few supporters aside from his relatives, then Beasley and his witnesses would have plenty of leeway in the stories they told the jury.

Granted, this is speculative, and it goes against Occam's first principle of rational deduction, which is to choose the simplest solution that requires the fewest assumptions.[*] But it does make as much sense as any possibility anyone has come up with thus far.

If there was a ransom deal, it would have been too risky for Beasley and Harrison to meet face to face. Someone might have witnessed them doing so. Or worse, someone might have started shooting. Far better to have the deal negotiated by a go-between, someone trusted to be discreet. Sam Beasley's legal counsel, perhaps?

---

[*] Attributed to William of Ockham—14th century English Franciscan friar, philosopher, and theologian—"Occam's razor" is a problem-solving principle suggesting the simplest solution tends to be the right one.

In his testimony, Beasley said he consulted an attorney before he swore out the criminal charges against Harrison. It is unknown who that was, or when the consultation happened, but it is known that Beasley had an attorney representing him in an unrelated civil matter that was pending at the same time his son was missing. It was Edwin Aydlett, the Grand Wizard himself.

It turns out that in December 1904, two months before Kenneth disappeared, Sam Beasley initiated a suit in Currituck County court on behalf of an orphaned teenager named William Dunton, for whom Beasley had been appointed legal guardian. That lawsuit had nothing to do with politics, liquor, or Harrison. It was a real estate case filed against a company that was allegedly trespassing on some farmland young Dunton had inherited from his father. But the law firm Beasley retained to represent him was Aydlett and Ehringhaus.[4]

It is no surprise that Beasley would have gone to Aydlett for advice on that case or any other legal matter. Not only did he have the most prominent law office in Elizabeth City, but the Grand Wizard was a political patron for Beasley and other candidates in the area. In August 1904, when Beasley had been chosen to run for the State Senate at the county Democratic convention, it was Aydlett who gave the nominating speech.[5]

After his son disappeared, Beasley seems to have let the Dunton case go. It was continued many times on the court docket, with no action being taken through the spring term of 1911. But throughout that time, Aydlett continued as Beasley's attorney of record even while he was defending Harrison in criminal court for kidnapping Beasley's child.[6]

And that was not the only matter in which Aydlett was representing Harrison. In September 1905, Harrison was sued by the Royster Guano Company of Norfolk.[7] Court records describe it only as a suit to collect a debt. Most likely, Harrison was purchasing farm fertilizer on account and fell behind on his payments. The Minute Docket clearly shows Aydlett and Ehringhaus as counsel for the defendant. The case lingered for a year but was settled on September 6, 1906, apparently upon payment of an undisclosed sum. That was the civil case that brought Harrison to Currituck

Courthouse, supposedly by coincidence, on the day the grand jury indicted him for kidnapping.[8]

Did all of these dealings amount to a conflict of interest on Aydlett's part? Not by the standards of the time, which illustrates how close-knit the legal community was, and to some extent still is, in small-town North Carolina. In rural counties, the same attorneys see each other in the same courtrooms every day, and there are always cases in which one attorney has a past or current relationship with an opposing party. Even today, some judges take the practical view that such conflicts are inevitable, and attorneys have to work around them as best they can.

In those eighteen months after Kenneth disappeared, Beasley told the press how badly he wanted to retrieve his son, and suspicion clearly was circling around Harrison. And during that time, both families were represented by the same law firm. If the child was still alive, would it really have been impossible to strike a deal?

Perhaps there was a deal, and perhaps it was facilitated by the Grand Wizard. Maybe Harrison's fertilizer debt and other debts he may have had were paid off by Beasley or by some other sympathetic party acting on his behalf. And if Beasley had saved his cash and paid the ransom in expectation of getting his son back, only to be hoodwinked, then he should be congratulated for his patience in not calling out the lynch mob. But he would at least have contacted his friend Solicitor Ward to make sure the grand jury indictment was ready to be served on September 6, when he knew Harrison would be at the courthouse.

Then again, maybe Aydlett did not facilitate the deal himself, so as to keep his hands clean and make sure he still could represent Harrison at trial if it came to that. If so, then who was the designated go-between?

T. C. Woodhouse is a mysterious figure in this narrative, and not just for his unlikely story about how he communicated back and forth between Harrison and Beasley and brought Harrison to tears in early September 1906. Think back to the 1904 and 1905 court sessions, when Harrison was found not guilty of selling liquor and "disposing of mortgaged property." The court records tell little but do offer a tantalizing, exasperating clue. The clerk noted that prior to the trials, each of those cases was continued at least once at the state's request because one of its prosecution witnesses was absent: someone named T. J. Woodhouse. Or did the clerk mean T. C. Woodhouse? Maybe the clerk wrote down the wrong initial, or maybe T. J. was a relative of T. C.[9]

But whichever Woodhouse it was, he did at least appear in court in February 1905, when he pled guilty to a charge of "affray."[10] Was that part of a deal? If Woodhouse was familiar with Harrison's liquor dealings and was cooperating with Ward and Beasley to prosecute Harrison as far back as 1904, then perhaps they used Woodhouse as their intermediary. They might have dispatched him to contact Harrison with a proposal for Kenneth's release, and done it much earlier than September 1906.

It is almost certain the answer will never be known. That eighteen-month gap was, and still is, the most perplexing question in the entire case. It is hard to come up with a plausible scenario for what transpired during that time—more difficult, in fact, than to imagine how the abduction took place. That part is relatively simple.

If Harrison did it, there must have been some premeditation in the way he met up with Kenneth alone in the woods. It is too much to assume that it happened coincidentally. Harrison, after he was indicted, protested he had never met Sam Beasley's children and would not have known any of them by sight. It was a fair point. The Harrisons and Beasleys lived in different communities, attended different churches, and certainly did not socialize. How would Harrison even have recognized Kenneth, much less arranged a meeting?

Chances are that someone set the boy up. Someone, likely a person he knew and trusted, encouraged Kenneth to venture into the woods by himself.

Imagine if one morning, after Kenneth arrived at school, he was taken aside for a moment by his charming young teacher, Miss Nina Pocahontas Harrison. She would have to be careful and make sure she was not overheard, especially by Professor Jennings, who was living at the Beasleys' house. She might have whispered something like, "Kenneth, a man lives in an old house back in the woods, and he has some mighty pretty puppies in a pen. Would you like to go back there and play with them?"

And Miss Nina would have cautioned him not to say anything about it to Benny, Irving, or the other boys, assuring Kenneth it would be their secret. In fact, she would let him go back there after recess, while the other children were in class. Maybe she pressed a pocketknife into Kenneth's hands as a token of sincerity. And she probably let him wander back there a couple of times, possibly on the Thursday or Friday before Valentine's Day, just to make sure he could find his way to the Yankee's cabin. And then on Monday, he ventured down the shadowy path, never to return. The day was probably chosen because everyone knew Senator Beasley would be in Raleigh, not able to take charge of searching for his son.

Secrecy would have been key. If Kenneth's schoolmates had known about the puppies, they would have wanted to come along. That would explain the evasive words Kenneth spoke to his cousin Benny—"I'm going back farther"—just as the bell rang to summon the rest of them back to class.

Many years later, Hallet Ward reflected on the case when he was interviewed by Manly Wade Wellman for *Dead and Gone*. Ward indicated he had forgotten Cassie Beasley told him Kenneth had mentioned the puppies as he walked out the door that Monday morning. The memory did not recur to him, in fact, until one day in the 1930s when he traveled through Poplar Branch and had a chance to explore the woods himself. Somewhere, someone had mentioned that the Yankee kept some dogs at his cabin in the woods.

For Ward, the story of the puppies filled a gap in his understanding of the case. It finally explained why Kenneth would have gone roaming the woods alone, and how Harrison would have known to be waiting for him. According to the former prosecutor, "All my misgivings were relieved."[11]

Well, maybe. It is understandable that Ward would have said that. By the time he spoke with Wellman in the 1950s, Ward was in his eighties and probably wanted to put to rest one of the few controversies that had marked his long career in public service. At the trial, he had assured the jury that Kenneth was alive and well and would be returned to his parents if they would find Harrison guilty. The jurors obliged, and yet the mystery only deepened with

Harrison's suicide. Some people probably resented Ward for that.

But if the puppies really were the clincher, why did Ward not bring it up during the trial? Why did he not get Mrs. Beasley to testify about it? Probably not because it slipped his mind but because it would have complicated the case needlessly. Any prosecutor wants his theory of the case to be simple, straightforward, and easy for jurors to grasp. To prove kidnapping, it was enough to present witnesses who saw Harrison driving away with the boy in his buggy, as well as evidence for Harrison's anger toward Beasley. If Ward tried to bring in too much detail, the jurors might have wondered if other people, whether the "Yankee" or Harrison's daughter Nina, were involved. That could have planted the seeds of reasonable doubt. Or the jurors might have ended up thinking someone in addition to Harrison should have been charged.

Imagine the spectacle of a father and his twenty-four-year-old daughter being indicted together for the kidnapping. That strategy could have backfired on Solicitor Ward, as some might have thought he was persecuting the entire Harrison family, and especially the young woman, for the sins of the patriarch. It was one thing to insinuate that Harrison's older daughter, Margaret, had helped conceal the boy after the fact, and quite another to accuse the young schoolteacher of conspiring to kidnap one of her students. It might have seemed ungentlemanly, which was the last way any North Carolina politician wanted to be seen.

As for Miss Nina, if the state did not want her to be the focus of the trial, neither did the defense. She did not even attend. Even though she was present at the scene of the disappearance and naturally would be a material witness, Nina was the only one of Joshua Harrison's five living children who did not testify at her father's trial. Her brothers Thomas and Joe testified that she was at home sick with the measles.[12]

Well, maybe. It is not impossible that Miss Nina happened to contract measles during the week her father was on trial for his life. But it is much more likely that her father's attorneys did not want her to take the stand, fearful she might let something slip or might buckle under the pressure of guilt and remorse.

In fairness to the young teacher, she probably never intended for her student to wind up dead. She just did as her father told her. From all indications, Joshua Harrison was the absolute ruler of his clan. And even he, as abusive and violent as he seemed, might not have intended murder in the beginning. Harrison may have believed he could pull off the kidnapping, collect the ransom quietly through back channels, and then release the boy, as in the Cudahy case. But within a few days, when the anonymous "letter" appeared in the *News & Observer*, Harrison knew he had been spotted in the act of carrying the boy away. After that, even if Kenneth was still alive, there would have been no way to let him return home, although demanding ransom was still not out of the question.

As for how Kenneth met his end, the elderly Hallet Ward had a theory about that as well. He remembered how the boy had left his coat and gloves in the schoolhouse closet. Ward figured that while Kenneth was driven in the open buggy on the long road to Norfolk through the rain and snow, wearing only his shirtsleeves, he probably caught his death of pneumonia.[13] That, too, is a comforting thought. It would have made Harrison's dirty work a little less so. He could have just allowed the boy to die, rather than strangling him or whacking him in the head.

There is also the chance Harrison shipped the boy away, maybe on a train headed west. Or he could have taken Kenneth to the Norfolk waterfront and dropped him on a ship headed out of the country. But for Harrison, it would have been too dangerous to let the boy go if there was even a remote chance of his returning to tell his story, so that probably is not what happened.

Consider the observation of Sam Walker, the closest relative of the Beasley family now living. As Cassie Beasley's grand-nephew, he has lived with the story all his life. "For years, I've imagined that someday, someone might tear down an old building in Norfolk, and find a set of bones sealed up in a wall," he says. "And then they'll call me up and ask for a DNA sample."[14]

Kenneth might be buried in some basement or, more likely, in some lonely spot in the woods on the outskirts of Norfolk. It would be deeply satisfying to know the truth, but this is a century-long cold case. A definitive conclusion would be too convenient.

Part V

Reckonings & Reassessments

Defense lawyer Charles Aycock, the former governor whose once-sterling legacy would be re-examined.

CHAPTER 20

HISTORY IN TRANSITION

If Hallet Ward spoke honestly when he was interviewed by Manly Wade Wellman, then it sounds like he eventually made peace with his involvement in the trial of Joshua Harrison. It is not clear that the same was true for Charles Aycock, who did not live nearly as long as Ward.

The newspaper accounts of Harrison's suicide do not include any remarks from his attorneys. Of course, even if reporters had sought out Aycock for comment, they could not have been surprised if he declined. The former governor had stuck out his neck for his client and made an impassioned case for his innocence, only to have the affair blow up in his face. If he wanted to put distance between himself and the memory of Joshua Harrison, he could hardly be blamed.

Aycock continued his legal practice with Frank Daniels in Goldsboro until 1909, when he and his family moved to Raleigh and he began a new partnership with Robert W. Winston, a former state judge. He kept up a diverse general practice, making a point not to become too closely identified with or financially dependent upon any individual or corporate client. In 1909, he traveled to Manhattan and obtained consent from the New York bar to represent John C. Lumsden, a young man from Raleigh who found himself charged with murder in the big city. Two years later, Aycock raised the eyebrows of some of his friends when he defended the Duke family's huge American Tobacco Company in an antitrust suit brought by the Ware-Kramer Tobacco Company, a small producer based in Wilson, North Carolina, just up the road from his boyhood home in Wayne County.[1] It seemed another unusual choice of battles for Aycock, who always prided himself as an advocate for the common man. The Dukes were not only mega-wealthy but staunch Republicans.

And then there was the case of Bertha Brown, a Raleigh woman of "notorious reputation." Brown had been found guilty in misdemeanor court of some unspecified public morals charge, and even though the case was tried without a jury, she received a long prison term. Aycock argued that any conviction that resulted in sending a lady to prison was not a misdemeanor and required a jury of one's peers. When the North Carolina Supreme Court rejected his reasoning, Aycock lost his temper, accusing the justices of "having ceased to be lawyers after having been elevated to the bench."[2]

On the political front, Aycock took part in the campaign for the statewide prohibition law when it was brought up for public vote in May 1908. He made at least ten speeches in favor of it, along with Governor Glenn and former governor Jarvis. Only a year had passed since Aycock and Jarvis were in court defending the alleged child-murdering bootlegger. But if the voters saw inconsistency on the distinguished gentlemen's part, they did not hold it against them at the polls. The act passed by a margin of 62 to 38 percent, making North Carolina the first state to adopt full prohibition.[3] The Democratic Party was now in full control of the state's political machinery and was united in favor of banning liquor.

But shortly afterward, cracks started to appear in the unified Democratic establishment that had begun with the 1898 campaign. Furnifold Simmons had orchestrated that campaign from behind the scenes and had served in the U.S. Senate since 1900, adroitly distributing federal jobs and patronage money to his favored local employees and sycophants. As North Carolina's undisputed political boss, he usually had no problem choosing the party's slate of candidates. But in 1908, a challenge arose from William W. Kitchin, a congressman from Roxboro who sought the governorship against Simmons's chosen candidate, Locke Craig. Kitchin alleged that Simmons and Aycock were trying to run a dictatorial political machine, which may have been a fair charge against Simmons but gave personal offense to Aycock, who never viewed himself as a candidate of anyone's "machine." Aycock deemed Kitchin's criticism of him "selfish, unpatriotic, and more or less vicious."

When Kitchin wrested the nomination from Craig, Aycock wrote to a friend, "I am hurt at present conditions in North Carolina, beyond the power of Emerson's mystical sayings to comfort." Privately, he confided to supporters that he wanted to withdraw from politics and not participate in any further campaigns beyond simply casting his vote at the polls.[4]

In one remarkable letter in early 1910, Aycock said that under no circumstances would he run for office again, and especially not a federal office such as the U.S. Senate. In explaining why not, he came as close as he ever did to expressing regret for the turmoil that had engulfed the state for the past dozen years.

The South, Aycock believed, needed to be represented in Washington by younger leaders, not men of his generation who had been influenced by the Civil War, Reconstruction, and all the consequent racial strife. North Carolinians like himself had been "compelled to devote ourselves to local issues." Such issues, particularly those of black corruption and black voting, "were vital but narrow, and in the discussion of them and in working them out, we imbibed passions and prejudices that unfitted us for great work on the stage of the nation."[5]

Profound words, and highly subject to interpretation. Regardless of all the schoolhouses he succeeded in building, was Aycock feeling remorse for having pressed the White Supremacy Campaign? Or maybe he just felt resigned to the brutal dynamics of race in the South, still believing he had no alternative but to preserve the social order by suppressing blacks, even if folks up north would never understand it.

As 1911 rolled around, some encouraged Aycock to run for the Senate anyway, despite his lack of interest. Simmons was up for re-election in 1912, and many North Carolina Democrats thought he had strayed from the Populist Party orthodoxy. Josephus Daniels, in particular, criticized Simmons for growing too close to Northern industrial interests, for not supporting antitrust legislation, and for voting for protective tariffs, which manufacturers tended to favor but which were opposed by farmers in the South and elsewhere. As of early 1911, only two candidates had declared they were willing to challenge Simmons: Governor Kitchin, whom Aycock obviously did not like, and North Carolina Supreme Court chief justice Walter Clark, who was less known and had little aptitude for the bare-knuckle campaign this promised to be.[6]

Aycock still did not want to do it. In late March 1911, he wrote again to Clarence Poe that his personal finances were not stable enough to devote time to a Senate campaign and that, even if he had more money, "I still would not do it, because I do not believe in such a fight."[7] But with more and more supporters urging him on, Aycock formally announced his candidacy in late May. Oddly enough, he said he would not barnstorm the state giving speeches, as he had so effectively in the past, nor would he spend big money on campaign infrastructure, as Simmons was sure to do. Instead, he said, "I shall make no campaign. . . . I shall . . . entrust my candidacy, without reservation, to the people of the State, and shall not seek to shape their selection by organization, or by personal appeals to them."[8] Aycock wanted it to be a campaign based upon principles.

And with that, the knives came out. Some, especially those supporting Kitchin, charged that Aycock was getting in the race to split the vote, thus ensuring victory for Simmons. And what was more, they accused Aycock of being, of all things, a drunkard.

If folks had taken a look back to Aycock's election as governor in 1900, it might have seemed a full-circle moment. His Republican opponent at the time, Spencer Adams, was a superior-court judge from Greensboro. Adams, like Aycock, came from a family of slave owners who supported the Confederacy. But Adams had cast his lot with the Fusionists, and that was enough for the Democratic campaign machine to paint him with the "Negro" and "liquor" brushes. The *News & Observer* ran a crudely drawn cartoon depicting Adams and some dark-skinned ape-like figures swilling jugs of booze in his hotel suite at the Republican National Convention.[9]

It is not clear where the whispers against Aycock began, but maybe with one of Kitchin's most vociferous supporters, Joseph J. Laughinghouse, the superintendent of the state prison in Raleigh. On official state letterhead addressed "Dear Friend," he circulated a letter stating that although he liked Aycock personally, "everybody knows of his terrible weakness," and "Damn a man who is making prohibition speeches today and drinking a pint or more during the twenty-four hours." The superintendent wondered "if Governor Aycock, with a wife and nine children dependent on him for

The race-baiting Raleigh *News and Observer* cartoon attacking Republican Spencer Adams, who would be defeated in North Carolina's 1900 gubernatorial election by Charles Aycock, later the object of a whispering campaign about his alleged drinking..

education and bodily comforts, cannot stay sober in North Carolina, how in the name of high heaven can we expect him to do so in Washington City?"[10]

Laughinghouse concluded his unsigned letter, "This is confidential." It is unknown how many people got wind of the whispering campaign, but apparently word got back to Aycock, who felt compelled to answer the rumors as discreetly as he could.

In January 1912, Aycock wrote to one of his supporters, J. R. Rodwell of Warrenton, with a mea culpa that sounds as if he were confessing some sick perversion: "It is a fact that at one time I did drink liquor and sometimes more than I ought to," but "for more than a month before the announcement of my candidacy, I have not touched a drop of liquor in any form, nor have I since." The accusations were "extremely painful" to him, and although he could never "publish such a letter as this, because it is too humiliating," Aycock urged Rodwell to spread the word that he was not an inebriate and was up to the challenge at hand. In conclusion, he said, "I am going to the Senate. I will not be beaten by a lot of calumniators."[11]

In all honesty, Aycock and his political associates were fond of socializing together, going back to before the 1890s. Drinking, cigar smoking, and tobacco chewing were all part of the scene. His law partner, Robert W. Winston, joked about it years afterward, saying, "All of us devoted to prohibition and equally devoted to a stiff highball!"[12] But in light of their public commitment to the anti-liquor campaign, they had to keep up appearances. Hypocrisy, one might say. As any politician knows, it is unavoidable in public affairs, human nature being what it is. The contradictions did not catch up with Aycock during the 1908 prohibition campaign, but they were definitely catching up now.

In March 1912, Aycock received several panicked letters from supporters who wondered why he was not campaigning harder and feared he might be struggling with demon drink. John Sentelle, the secretary to Congressman J. M. Gudger, told Aycock, "Some of your opponents are making the statement that you are physically unable to make the race, and that you are a drunkard." But Sentelle urged that he could still win "if you will only get busy and let your friends know you are in the fight to the finish." Former governor Glenn also wrote, encouraging Aycock to work hard and prove the doubters wrong. But he also mentioned a troubling detail. Glenn had heard that Aycock was recently hospitalized, a fact his opponents might misrepresent as a stay in a sanitarium.[13]

The truth was that Aycock had spent much of February and March not in a sanitarium but at the University of Pennsylvania Hospital in Philadelphia. It had nothing to do with alcohol. For several years, he had been sick with what likely would be diagnosed today as congestive heart disease, a condition that had no effective treatment at the time. He had several minor heart attacks and frequent angina that caused chest pains.[14] He probably knew he was dying when he announced his candidacy in 1911, which would explain his reluctance. And yet he went ahead, only to end up being attacked by people who supported him in his campaigns a decade earlier.

Charles Aycock wrote his last letter, dated April 1, 1912, to Hugh G. Chatham, a manufacturing executive from Winston-Salem who was active with the national Democratic Party. He thanked Chatham for inviting him to the Democratic National Convention in Baltimore, scheduled for June, which would nominate Woodrow Wilson for president. He said, "The statement that I declined your invitation on account of ill health is absolutely a false one, made out of whole cloth. If the advocates of my opponents continue their campaign of falsehood, the majority which I shall get in the state will be phenomenal."[15]

He kept up appearances to the end.

At the moment, he was headed out the door to catch a train for a prior engagement. Back in December, Aycock had agreed to give a speech on school policy to the Alabama Educational Association at its meeting in Birmingham on April 4, 1912. Once there, he received a warm ovation from the assembly and was partly through his speech when "abruptly his voice stopped and his face grew rigid. Turning aside, he raised one hand, staggered slightly, tried vainly to straighten, and sank slowly to the floor." Only fifty-two, he had suffered a massive heart attack and was probably dead before he hit the stage. Witnesses recalled that "education" was the very last word he spoke.[16]

It is anyone's guess how the Senate contest might have shaken out had Aycock lived. As it happened, Furnifold Simmons won easily after being relieved of his strongest opponent. He also would be re-elected with little difficulty in 1918 and 1924. Throughout that period, he became one of the most influential power brokers in Washington.

Simmons was a member of the Commerce Committee, and he chaired the Finance Committee, shepherding the legislation that enabled Woodrow Wilson to fund the army and navy through World War I. He worked hard to finance public works such as the Atlantic Intracoastal Waterway, and he got several military training facilities to be placed in North Carolina, one of which developed into Fort Bragg; Josephus Daniels, whom Wilson had appointed secretary of the navy, was also instrumental. All along the way, Simmons was a master of political patronage, doling out federal money to his supporters back home, from postmasters to census takers to tax collectors.[17] And through it all, he kept up his political base with his tried-and-true 1898 playbook of railing against Negroes, liquor, Catholicism, and Northern agitators who advocated for women's suffrage. For years, Simmons was respected and feared as North Carolina's "Great White Chieftain."[18]

But by 1930, it was a different story. Simmons was now in his seventies and starting to look it. Women were now voting, thanks to constitutional amendment. And worst of all, the Great Depression was in full swing. Two years earlier, Simmons had broken with his party and endorsed Republican Herbert Hoover for president, over Governor Al Smith of New York. Smith, an Irish Catholic who opposed prohibition, was easy for Simmons to portray as a Yankee foreigner. He helped Hoover carry North Carolina, but after the stock market crashed, Simmons was now bound at the hip to a president everyone blamed for massive unemployment and shuttered banks.

In his final campaign, Simmons kept up with white supremacy and prohibition, themes that had served him well for so long. He and his lieutenants circulated thousands of fliers claiming that his primary opponent, Josiah Bailey, was supported by blacks. One was entitled, "Tammany and North Carolina Negroes Would Defeat Simmons." But Bailey won in the end, crushing Simmons in a landslide, 61 to 39 percent.[19] For some, it seemed like the aging serpent had finally choked on his own venom.

As Simmons departed the political scene in shame, some in North Carolina thought back to Charles Aycock and had a sense that the better man had been shortchanged by history. The new governor, O. Max Gardner, was a dynamic young businessman determined to reshape state government, make it more efficient, and promote economic development to lead the state out of the Depression. Improved schools were an essential part of the formula, and Gardner admired the legacy of Aycock, who had promoted the cause of education to his dying breath.

Starting in the 1930s, as New Deal money financed construction on campuses all over North Carolina, it became routine for colleges to name new buildings after Charles Aycock. Several elementary and high schools also bore his name. And in 1932, North Carolina commissioned a bronze statue of him and placed it in the Statuary Hall collection in the U.S. Capitol. Max Gardner spoke at the statue's dedication and did not ignore the travails of Aycock's final years, noting that "most of our great public men have been victimized by both their enemies and their friends." But he expressed pride and confidence in his state's choice to honor Aycock, noting, "It has a finality about it that is subject to all the discounts of history. But I dare say that if there ever comes a time when North Carolinians repudiate the decision of our own day, the Commonwealth itself will have degenerated so that it will be interested in no great past, without which interest there can be no great future."[20]

Well, fast-forward eighty-some years to another full-circle moment. In 2015, the North Carolina General Assembly *did* repudiate the decision of 1932 and passed a bill to remove Aycock's statue from the Capitol and replace it with one of the Reverend Billy Graham.[21] This was one step in a still-developing trend, and whether it signals a degeneration in the civic body is a matter of perception.

Starting in the late 1990s, new scholarship began to focus on the White Supremacy Campaign. In 1998, Timothy B. Tyson and David S. Cecelski edited and published a collection of essays on the Wilmington race riot, which led in part to a state-appointed commission to study the event and the years surrounding it. The commission's report, issued in May 2006, concluded that the dark aspects of the 1890s and early 1900s have been downplayed in the commemoration of North Carolina history. For all of Southern progressivism's educational achievements, its racial character and violent undertones too often have been glossed over in the history books.[22]

After the 2008 election of the first African-American president, activists became even more vocal about redressing history's injustices. In 2011, the North Carolina Democratic Party was pressured to remove Aycock's name from its annual Vance-Aycock Dinner. Between 2014 and 2016, three universities—Duke, East Carolina, and UNC-Greensboro—renamed buildings that were named for Aycock, and one elementary school in Greensboro removed his name from campus entirely.

All this was part of the broad political tenor of the Obama years. It meant greater attention to issues of wealth inequality, racial discrimination in law enforcement, and the need for immigration reform, among others. But the Obama administration was followed by the election of America's first reality-show president in 2016, which many interpreted as white backlash against multiculturalism and political correctness. After Donald Trump's victory, pundit Ta-Nehisi Coates, in *We Were Eight Years in Power: An American Tragedy*, compared the Obama administration with the short-lived Reconstruction/Fusionist experiments.

The full effects are yet to be seen, much less chronicled. But perhaps the progressive activists overplayed their hand again.

The Republican resurgence in North Carolina, which began before Trump—in 2010, when the party took full control of the General Assembly for the first time since the 1890s—has even brought into question whether North Carolina is still committed to the concept of public schools, Charles Aycock's signature passion. Recent years have seen bitter debates in Raleigh over funding, charter schools, private school vouchers, and teacher pay raises. Democrats charge that Republicans are scheming to wreck the system in order to justify privatizing it. Even mainstream publications including the *Washington Post* have run opinion pieces with titles such as, "The Assault on Public Education in North Carolina Just Keeps on Coming."[23]

And the legacy of Charles B. Aycock just keeps on taking a beating from both right and left. One night in January 2016, unidentified persons broke into Raleigh's historic Oakwood Cemetery and desecrated several monuments, including Confederate veterans' graves. On Charles Aycock's tombstone, they spray-painted the words WHITE SUPREMACIST in bold black letters.[24]

Samuel M. Beasley, 1863-1910.

CHAPTER 21

TO THE FOUR WINDS

It might be too much to assume that Charles Aycock's defense of Joshua Harrison led to the rumors that he was soft on alcohol or an alcoholic himself. That is the tricky thing about rumors—they can be hard to trace, and even if the gossip is preserved in writing, the motivation is not always clear.

As for the other attorneys involved in the case, it does not appear that any were damaged politically by it. Hallet Ward remained in office as solicitor until 1910. After returning to private practice for a while, he served two terms in Congress from 1921 to 1925 and served briefly in the State Senate in the early 1930s. His good friend William M. Bond, who assisted in prosecuting Harrison, was a superior-court judge from 1913 through 1928.

Thomas Jarvis enjoyed his role of educational patriarch, raising money and serving on the board of trustees for what is now East Carolina University from its inception in 1908 until his death in 1915. There remains today a Jarvis Residence Hall on the Greenville campus. Unlike its former Aycock Residence Hall, the university has not yet faced pressure to rename it, even though Jarvis also gave speeches for the White Supremacy Campaign.[1]

Although he was a Republican in a town that was growing less and less so, Isaac Meekins continued to have a prestigious career. In those days, when a Republican president needed to choose a federal official in eastern North Carolina, he did not have a wide pool from which to select. In 1910, William Howard Taft appointed Meekins an assistant U.S. attorney for eastern North Carolina, a position he held until 1914. He also was the Republican nominee for governor in 1924, although he could not have expected to win; Democrat Angus McLean took the election handily. The following year, Calvin Coolidge appointed Meekins to a federal district-court judgeship, which led to an interesting opportunity out of town. Former president Taft, now the chief justice of the U.S. Supreme Court, assigned him to a special judge position that took him to New York City to try federal prohibition cases. As Meekins himself would tell it, he had no problem sentencing bootleggers to prison.[2]

Edwin Aydlett continued as the Grand Wizard of Elizabeth City politics, often with the help of pliant local journalists. One of them was Walter Cohoon, his former opponent in the Harrison trial. Cohoon was the owner of the *Daily Star*, which functioned as a mouthpiece for Aydlett, promoting his chosen candidates and advertising the businesses he favored.

But their primacy was challenged in late 1907, when Cohoon hired twenty-four-year-old W. O. Saunders to be his editor. On one occasion, just two weeks after Saunders came on the job, he was preparing to run a story about a criminal assault charge pending against an Aydlett crony. Aydlett called Saunders and instructed him not to print the story, yet Saunders did so anyway. Furious, Cohoon fired Saunders, who immediately swore he would "publish a free-speaking newspaper of his own in Elizabeth City, and write what he damn well pleased."[3]

So began Saunders's *Independent*, which became the regional hornet's nest poker and a great annoyance to Cohoon, Aydlett, and anyone else Saunders viewed as part of the corrupt political establishment. Saunders was not just in favor of civil rights for blacks. He also spoke out against anti-Semitism, for teaching evolution, and even for birth control for women. For twenty-five years, the *Independent* proudly wore its moniker as the most "cussed" newspaper in North Carolina.[4] H. L. Mencken, the legendary snobbish cynic from Baltimore, said, "If the South had forty editors like W. O. Saunders, it would be rid of most of its problems in five years."[5]

As soon as Saunders got his fledgling paper off the ground, Cohoon tried to squelch him, calling him "a mugwump, a Republican in disguise, and a jailbird." Saunders replied by castigating Cohoon as a "braying ass" and Aydlett's entire Democratic Party machine as "a veritable omnium-gathrum of political odds and ends huddled together under the party blanket like household goods and barnyard refuse after a hurricane; a party controlled by grafters and mongrels, nincompoops and duds."[6]

Saunders claimed he lost count of the number of libel suits that Aydlett and Cohoon filed against him—maybe as many as forty over the next fifteen years. They tried to bankrupt him by suing in far-flung counties such as Washington and Beaufort, anywhere they could find a copy of the *Independent*, forcing him to take time and money away from his paper. And yet "a fair-minded citizenry was quick to resent the Grand Wizard's highhandedness and to side with the scrappy underdog of a newspaperman who dared to do battle with the formidable E. F. Aydlett."[7] Nevertheless, Aydlett held on to his wealth and political influence. He passed away in 1930, just two years before his former protégé, John C. B. Ehringhaus, was elected governor.

Suffice to say that the local attorneys who participated in the Harrison trial came out no worse for it.

The same cannot be said for the families who were most impacted by the case: those of the victim and the accused. In particular, it is hard to remain dry eyed when reading about the fate of the Beasleys in the following years. There is no question that the loss of their youngest child, and the repercussions from it, wrecked their family.

It is clear Sam Beasley decided, not long after Kenneth went missing, that he did not want his family to remain in Poplar Branch.

Perhaps the memories were too painful, or they might have feared reprisals from relatives and friends of the Harrisons. In October 1905, the Beasleys purchased a house on Brown Avenue in Norfolk. It was in the new Brambleton district a couple of miles east of downtown, where Harrison's daughters were still living.[8] The city became their primary residence, although they did not sell their property in Currituck until 1908.[9]

The former state senator tried to stay in the commercial fishing business, although it appears he did not have an easy go of it. Given more time, he might have reestablished financial security for his family. Tragically, it was not to be.

One day in late July 1910, Sam Beasley was working on a fishing boat that traveled down the Back Bay from Norfolk and was anchored in Currituck Sound just offshore from his former homestead at Poplar Branch. Somehow, his right foot became entangled in some of the onboard machinery, possibly a motor or a fishing net crank. Several of his toes were torn off, and his foot was nearly severed at the ankle.[10]

His crew telegraphed for help, and in a cruel replay of Beasley's return to Poplar Branch from Raleigh five and a half years earlier, another "special train" was dispatched from Norfolk to Snowden station to rush the injured man to the city. He was taken to St. Vincent's Hospital, the same one where Joshua Harrison had breathed his last. The doctors did what they could, which without antibiotics was not much. They amputated both of his legs in a desperate attempt to stop the onset of blood poisoning. But after lingering in agony for

Sam Beasley's headstone in Elmwood Cemetery, Norfolk, Va.

ten days, Sam Beasley died at the age of forty-seven.[11]

His fellow Masons took charge of the funeral, laying Beasley to rest in Norfolk's Elmwood Cemetery beneath a granite column engraved with the rulers and compasses. Newspapers mentioned that this was the second unspeakable loss to strike the family within six years, and profound sympathy was extended by all to the sorrowing Mrs. Beasley and the surviving children. Their older son was now twenty-three and their daughter sixteen.

Kenneth's brother, Moran, had probably been struggling with grief even prior to his father's death. Back in 1905, he had been the teenage older son with two elementary-age siblings. Although he was away at school when Kenneth disappeared, he probably shared in whatever guilt or remorse his parents felt.

Census records show that when his father died, Moran also was working on the water, as an oiler on a tugboat based in Norfolk, while still residing at his parents' home. But he does not appear to have stayed around long. He headed for New York to embark on the solitary life of a longshoreman and sailor. For a year, he served on the USS *Hector*, a navy coal-supplying ship. When the United States entered World War I in 1917, he enlisted as a private first class in the U.S. Army Quartermaster Corps, the military's stateside supply chain, and was honorably discharged in 1919.[12]

During the 1920s, shipping records show Moran working as a sailor on merchant vessels bound for ports such as Vancouver, Panama, Manila, and many others in between. In 1930, the census had him living in an apartment in Manhattan, working as a window cleaner at the Metropolitan Hospital on Roosevelt Island, or Welfare Island, as it was known then, due to several hospitals and asylums located there. In 1940, he was living in the same area, doing essentially the same thing, working now as a "hospital helper." If he ever had a wife or children, the records do not reveal them.[13]

When it comes to these old, obscure documents, small details can reveal a lot. In April 1942, although he was fifty-five, Louis Moran Beasley dutifully filled out his World War II draft registration card. Each registrant was asked for contact information for his next-of-kin. Even though his mother and sister were still alive at that time and living in the old house on Brown Avenue, Moran wrote that he had none.[14]

Moran died in 1945 and was buried in a veterans' cemetery on Long Island, one of thousands of servicemen resting in neat rows with standard marble grave markers. Although he is surrounded by so many others, it seems a lonely way to spend the hereafter, with no family around. Yet he is the only one of Sam and Cassie Beasley's three children who has a tombstone at all.

His mother outlived him by a year and a half, passing away in 1947 at eighty-one. Cassie Beasley never remarried. She lived in the Brambleton house to the end, no doubt haunted by sad memories. But at least she does not appear to have held on to forlorn hopes that her younger son would return home one day, as the parents of some missing children do. There may have been some false alarms over the years, as in 1913 when the press reported a rumor that a teenage Kenneth was seen alive in Currituck County. But when visited by a Norfolk reporter, Mrs. Beasley gave him no display of emotion, no hopeful sentiments to quote. She brushed the reporter aside, saying she had accepted that Kenneth was no longer living and had been "killed in some manner" by Harrison.[15]

Cassie Beasley is buried beside her husband at Elmwood, yet she has no grave marker of her own, not even a new inscription added on Sam's tombstone. It seems an odd omission unless money was tight, which it probably was.

If the census records are correct, daughter Ethel stayed with Cassie most of the intervening years, sharing the home with her, as well as some boarders from time to time. Ethel married at some time prior to 1920. Her husband was a fellow named William Porter, who worked as a salesman for a paper company. But it did not last, and no children were born to the marriage. In 1930 and 1940, Ethel was back with her mother on Brown Avenue, divorced and working as a packer in warehouses.[16]

Cassie willed the house to Ethel, who continued to live there until her death in 1975, also at eighty-one.[17] But if her death certificate is correct, Ethel did not pass away in Norfolk, but miles to the west at the Central State Hospital in Petersburg, Virginia. It was a notorious facility started in 1869 by the Freedmen's Bureau as a hospital to serve, if that is the proper word, African-American patients who were "mentally ill, mentally retarded, geriatric, and criminally insane."[18] Following the Civil Rights Acts of the early 1960s, the hospital was integrated to serve the neglected and indigent of all races. But it was always overcrowded and understaffed, and not a place where any self-respecting white Virginian of Ethel's generation would want to be. Chances are she ended her life lonely and impoverished. She was returned to Norfolk for burial beside her parents, also in a grave that remains unmarked even now.

With no near relatives to inherit it, the house on Brown Avenue remained in Ethel's name for thirty more years. It was not until 2005 that the city of Norfolk finally took note of the property taxes that had gone unpaid since her death and filed a condemnation action to take title to the land. The city's complaint alleged, in routine legal parlance, that it was unknown whether Ethel Beasley was living or dead, and if dead, who her legal heirs were.[19] As to the first question, the city apparently did not check the Elmwood Cemetery records prior to filing. Today, the site of the house is a vacant lot.

As for the Harrison family, they also went their separate ways after the death of their patriarch. Even at death, most of them did not gravitate back.

Little information aside from spare bureaucratic details can be found regarding Joshua Harrison's three sons. No one seems to know what became of the eldest, Joe. The middle son, Marvin Hoge, moved to Detroit and was working in real estate when he filled out his World War I draft registration. He was still in Detroit in 1937 when, at fifty-nine, he married a lady thirty-four years younger; according to the marriage certificate, it was the first marriage for each of them. Despite the age difference, he appears to have outlived her. Hoge died in 1972 in Wilmington, North Carolina, at ninety-five; his death certificate lists him as a retired salesman and a widower. Youngest son Thomas lived in New Bern, North Carolina, most of his life. He served as an infantry sergeant during the Great War, worked as a justice of the peace, if his death certificate is correct, and like his brother had an affinity for May-December marriage. When he died in 1960, he was survived by a wife who was twenty-six years younger, and who outlived him by twenty-four.[20]

Although Thomas served in the war, he requested an exemption when he registered for the draft because he had a "widowed sister to support."[21] Presumably, that was Margaret Gallop, the mother of three sons and the keeper of Lord knows how many dark secrets dating from her time as proprietress of the boardinghouses in Norfolk.

Margaret lived until 1954, spending her last years at a retirement home in Greensboro, North Carolina.[22] By all accounts, she was a charmer. She had tried to captivate the jury at her father's trial, although most observers apparently were not taken in. Even in her old age, she had a talent for drawing people near and holding their attention.

One family friend who visited her described it this way: "I met this elegant lady in her seventies when she was staying for awhile with a relative. . . . She was an excellent conversationalist, well-educated, warm and gracious in every way. She related to me that all of her sons had died tragic deaths—one while horseback riding, one in a plane crash, and one as a young man from an unusual illness."[23]

The plane crash and the riding accident may or may not have occurred, but all three of the Gallop boys did in fact predecease their mother and are buried alongside their parents in Norfolk's Forest Lawn Cemetery. The oldest of them, Harold, was a distinguished army flier during the Great War, winning decorations from both the American and French governments. He died "after a long illness" of unspecified nature in 1943 at age forty-eight.[24] That means he was not quite ten in February 1905.

Did Harold carry with him a vague memory from those days, of a mysterious boy just a little younger than he, brought to his mother's house? Maybe the boy was introduced to Harold as a new playmate, or maybe he was just shut away in an attic room, out of sight. It will never be known.

Margaret's younger sister, Miss Nina, left her teaching position in Poplar Branch soon after Kenneth Beasley disappeared and went to live with Margaret in Norfolk. By 1910, Nina married William Cleve, and they moved to a rented home on Bute Street, just a few blocks from the old Glisson-Biggs house on Duke Street. For a time, they were joined there by Nina's youngest brother, Thomas, as well as their mother, Ann, who had disposed of the family property in

Currituck after Joshua's suicide.[25]

Mrs. Harrison understandably did not want to continue living alone in Currituck after her husband's shocking end. She probably remained in Norfolk with her children until her death in 1916. Nina and her husband continued living there until at least 1920, by which time they had three daughters.[26] Surprisingly Nina, who may have been the most culpable of all the Harrison children in Joshua's crime—again, if he in fact did it—later moved back to Poplar Branch. If she felt remorse about any role she played in Kenneth Beasley's disappearance, it did not keep her from living again near the scene of the crime.

Nina and her husband, William Cleve, operated a "floating luxury hotel" mounted on a barge they kept anchored at Poplar Branch Landing, the very place Sam Beasley once did business. Where they got the money to purchase such a vessel, and who their clientele may have been, is not clear. But it apparently kept operating until 1933, when a hurricane blew the barge onto shore, damaging it beyond repair.[27] Nina and Cleve divorced in 1936 in the court of Polk County, Florida. She moved to New York City with at least one of her daughters, Florence.[28]

Nina Harrison Cleve died in New Jersey in 1963, but not until after she and Florence made an interesting contribution to North Carolina's history museum. In November 1945, mother and daughter donated a portrait of their uncle and grand-uncle, the late governor Jarvis, to the state. The painting was presented in a grand ceremony held in the chamber of the House of Representatives in Raleigh, attended by Governor R. Gregg Cherry.[29] By that time, if anyone in Raleigh remembered the Harrison kidnapping case, and if any whispers of Nina's involvement lingered, they did not prevent the state from accepting this act of philanthropy.

Although their children were flung far and wide during their lives, Joshua and Ann Harrison lie together in death, in the sandy soil of Currituck County barely a mile from the farm where they made their home. Despite all the controversy and shame, the Jarvis family did not abandon Joshua in death. They buried him in their family cemetery only a few feet from his revered father-in-law, the Methodist pastor. The burial ground is still there, forty or so graves

Joshua Harrison's grave in the Jarvis-Forbes Cemetery (below), Jarvisburg, N.C.

in the middle of an old cornfield on the edge of Highway 158 in Jarvisburg. Joshua's grave is marked with an upright marble slab bearing his name and the dates of his birth and death, along with the simple epitaph, "Rest in Peace." Considering the manner of his departure from this world, it may be the most hopeless prayer that has ever been carved on a stone.

On the highway, beach-bound cars continue to whiz by. And on a tract of former Jarvis land adjacent to the old cornfield and cemetery, there now stands an entirely new business. It is a modern vineyard and winery that opened within the past few years. On most days, it offers wine tastings and tours of its acres of manicured grapevines, which include European varieties such as Chardonnay and Cabernet, as well as native scuppernongs. Now, unlike a century ago, the wine is produced well within the law.

Times definitely have changed in Currituck County, and mostly for the better, even considering all the traffic, sprawl, and gentrification. The vineyard puts forth a sweet, sophisticated product locals and visitors alike can savor openly, even if some aspects of the community's history are more challenging to digest.

The land still produces, as at least one witness testified under oath, "good wine."

ACKNOWLEDGMENTS

No one will ever find a way to make writing a book a simple task. It is a long endeavor that involves advice and input from many sources. It's a learning process, and any author has to go through it with a blank slate and an open mind. For a first-time author who has not previously written anything more creative than a legal brief, that is especially true.

Throughout this journey, I was blessed with wonderful guidance from many people. If the quality of my work does not reflect it, the fault is mine.

My first, and best, thanks must go to my family, to whom this book is dedicated. To my parents, Charles and Martha Oldham, who have always had a love for history and who have encouraged me, whenever I find a story that fascinates me, to run with it. To my brother Eric and my aunt Pamolu, who along with my parents have been the best proofreaders imaginable, always helpful with suggestions, constructive criticism, and snide remarks (where appropriate).

Ray McAllister of Beach Glass Books, who was willing to take on this project for publication, has my undying gratitude. From the beginning, he recognized that Kenneth Beasley's story had potential, and he saw how much I cared about telling it the right way. As we worked together, Ray calmed my anxieties and answered all my questions, whether intelligent or not. For his expertise with editing the manuscript, I must also credit Steve Kirk. The finished product is due in large part to their caring and diligence.

When it came to historical research, I had a wealth of written resources to call upon. In finding them, I was honored to meet wonderful folks who guided me through the motions and minutiae. In particular, I remember the staff at the Charlotte Mecklenburg Library, especially Thomas Cole, who introduced me to its historical collection and turned me on to newspapers.com and other online resources. I found another wonderful set of sources at the Slover Library in Norfolk; there, special thanks go to Troy Valos, who showed me a fascinating set of Norfolk's land records I could not have found elsewhere.

At the State Archives of North Carolina in Raleigh, I found the most indispensable sources, dealing with the genealogical and court records of Pasquotank and Currituck Counties. Many thanks to the staff, who kept me pointed in the right direction and provided consent to use photographs of some of the historic figures pictured here. The same goes for the folks at the Wilson Library of the University of North Carolina at Chapel Hill, with its incomparable Southern Historical Collection. There, I was able to find the original Record on Appeal in Joshua Harrison's trial, as well as the Tar Heel newspaper's coverage of the trial. There is no way this book could have been written without them.

Katherine Cartwright and Ray Matusko, the clerks of superior court of Pasquotank and Currituck Counties, respectively, as well as their staff members, were helpful in my research. The same goes for the Office of the Register of Deeds in Currituck and the Offices of the Circuit Court and Land Records in Norfolk. In a case like this, you just

Acknowledgments

never know what obscure details might be found in those old ledger books. I'm happy to say that, with some help, I unearthed a few gems.

The Currituck County Historical Society was generous in allowing consent to publish photos from its collection, including those of the now-disappeared Beasley and Harrison farmhouses. Keith Vincent permitted me to use photos of the Pasquotank and Currituck County Courthouses, from his collection at www.courthousehistory.com. Also, many thanks to Matthew Davis of The Map Shop in Charlotte, who prepared a wonderful map of the Currituck Sound region, showing the locations important to the story.

Since I still flatter myself as being a relatively young attorney, I am grateful to colleagues who were willing to share their experience and wisdom. J. Norfleet Pruden, whose great-grandfather was one of the prosecutors in the Harrison trial, was kind enough to speak with me about his family memories of northeastern North Carolina. Likewise Samuel B. "Sambo" Dixon, whom many Tar Heels know as a talented writer and historian as well as a trial lawyer, for taking the time to respond to my curiosity.

Early on, I discovered that when it comes to Currituck County, any research project should begin with Barbara Snowden, the acknowledged dean of local historians. She welcomed me into her beautiful home and shared her amazing collection of materials. She also was kind enough to give me a tour of the historic courthouse where rumors of lynching once fluttered around Joshua Harrison. I'm also grateful to the late Travis Morris, another chronicler of Currituck history, for sharing his memories.

Roy Sawyer, Charles Griggs, and Stanley Griggs took the time to speak with me about the history of Poplar Branch and the legacy of the Beasley family. Walter Gallop, who compiled a genealogy of the Harrison family, answered my questions and pointed me along as best he could. The late Ms. Murden Snow Newbern allowed me to explore the old Jarvis-Forbes Cemetery, where the Harrisons lie buried. I recognize that, for people who still reside in the community, it is not an easy subject to discuss, so I thank them all for their expressions of trust.

And that goes most of all for Sam Walker and his wife, Linda, who provided a testimonial link to the Beasley family. I cannot thank them enough for their willingness to speak openly, even after so many years, with a newly minted writer about a tragedy that struck so deeply into their family. They also provided use of the invaluable Beasley family photos, including one of Kenneth. The story just would not be the same otherwise. However good this book might be, it is due to them.

If I have made any omissions, they are inadvertent, and I apologize.

Finally, I owe a tremendous debt—not only as a writer but as a North Carolinian—to modern historians David Cecelski and Timothy Tyson*, who in recent years have brought new awareness to that inconvenient chapter in our state's history, the white supremacy campaign of the 1890s and 1900s. Their work, as well as that of Rob Christensen and Lee A. Craig, has done a great deal to hold up the mirror to show us who we are and where we come from. The image is not always pretty, but it is important to see.

The process of unraveling that history is not complete and surely will go on. And so it may be with my own work. It is possible that other undiscovered clues to the disappearance of Kenneth Beasley may exist somewhere in an obscure clip folder or in a trunk in the corner of someone's basement. Someone might come along and prove my telling of the

---

*   On a personal note, Tim's legendary father, the Reverend Dr. Vernon Tyson, has been a friend to my family for many years, dating back to the eventful 1960s in Lee County. I can attest myself that the Reverend Tyson is, as Tim notes in Blood Done Sign My Name, "the best damn preacher who ever beat on the Book."

Acknowledgments

story to be incomplete. If it happens, then it goes with the territory, and I can live with it.

But this much, at least, needed to be told.

ENDNOTES

Part I: The Disappearance

Chapter 1: The Scene, Set

1   U.S. Decennial Census, www.census.gov.
2   *Ibid.*
3   "Poplar Branch," by Vickie Brickhouse; *Journal of the Currituck County Historical Society*, 1977, pp. 172-73.
4   *Ibid., p. 172.*
5   *Norfolk: A Pictorial History*, from the "Those Were the Days" collection by Carroll White, ed. by Linda G. Fates; Donning Co. Publishers, Virginia Beach, VA, 1975, p. 91.
6   "Poplar Branch," by Vickie Brickhouse; *Journal of the Currituck County Historical Society*, 1977, p. 175
7   Storms had long been a fact of life on the sound and shaped the lives of everyone there. Henry Beasley Ansell, a surveyor who served as the Currituck County clerk of court in the late 1800s, wrote an unpublished memoir in 1907 recounting his life in the area. He recalls his boyhood days in the 1830s, when waterfowl

hunting first became big business on Currituck Sound. One of the nearby inlets had filled with sand, restricting the flow of ocean water. It encouraged the growth of freshwater marsh grass, which the ducks and geese loved to eat, attracting huge flocks for decoy gunners to harvest. But then came the great nor'easter of 1846. The wind blew ceaselessly for two days, washing away homes, fences, and graveyards all over the Currituck shore. "Such a sight was never seen before. No marsh, no beach, nothing [was] to be seen oceanward except a few tops of the large mounting sandhills. The great salt waves were breaking at our feet." The storm surge was high enough that the ocean waves washed over the Outer Banks, inundating the sound with salt water, killing most of the marsh grass that the ducks and geese depended on for food. It was enough to wipe out the hunting business for several years, although the birds eventually returned. *A Historian's Coast: Adventures into the Tidewater Past* by David S. Cecelski, John F. Blair, Publisher, Winston-Salem, NC, 2000, pp. 21-26; citing "Recollections of a Life Time and More" by Henry B. Ansell, 1907, Southern Historical Collection, University of North Carolina at Chapel Hill.

8   "Poplar Branch," by Vickie Brickhouse; *Journal of the Currituck County Historical Society*, 1977, p. 175.

9   The house originally might have been two stories tall. Later, as some witnesses would testify in court, it consisted of an upper school and lower school. It is not clear whether that referred to different floors of the building or just groupings of the students by age. Record on Appeal, *State v. Harrison*; trial transcript, testimony of Minuard P. Jennings.

10   "The Introduction of Modern Education into Currituck County, North Carolina," by Gordon Cowley Jones, Aug. 1971; *Journal of the Currituck County Historical Society* 1, No. 2, 1974, p. 63.

11   *The Paradox of Tar Heel Politics*, by Rob Christensen, University of North Carolina Press, Chapel Hill, 2008, p. 42.

12   *Josephus Daniels: His Life and Times*, by Lee A. Craig, University of North Carolina Press, Chapel Hill, 2013, p. 205; *Old South, New South: Revolutions in the Southern Economy Since the Civil War*, by Gavin Wright, Basic Books, New York, 1986; *The Paradox of Tar Heel Politics*, p. 44; Charles Brantley Aycock, by Oliver H. Orr Jr.,

University of North Carolina Press, Chapel Hill, 1961, pp. 320-21.
13   *The Paradox of Tar Heel Politics*, p. 44; Charles Brantley Aycock, p. 329; "The Introduction of Modern Education into Currituck County, North Carolina," p. 67.
14   "Some Memories of Currituck County, North Carolina 1908-1957," by Carrie Parker Walker, *Journal of the Currituck County Historical Society*, Vol. 1, No. 2, 1974, pp. 43-45.
15   *N&O*, Raleigh, NC, Aug. 24, 1899, section 4, p. 25.
16   Deed reference: Book 51, p. 150, Currituck County Public Registry.
17   Interview with Charles Griggs, Nov. 14, 2015.
18   "Complete Story of the Lost Beasley Boy," *Weekly Economist*, Elizabeth City, Feb. 17, 1905, p. 1.
19   *Dead and Gone: Classic Crimes of North Carolina*, by Manly Wade Wellman, University of North Carolina Press, Chapel Hill, 1954, p. 88.

Chapter 2: Shadows Descend

1   Trial transcript, testimony of Prof. M. P. Jennings.
2   *Ibid.*, testimony of Samuel M. Beasley.
3   *Ibid.*, testimony of Samuel M. Beasley; "This Booklet Contains the Evidence of the Beasley-Harrison Kidnapping Case," *Tar Heel*, Elizabeth City, NC, 1907.
4   *Tar Heel* booklet, testimony of Prof. M. P. Jennings.
5   "Thomas Jordan Jarvis, 1836-1915," *Documenting the American South*, www.unc.edu.
6   *Tar Heel* booklet, testimony of Thomas Harrison.
7   *Ibid.*; trial transcript, testimony of Samuel M. Beasley.
8   "Search Abandoned; New Clues Indicate That Kenneth Beasley Was Kidnapped," *N&O*, Feb. 26, 1905, p. 12.
9   Trial transcript, testimony of Bennett Walker.
10   *Ibid.*, testimony of Bennett Walker.
11   *N&O*, Feb. 26, 1905, p. 12.
12   *N&O*, Feb. 26, 1905, p. 12; trial transcript, testimony of Prof. M. P. Jennings; *Tar Heel* booklet, testimony of Prof. M. P. Jen-

nings

13   *Electrical Review* "The Pioneer Electrical Weekly of America," New York, Vol. 43, No. 17, Oct. 24, 1903, p. 608

14   As rural as it was, Currituck County, due to its proximity to Norfolk, was probably ahead of the game when it came to phone coverage in eastern North Carolina. Although Southern Bell and Carolina Telephone and Telegraph had extended service to almost all towns in the region by 1927, many outlying farms were without it until much later. Former U.S. senator Lauch Faircloth, who spent his boyhood on a farm in Sampson County in the 1930s, recalled having to drive seven miles to the drugstore in Clinton to make phone calls. His family did not get its own phone until 1941, and the first call his father received was from the sheriff, informing him of the Pearl Harbor attack. "Party on the Line: Recalling Southern Bell and Carolina Telephone" by Susan Stafford Kelly, *Our State*, Feb. 26, 2014.

15   "Complete Story of the Lost Beasley Boy," *Weekly Economist*, Feb. 17, 1905, p. 1; trial transcript, testimony of J. W. Poyner; *Tar Heel* booklet, testimonies of J. W. Poyner and D. W. Woodhouse.

16   *Dead and Gone*, p. 89.

17   Trial transcript, testimonies of Prof. M. P. Jennings, J. W. Poyner; *Tar Heel* booklet, testimonies of Prof. M. P. Jennings, J. W. Poyner, D. W. Woodhouse

18   *Ibid.*, testimonies of J. W. Poyner, D. W. Woodhouse.

19   "From Cape Henry to Currituck Beach Including the Albemarle and Chesapeake Canal," U.S. Coast and Geodetic Survey, 1913; "Soil Map, North Carolina, Camden and Currituck Counties," A. Hoen & Co., Baltimore, MD, 1923.

20   *Tar Heel* booklet, testimony of D. W. Woodhouse.

21   Trial transcript, testimony of E. B. Gallop

22   *Tar Heel* booklet, testimonies of J. W. Poyner, D. W. Woodhouse.

23   *Ibid.*, testimony of Samuel M. Beasley; trial transcript, testimony of Samuel M. Beasley; "Hundreds Now in Search of the Lost Boy," *N&O*, Feb. 16, 1905, p. 1.

24   *Ibid.*

25 *Ibid.*; *Tar Heel* booklet, testimony of W. A. Doxey.
26 "Where Is the Boy: Has Senator Beasley's Son Been Kidnapped?" *N&O*, Feb. 15, 1905, p. 1.
27 "Hundreds Now in Search of the Lost Boy," *N&O*, Feb. 16, 1905, p. 1
28 "Missing Boy Found," *Winston-Salem Journal*, Feb. 19, 1905, p. 1; "The Lost Boy Found: In an Abandoned Cabin with a Man in a Drunken Stupor," *Weekly High Point Enterprise*, High Point, NC, Feb. 22, 1905, p. 1.
29 *Dead and Gone*, pp. 90, 101.
30 "Kidnapped? Theory About the Young Son of Senator Beasley," *N&O*, Feb. 24, 1905, p. 1; *Windsor Ledger*, March 2, 1905, p. 1; *French Broad Hustler*, Hendersonville, NC, March 2, 1905, p. 1; *Weekly High Point Enterprise*, March 1, 1905, p. 1.
31 *Ibid.*
32 *Ibid.*
33 *Ibid.*
34 *Ibid.* Although the *News & Observer* article was widely reprinted, some papers, possibly to avoid liability, did not include the portion of the letter that pointed the finger at Joshua Harrison. "Senator Beasley's Son: It is Believed Now That He Was Kidnapped," *Weekly High Point Enterprise*, March 1, 1905, p. 1.

Chapter 3: An Aggressive Breed

1 *Fantasy Voices: Interviews with American Fantasy Writers*, by Jeffrey M. Elliot, Borgo Press, 1982.
2 *Dead and Gone*, p. 87.
3 "Descendants of Zorababel Harrison," genealogy compiled by Walter Gallop, June 21, 2007.
4 *Record of Marriages, Book A* (1851-1867), copied from the Register of Deeds Office, Currituck County, 1998, Albemarle Genealogical Society.
5 Interviews with Roy Sawyer, July 26, 2014, and Charles Griggs, Nov. 14, 2015.
6 "Lawyers Get on Harrison's Alibi," *N&O*, March 20, 1907,

p. 1.
7 Currituck County Superior Court Minute Docket, p. 208.
8 *Ibid.*
9 U.S. Decennial Census, Currituck County, 1860.
10 Currituck County Superior Court Minute Docket, p. 268.
11 "Lawyers Get on Harrison's Alibi," p. 1.
12 Currituck County Superior Court Minute Docket, p. 268.
13 The Currituck County censuses of 1880 and 1900 show a Thomas B. Jarvis living in Poplar Branch and a Thomas L. Jarvis living in Moyock in the northern part of the county.
14 *The Heritage of Currituck County North Carolina 1985*, ed. by JoAnna Heath Bates, Albemarle Genealogical Society in cooperation with Currituck County Historical Society and Hunter Publishing Co., Winston-Salem, 1985, pp. 329-30.
15 "Descendants of Zorababel Harrison."
16 *Daily Standard*, Raleigh, Sept. 5, 1870, p. 3.
17 Currituck County Superior Court Minute Docket.
18 Currituck County Public Registry: Book 33, p. 181.
19 Currituck County Public Registry: Book 34, p. 250; Book 34, p. 539; Book 37, p. 500; Book 38, p. 22; Book 38, p. 529.
20 Currituck County Public Registry: Book 48, p. 214.
21 U.S. Decennial Census, www.census.gov.
22 Currituck County Superior Court Minute Docket; Criminal Docket, Superior Court, 1889-1913.
23 "Mr. Harrison in Jail Here," *Daily Economist*, Sept. 7, 1906, p. 1.
24 *North Carolina Lighthouses and Lifesaving Stations*, by John Hairr, Arcadia Publishing, Charleston, SC, 2004, p. 118.
25 "H. M. Gallop Dead," *Tar Heel*, May 9, 1902, p. 8; "Poyner's Hill—Death of Capt. H. M. Gallop," *Tar Heel*, May 16, 1902, pp. 2, 5.

Chapter 4: Will-o'-the-Wisp Clews

1 Approximately $13,000 in 2015 dollars, based upon historical rates of inflation; www.intodaysdollars.com.

ENDNOTES

2   For example, *N&O*, Feb. 28, 1905, p. 8.
3   *Kidnapped: Child Abduction in America*, by Paula S. Fass, Oxford University Press, New York, 1997, p. 27.
4   *A Murder in Virginia: Southern Justice on Trial*, by Suzanne Lebsock, W. W. Norton & Co., New York, 2003, p. 126.
5   "Search Abandoned: New Clues Indicate That Kenneth Beasley Was Kidnapped," *N&O*, Feb. 26, 1905, p. 12; "Search for Lost Boy Has Been Abandoned," *Weekly Economist*, Feb. 24, 1905, p. 1.
6   *Ibid.*
7   Trial transcript, testimony of J. J. Pierce; *Tar Heel* booklet, testimony of J. J. Pierce.
8   *Ibid.*
9   "Kenneth Beasley Found?" *Charlotte Observer*, Apr. 6, 1905, p. 1; "Kenneth Beasley Located," *Wilmington Messenger*, Apr. 6, 1905, p. 1; "Found! And Alive! Young Beasley in Norfolk," *N&O*, Apr. 6, 1905, p. 1.
10   "Investigation Proves Him Negro, Not Beasley Boy; Excitement Caused in City Monday Night and Tuesday by Report of Finding Kenneth Beasley in Negro Hut; Hundreds of People Visited the House to Investigate," *Weekly Economist*, May 24, 1905, p. 3.
11   "Reward of $1,000.00 Offered for Kenneth Beasley," *Weekly Economist*, Apr. 21, 1905, p. 3.
12   "Futile Efforts at Rocky Mount to Locate Beasley Boy—Father Returns," *Weekly Economist*, Apr. 14, 1905, p. 1; "Claims Not Guilty—Will-o'-the-Wisp Clews," *Roanoke Beacon*, Plymouth, NC, Sept. 27, 1907, p. 1.
13   "Search Abandoned: New Clues Indicate That Kenneth Beasley Was Kidnapped," *N&O*, Feb. 26, 1905, p. 12.
14   *Ibid.*
15   *Dead and Gone*, p. 92.
16   "Statement Analysis: What Do Suspects' Words Really Reveal?" by Special Agent Susan H. Adams, Federal Bureau of Investigation, Oct. 1996
17   "Father Yet Believes That Kenneth Beasley Is Alive," *Daily Economist*, Sept. 18, 1905, p. 1.

18   "Beasley Case Yet Unsolved," *Daily Economist*, Nov. 22, 1905, p. 1.
19   *Ibid.*

Part II: The Times

Chapter 5: The Charley Ross Case

1   *We Is Got Him: The Kidnapping that Changed America*, by Carrie Hagen, Overlook Press, New York, 2011, p. 17.
2   *Almost a Miracle: The American Victory in the War of Independence*, by John Ferling, Oxford University Press, New York, 2007, pp. 250-58. Despite the defeat, North Carolina troops fought valiantly at Germantown. Nine regiments were led by Brigadier General Francis Nash (brother of future governor Abner Nash), who became a casualty when one of his legs was shot away by a cannonball. General Washington and several of his senior officers attended Nash's burial days later at the nearby Towamencin Mennonite Meeting House. "General Francis Nash: An Address Delivered at the Unveiling of a Monument to General Nash," by Alfred M. Waddell, 1906; www.ncpedia.org.
3   *We Is Got Him*, pp. 17-18.
4   *Id.*, pp. 21-23.
5   This case was the origin of the classic parental instruction, "Don't take candy from strangers."
6   *Kidnapped*, pp. 21-22.
7   *We Is Got Him*, pp. 18-19, 21-22; *Kidnapped*, pp. 21-22.
8   *We Is Got Him*, p. 22; *Kidnapped*, p. 22.
9   *We Is Got Him*, pp. 23-24.
10   *Ibid.* pp. 24-25.
11   Walter remembered the two men drinking from a "dark bottle" they kept in the floorboard of the buggy. *Kidnapped*, p. 22.
12   Telegraph was the quickest means of communication available. The telephone was not yet a factor, even in large cities such as Philadelphia.
13   *Kidnapped*, pp. 26-27; *We Is Got Him*, pp. 25-27.

14   *Kidnapped*, pp. 26-27; *We Is Got Him*, p. 29.
15   *We Is Got Him*, p. 33.
16   Ibid., p. 36.
17   *Kidnapped*, p. 28, citing *The Father's Story*, by Christian Ross, pp. 46-48.
18   Ibid., p. 28, citing *New York World*, July 15, 1874, cited in *Philadelphia Inquirer*, July 17, 1874, p. 3.
19   "The Story Behind the First Ransom Note in American History," by Carrie Hagen, *Smithsonian*, Dec. 9, 2013.
20   *We Is Got Him*, p. 46; *Kidnapped*, p. 29.
21   *We Is Got Him*, pp. 47-48; *Kidnapped*, p. 30.
22   *Kidnapped*, p. 29.
23   *Id.*, p. 32.
24   *We Is Got Him*, pp. 45-46.
25   *Id.*, p. 48.
26   *Kidnapped*, p. 28.
27   *We Is Got Him*, p. 52.
28   *Id.*, pp. 53-54.
29   *Id.*
30   *Kidnapped*, p. 30, citing *The Father's Story*, pp. 87-88, 94; *Philadelphia Inquirer*, July 27, 1874, p. 2; *New York Herald*, July 25, 1874, p. 4; *New York Times*, Dec. 15, 1875, p. 6, Dec. 24, 1875, p. 4, and Jan. 12, 1876, p. 4.
31   "A Historic Philadelphia Kidnapping," by Bill Kent, *Philadelphia Inquirer*, Sept. 4, 2011, www.philly.com. Review of *We Is Got Him*.
32   *Id.*
33   *Kidnapped*, pp. 37-38; *We Is Got Him*, pp. 171-74.
34   *Id.*
35   *We Is Got Him*, pp. 177-78.
36   *Kidnapped*, p. 38.
37   *Id.*, pp. 38-39.
38   *We Is Got Him*, pp. 181-83; *Kidnapped*, pp. 48-51.
39   There was also the case of John Conway, a five-year-old son of a railroad dispatcher, kidnapped from near his home in Albany, New York, in August 1897. The abductor left a note demanding a three-thousand-dollar ransom, or John "would be killed the same as Charley Ross." However, this crime was not really comparable to

the Ross case and is not believed by most analysts to have been a ransom kidnapping. John was recovered by police after three days, and the orchestrator of the crime was found to be the boy's uncle. In all likelihood, this crime was motivated by family resentment and the ransom demand was not serious, as a railroad dispatcher would not have been able to come up with three thousand dollars. *Kidnapped*, p. 29; *The Encyclopedia of Kidnappings*, by Michael Newton, Facts on File, New York, 2002, p. 70.

Chapter 6: The Eddie Cudahy Case

1   " 'A Really Spectacular and Truly Named Desperado': Pat Crowe and the Cudahy Kidnapping Case," by Garneth Oldenkamp Peterson, *Nebraska History*, 57 (1976), pp. 331-58, 332; *Mobile Americans*, by Howard P. Chudacoff, Oxford University Press, New York, 1972, pp. 18-19.
2   *The Gate City: A History of Omaha*, by Lawrence Larsen and Barbara Cottrell, University of Nebraska Press, Lincoln, 1997, pp. 43, 135.
3   A Really Spectacular and Truly Named Desperado," p. 333.
4   *Ibid.*, p. 333.
5   *Ibid.*, p. 333.
6   *Ibid.*, pp. 353-54; *Kidnapped*, pp. 33-34.
7   "A Really Spectacular and Truly Named Desperado," p. 336; *Kidnapped*, p. 34.
8   "A Really Spectacular and Truly Named Desperado," pp. 335, 339.
9   "Patrick Crowe: The Friendly Kidnapper," by Jay Robert Nash, Jay Robert Nash's Annals of Crime, www.annalsofcrime.com.
10 "A Really Spectacular and Truly Named Desperado," pp. 335-36.
11 *Ibid.*, p. 336.
12 *Ibid.*, p. 338.
13 *Ibid.*, p. 339.
14 Or at least that was the story Crowe himself later told to

the sensationalistic press. As with everything else in his life story, it seems heavy with embellishment. *Ibid.*, p. 332; "Patrick Crowe, The Friendly Kidnapper."

15   *Ibid.*, pp. 332-33; "Patrick Crowe, The Friendly Kidnapper."
16   *Ibid.*, pp. 341-43; "Patrick Crowe, The Friendly Kidnapper."
17   *Ibid.*, p. 343.
18   "A Really Spectacular and Truly Named Desperado," pp. 341, 343.
19   *Ibid.*, pp. 343-44.
20   *Ibid.*, p. 346.
21   *Ibid.*, pp. 346-47.
22   February 1906 also saw the publication of *The Jungle*, Upton Sinclair's classic muckraking novel that depicted the filthy conditions in Chicago's meat packinghouses, similar to those run by Cudahy. Some elements of the story were exaggerated, such as workers drowning in vats of lard and child laborers being eaten alive by rats. But everyone who read it was appalled to think of where the meat on their tables was coming from. Even Theodore Roosevelt, who privately thought Sinclair was a liar and rabble-rouser, felt political pressure. Within a year, Congress passed, and the president signed, two landmark pieces of legislation, the Federal Meat Inspection Act and the Pure Food and Drug Act.
23   *Ibid.*, pp. 347-50.
24   *Ibid.*, p. 351; "Patrick Crowe, The Friendly Kidnapper."
25   "Omaha Kidnappers: A Millionaire's Son Missing From Home," *Virginian-Pilot*, Norfolk, Dec. 20, 1900, p. 11; "The Cudahy Kidnappers: Boston Police Think They Are en Route to Boston," *Virginian-Pilot*, Dec. 28, 1900, p. 6; "Lost Boy Returns: Kidnappers Work Cudahy for $25,000.00 in Gold: The Detectives Foiled," *Morning Post*, Raleigh, Dec. 21, 1900, p. 1; "Callahan Again Released: His Second Trial in the Cudahy Kidnapping Case Fails of Conviction," *Charlotte Observer*, Nov. 9, 1901, p. 4; "A Jury to Try Pat Crowe: Young Cudahy Unable to Identify Pat as His Kidnapper," *N&O*, Feb. 9, 1906, p. 1; "Pat Crowe's Own Story: Why He Kidnapped Cudahy Boy," Charlotte Observer, Apr. 1, 1906, p. 24.
26   "Beasley Case Yet Unsolved: Nine-Tenths of Currituck People Adhere to Kidnapping Theory, Among Them the Missing

Boy's Parents," *Daily Economist*, Elizabeth City, NC, March 23, 1906, p. 1; "The Boy Still Missing," *Charlotte Observer*, March 26, 1906, p. 2.

27   *State v. Harrison*, 145 N.C. 408, 59 S.E. 867 (1907). When the North Carolina Supreme Court was finally called upon to define the crime of kidnapping, it had only common law to rely upon; there was no North Carolina statute or case law on point. The defense argued, based upon Blackstone and other ancient English legal texts, that only the "forcible abduction or stealing away of a man, woman or child from their own country and sending them to another" could qualify as a kidnapping; if so, then in the 1905 context, the state would have to prove the victim was transported across a national border to establish a kidnapping. The court decided against that. Instead, it defined kidnapping more generally as "false imprisonment, aggravated by conveying the imprisoned person to some other place." But to do so, the court had to rely on case law from New Hampshire, Indiana, Iowa, and New York.

Chapter 7: Delayed Reckoning

1   " 'A New Court House of Brick': A Documentary History of the Currituck County Courthouse, Currituck, North Carolina," with an addendum, "Establishing a Date for the Currituck County Jail," prepared for the County of Currituck, North Carolina, and the Currituck County Historical Society, by John B. Green III, historic preservation consultant, New Bern, NC, 1998.

2   As striking and evocative as they are, neither the historic courthouse nor the old jail is still used for its original purpose. Several years ago, the county built a modern judicial complex beside the highway just north of the old courthouse community. The old jail is far too small and rustic to be used for anything other than a sightseeing curiosity, although the courtroom in the historic courthouse is still used sometimes for board meetings.

3   "Mr. Harrison Arrested," *Daily Economist*, Sept. 6, 1906, p. 1; "Mr. Harrison in Jail Here," *Daily Economist*, Sept. 7, 1906, p. 1.

4   *Ibid.*

Endnotes

5   *Ibid.*
6   *Ibid.*
7   *N&O*, Sept. 8, 1906, p. 1
8   Aydlett's younger partner, John C. B. Ehringhaus, would go on to a distinguished legal and political career, serving for several years in the General Assembly. In 1932, he would be elected governor.
9   *The Heritage of Currituck County 1985*, p. 143
10 *Ibid.*, pp. 329-30; "Descendants of Zorababel Harrison," compilation of Harrison family genealogy by Walter L. Gallop, Harbinger, NC, 2007.
11 "Harrison Makes Complete Denial; Had Nothing to Do With Kidnapping; Sets Up an Alibi," *N&O*, Sept. 11, 1906, p. 1; "Mr. Harrison Out on Bail," *Daily Economist*, Sept. 12, 1906, p.1.
12 *Ibid.*; "Harrison Out under Bond; He Gives Out Statement Tending to Prove Alibi," *Raleigh Times*, Sept. 11, 1906, p. 2.
13 Record on Appeal, *State v. Harrison*; Defendant's Affidavit for Removal of Cause, filed Feb. 25, 1907.
14 Record on Appeal, *State v. Harrison*; Answer to Defendant's Affidavit for Removal, filed Feb. 26, 1907.
15 Record on Appeal, *State v. Harrison*; Affidavit of Solicitor, filed Feb. 26, 1907.
16 *The Heritage of Currituck County 1985*, p. 331.
17 *Ibid.*, p. 23; Record on Appeal, *State v. Harrison*; "Mr. Harrison Arrested," *Daily Economist*, Sept. 6, 1906, p. 1; "Mr. Harrison in Jail Here," *Daily Economist*, Sept. 7, 1906, p. 1.
18 *Tar Heel* booklet, testimony of Lee Thomas.
19 "Lynching Party Foiled," *Washington Post*, Washington, DC, Sept. 8, 1906, p. 1.
20 "Claims Not Guilty," *Roanoke Beacon*, Plymouth, NC, Sept. 27, 1907, p. 1.

Chapter 8: A Culture of Lynching

1   *Watering the Sahara: Recollections of Paul Green from 1894 to 1937*, by James R. Spence, ed. by Margaret D. Bauer, Office of Archives and History, NC Dept. of Cultural Resources, Raleigh, 2008,

pp. 2-4, 9.

2   *Ibid.*, p. 19, citing interview by Billy Barnes, March 5, 1975, pp. 40-41, # B-0005-1, Southern Oral History Program Collection # 4007, Southern Historical Collection, Wilson Library, UNC at Chapel Hill.

3   *Lynching in North Carolina: A History, 1865-1941*, by Vann R. Newkirk, McFarland & Co.., Jefferson, NC, 2009, p. 171. In the same forty years between 1890 and 1930, 152 documented lynchings occurred in South Carolina, 214 in Tennessee, and a whopping 458 in Georgia.

4   "History of Lynchings in the South Documents Nearly 4,000 Names," by Campbell Robertson, *New York Times*, Feb. 10, 2015.

5   *Hunger Pains in Our Heads: The Story of the Non-Violent Student Sit-In Movement and the Black Struggle for Equality*, by Mansel P. McCleave, Tavine'ra Publishing, Birmingham, AL, 2008, pp. 29-33; citing "Harpers Crossroads Folks Recall 1898 Lynching," *Chatham County Herald*, Siler City, NC, Nov. 26, 1980.

6   *Lynching in North Carolina*, p. 169.

7   *Ibid.*, p. 162, citing "Lynching at Carthage," *Landmark*, Statesville, NC, March 12, 1901.

8   In April 1901, Aycock played host in Winston-Salem to the Conference for Southern Education, a meeting of educators, ministers, politicians that intended to sell Northern industrialists on the benefits of expanding schooling in the South. John D. Rockefeller Jr. was among the attendees. *The Paradox of Tar Heel Politics*, pp. 42-43.

9   *Ibid.*, p. 42.

10 *Democracy Betrayed: The Wilmington Race Riot of 1898 and Its Legacy*, ed. by David S. Cecelski and Timothy B. Tyson, University of North Carolina Press, Chapel Hill, 1998, introduction pp. 7-8, citing "The Two Faces of Domination in North Carolina, 1800-1898," by Stephen Kantrowitz

11 *Troubled Ground: A Tale of Murder, Lynching, and Reckoning in the New South*, by Claude A. Clegg III, University of Illinois Press, Urbana, 2010, p. 42.

12 *Lynching in North Carolina*, pp. 14-15, 169.

Endnotes

13   *Charles Brantley Aycock*, p. 239.
14   *Troubled Ground*, pp. 86-88.
15   Two recent books have addressed the Lyerly murders, each arguing that the lynched sharecroppers were innocent of the crime. *A Game Called Salisbury: The Spinning of a Southern Tragedy and the Myths of Race*, by Susan Barringer Wells, Infinity Publishing, West Conshohocken, PA, 2007. One of them, in fact, asserts that the crime was committed by a train-hopping mass murderer who killed dozens of victims nationwide. *The Man from the Train: The Solving of a Century-Old Serial Killer Mystery*, by Bill James and Rachel M. James, Simon & Schuster, New York, 2017.
16   *Troubled Ground*, pp. 89-105; *A Game Called Salisbury*, 2nd ed., 2010.
17   *The Paradox of Tar Heel Politics*, p. 7.

Chapter 9: Race and Politics

1   *The Paradox of Tar Heel Politics*, pp. 2-3.
2   *Liquor in the Land of the Lost Cause*, by Joe L. Coker, University Press of Kentucky, Lexington, 2007, pp. 124-25.
3   *Ibid.*, pp. 125-26, 129.
4   "Jim Crow Comes to Mecklenburg County," by Dr. Dan L. Morrill, UNC-Charlotte, www.cmhpf.org.
5   "Jim Crow Comes to Mecklenburg County."
6   *The Paradox of Tar Heel Politics*, pp. 13-14.
7   "Jim Crow Comes to Mecklenburg County."
8   *Josephus Daniels*, pp. 149-50.
9   *Ibid.*, p. 153.
10   *Ibid.*, p. 158; *The Paradox of Tar Heel Politics*, pp. 10-11.
11   Bryan was the nominee of both the Populist and the Democratic Parties on the national level, while in North Carolina the two parties were in opposition to each other. Partisan labels in that era were, to say the least, confusing.
12   *The Paradox of Tar Heel Politics*, p. 11.
13   *Josephus Daniels*, p. 178, citing *The Mind of the South*, by W. J. Cash, Vintage Publishing, New York, 1941, p. 66.

14   *The Paradox of Tar Heel Politics*, pp. 14-15; *Charles Brantley Aycock*, pp. 6-7.
15   *Josephus Daniels*, p. 180, citing *Editor in Politics*, by Josephus Daniels, University of North Carolina Press, Chapel Hill, 1941, p. 297.
16   *Ibid.*, at pp. 178-79; *The Paradox of Tar Heel Politics*, p. 37.
17   *Josephus Daniels*, pp. 181-82.
18   *The Paradox of Tar Heel Politics*, pp. 23-24.
19   "Jim Crow Comes to Mecklenburg County"; "We Have Taken a City: A Centennial Essay," by Leon H. Prather Sr., *Democracy Betrayed*, p. 22. Bellamy, in his college days in the early 1870s, had been a close personal friend of young Thomas Woodrow Wilson, the son of the pastor of Wilmington's First Presbyterian Church. Wilson, of course, was destined to become president of Princeton University and later of the United States. *Wilson*, by A. Scott Berg, G. P Putnam's Sons, New York, 2013, p. 49.
20   *Ibid.*, pp. 17-18; *Josephus Daniels*, pp. 184-85; *Democracy Betrayed*, pp. 17-18.
21   *Down the Wild Cape Fear: A River Journey through the Heart of North Carolina*, by Philip Gerard, University of North Carolina Press, Chapel Hill, 2013, pp. 132-33.
22   *The Paradox of Tar Heel Politics*, p. 20; *Josephus Daniels*, pp. 185-86.
23   *The Paradox of Tar Heel Politics*, p. 19, citing *Editor in Politics*, p. 293.
24   *Ibid.*, p. 23.
25   Waddell served in Congress from 1871 to 1877, when he was defeated for re-election by Russell, the future governor. He would become known in later years as a popular public speaker, especially at events commemorating North Carolina's military history. In 1906, he gave a patriotic speech dedicating the memorial to General Francis Nash and the other North Carolina troops who fought at Germantown in the American Revolution.
26   "We Have Taken a City"; *Democracy Betrayed*, pp. 29-37.
27   "Lewin Manly: The Injustice We Never Forget," by Eric Frazier, *Charlotte Observer*, Nov. 19, 2006.
28   *Josephus Daniels*, p. 187.

ENDNOTES

29   "White Men's Union Organized," *Weekly Economist*, Sept. 30, 1898, p. 3.
30   "Lieut. Barrington of the Republican Pie Brigade," *Weekly Economist*, Sept. 30, 1898, p. 3.
31   "Local News," *Weekly Economist*, Sept. 30, 1898, p. 3.
32   *Democracy Betrayed* introduction, p. 11n, citing *Weekly Economist*, Sept. 30, 1898, and Nov. 11, 1898.
33   Incidentally, the candidate who was elected to the House in 1894 and 1896—but for unknown reasons was not re-nominated in 1898, thus clearing the way for Sam Beasley—had family ties to Joshua Harrison's clan. Representative Willis Gallop, who lived near Jarvisburg, had two brothers who were married to daughters of Joshua and Ann Harrison. Parron Gallop was married to Bettie Harrison, who died in 1901, and Hodges Gallop was the husband of Margaret Ann "Maggie" Harrison, who ran the boardinghouse in Norfolk after her husband's death in 1902. *Currituck County Record of Elections*, 1894 and 1896; *The Heritage of Currituck County 1985*, "Willis H. Gallop and Descendants," by Alyce Sumrell, p. 236.
34   *Currituck County Record of Elections*, 1896 and 1898.
34   The 1900 census recorded 1,228 white males over age twenty-one living in Currituck County (1,029 of them literate, 199 not), compared with 418 black males over twenty-one (208 literate, 210 not). U.S. Department of Commerce, Bureau of Census, Twelfth Census.
35   *Josephus Daniels*, pp. 190-91; *The Paradox of Tar Heel Politics*, pp. 27-28.
37   *The Paradox of Tar Heel Politics*, pp. 29-30.
38   *Ibid.*, p. 39, citing *North Carolina Votes: General Election Returns by County*, ed. by Donald R. Matthews, University of North Carolina Press, Chapel Hill, 1962.

Chapter 10: The Anti-Liquor Crusade

1   "Kidnapper Put Behind the Bars, Harrison in Pasquotank County Jail, Feeling is Strong," *N&O*, Sept. 8, 1906, p. 1.
2   *N&O*, Sept. 8, 1906, p. 1.

3   *Liquor in the Land of the Lost Cause*, pp. 132-33.
4   *Prohibition in North Carolina, 1715-1945*, by Daniel Jay Whitener, University of North Carolina Press, Chapel Hill, 1945, p. 121, citing *Fayetteville Observer*, Jan. 12, 1899.
5   *Josephus Daniels*, pp. 198-200, quoting *Editor in Politics*, pp. 422-23.
6   *Ibid.*, p. 200.
7   *Prohibition in North Carolina*, pp. 135-36
8   *Liquor in the Land of the Lost Cause*, p. 167.
9   *The Paradox of Tar Heel Politics*, pp. 136, 140-41.
10 *Prohibition in North Carolina*, p. 141, citing *Winston Union Republican*, March 26, 1903, and *Asheville Register*, July 2, 1903.
11 *Public Laws of the State of North Carolina*, session 1903, chapters 318, 319.
12 *Carolina Moonshine Raiders*, by Frank Stephenson Jr., Meherrin River Press, Murfreesboro, NC, 2001, p. 1.
13 *Ibid.*, p. 2.
14 "The Rise and Fall of a Moonshine Capital," *Our State*, Feb. 28, 2011.
15 *Public Laws of the State of North Carolina*, session 1905, chapter 2.
16 *State v. Harrison*, 1907; trial transcript, testimony of Samuel M. Beasley.
17 *Currituck County Criminal Docket, Superior Court, 1889-1913*.
18 *Prohibition in North Carolina*, p. 159.
19 "Schools vs. Saloons: Governor Jarvis on the Eternal Conflict That Is Raging between the School-Room and the Bar-Room, That Is the Reason for the Election in May," Edwards & Broughton Printing Co., Raleigh, NC, *Documenting the American South*, http://docsouth.unc.edu
20 Aus Watts had an influential career in the General Assembly, and in 1921 was appointed the state's Revenue Commissioner, where he had wide influence in distributing patronage money for Senator Simmons. But in 1923, he was caught up in a prostitution sting. Three officers from the Raleigh Police vice squad barged into his Fayetteville Street apartment and found a woman hiding under his bed. Worse, for the times, it was a black woman. Watts did not

even attempt to defend himself. He immediately resigned from office, saying, "I'm ruined. I'll not lie. I'll take my medicine." *The Paradox of Tar Heel Politics*, pp. 56-57.

Part III: The Trial

Chapter 11: Battle Lines Drawn

1   "Thomas Jordan Jarvis, 1836-1915," *Documenting the American South*, http://docsouth.unc.edu.
2   *The Independent Man: The Story of W. O. Saunders and His Delightfully Different Newspaper*, by Keith Saunders, Saunders Press, Washington, DC, 1962, p. 15.
3   *Legendary Locals of Elizabeth City*, by Marjorie Ann Berry, Arcadia Publishing, Charleston, SC, 2014, pp. 69, 73.
4   The U.S. Supreme Court banned the practice at the federal level in *Young v. United States ex rel. Vuitton et Fils S.A.*, 481 U.S. 787 (1987). For a study of the history and development of law on this subject, see "The Public Interest and the Unconstitutionality of Private Prosecutors," by John D. Bessler, *Arkansas Law Review* 47, no. 3 1994, p. 511.
5   *Dead and Gone*, p. 95; "Little Known Stories About Well-Known People," by Fred Kelly, *The State* 39, no. 11, Nov. 1, 1971, p. 25.
6   *The Paradox of Tar Heel Politics*, pp. 44-45, citing *Separate and Unequal: Public School Campaigns and Racism in the Southern Seaboard States*, 1901-1905, by Louis R. Harlan, University of North Carolina Press, Chapel Hill, 1958, p. 104
7   *Ibid.*; also, speech delivered by former U.S. senator Frank Porter Graham before joint session of North Carolina General Assembly on Apr. 9, 1951, on occasion of the unveiling of the Howard Chandler Christie portrait of Governor Aycock
8   By 1915, North Carolina was spending $3.22 per year on the education of each white child and only $1.00 for each black child. *The Paradox of Tar Heel Politics*, p. 45.
9   *Charles Brantley Aycock*, pp. 335-36.

10   *Ibid.*, pp. 205, 219, 237.

11   The defense asked that the trial be held in Manteo, the seat of Dare County, located across the sound on Roanoke Island. But in the days before highway bridges, that would have required boat travel for all the attorneys and witnesses, which the court deemed too costly and inconvenient. The court deemed the twenty-five-mile distance between Currituck and Elizabeth City sufficient to eliminate any local prejudices. This was despite the wide readership of the *News & Observer*, a point the defense emphasized in its motion. The state countered that few people in Currituck actually subscribed to the *N&O*; according to its affidavits, only six copies of it were mailed to box holders at the Poplar Branch post office. Record on Appeal, *State v. Harrison*, defendant's Affidavit for Removal and Senator Beasley's answer.

12   U.S. Decennial Census.

13   *On the Shores of the Pasquotank: The Architectural Heritage of Elizabeth City and Pasquotank County, North Carolina*, by Thomas R. Butchko, Museum of the Albemarle, Elizabeth City, 1989, pp. 172-73.

14   This is an example of the hardships out-of-town attorneys must have encountered in trying to interview witnesses and prepare a case in the days before the internet, fax, and even telephone and automobile.

15   Trial transcript; *Tar Heel* booklet; "Kenneth Beasley Kidnapping Case: Harrison on Trial Charged with the Crime," *Farmer and Mechanic*, Raleigh, NC, March 19, 1907, p. 5.

16   "Witnesses Saw Boy in Blue Cap: Kidnapping Theory Is Gaining Credence," *N&O*, March 16, 1907, p. 1.

17   "Kenneth Beasley Kidnapping Case."

18   *Tar Heel* booklet.

19   From all appearances, Beasley had no trouble evoking the jury's sympathy. He had declined to run for re-election to the State Senate in 1906, and he and his family now were living primarily in Norfolk, visiting their property in Poplar Branch only occasionally to tend to business. Mrs. Beasley's health had been fragile since Kenneth disappeared, and they needed to stay in the city because she was often under doctors' care. Beasley said on the stand that he

was still "anxious" about his wife's condition, and he wanted her to avoid having to testify. *Tar Heel booklet*, testimony of Samuel M. Beasley

20 *Ibid.*
21 *Ibid.*
22 *Dead and Gone*, pp. 95-96.
23 Trial transcript, testimony of Samuel M. Beasley; "Kenneth Beasley Kidnapping Case."
24 Trial transcript, testimony of Samuel M. Beasley.
25 *Ibid.*
26 *Ibid.*; *Dead and Gone*, pp. 92-93.
27 Trial transcript, testimony of Samuel M. Beasley; "Kenneth Beasley Kidnapping Case."
28 Trial transcript, testimony of Samuel M. Beasley.
29 *Ibid.*
30 *Public Laws of the State of North Carolina, Session 1905*, Chapter 2: An Act to Amend Chapter 378, Public Laws of 1903.
31 Trial transcript, testimony of Samuel M. Beasley. If those were Harrison's exact words, he could be commended for his perfect diction, free of profanity, unlike his previous conversation with Beasley.
32 *Ibid.*
33 *Ibid.*
34 Trial transcript, testimony of M. P. Jennings.
35 Trial transcript, testimonies of D. W. Woodhouse, J. W. Poyner, W. A. Doxey, E. B. Gallop; *Tar Heel* booklet; "Kenneth Beasley Kidnapping Case"; "Witnesses Saw Boy in Blue Cap"; "Harrison Admitted Deed," *Charlotte Observer*, March 16, 1907, p. 1; "Trial of Joshua Harrison," *Chatham Record*, Pittsboro, NC, March 21, 1907, p. 1; "On Trial for Kidnapping," *Concord Daily Tribune*, Concord, NC, March 16, 1907, p. 1; "The Trial of Harrison," *Caucasian*, Clinton, NC, March 21, 1907, p. 1; "Trial of Joshua Harrison," *French Broad Hustler*, Hendersonville, NC, March 21, 1907, p. 1.
36 Two of them, Morrisette and Berry, are shown in the Record on Appeal to have been among the witnesses who testified before the grand jury that brought the indictment against Harrison back in September 1906.

37   Interestingly, none of these four men was among the three people (Ansell, Barco, and Griggs) mentioned as witnesses in the *N&O* letter.
38   Trial transcript, testimonies of Millard Morrisette, J. L. Turner, John Berry, Lemuel Civillis; *Tar Heel booklet*; "Kenneth Beasley Kidnapping Case"; "Harrison Admitted Deed"; "Witnesses Saw Boy in Blue Cap."
39   *Ibid.*
40   "Witnesses Saw Boy in Blue Cap."
41   *Ibid*; "Harrison Admitted Deed."
42   Trial transcript, testimony of Millard Morrisette.

Chapter 12: Revenge on Him or His Family, One

1   Trial transcript, testimony of J. J. Pierce; *Tar Heel* booklet, testimony of J. J. Pierce; "Kenneth Beasley Kidnapping Case"; "Witnesses Saw Boy in Blue Cap"; "Harrison Admitted Deed."
2   *Tar Heel* booklet. This pattern would be repeated many times during the trial. Character witnesses would be called to give quick opinion testimony as to whether a particular witness had a good or bad reputation for trustworthiness.
3   Trial transcript, testimonies of Balance, Dudley, Levin.
4   Trial transcript, testimony of A. B. Parker; *Tar Heel* booklet, testimony of A. B. Parker.
5   Trial transcript, testimony of Bunch.
6   If Harrison really did claim he was safe from hanging, he might have been speaking of either vigilante lynching or judicial punishment. At the time, hanging was still the method of legal execution for murder in North Carolina, and executions typically took place on or near the courthouse lawn. It was not until 1910 that the electric chair was installed at Central Prison in Raleigh and the state took over from the counties the responsibility of administering capital punishment.
7   Trial transcript, testimony of T. L. Baum; *Tar Heel* booklet, testimony of T. L. Baum; "Kenneth Beasley Kidnapping Case"; "Witnesses Saw Boy in Blue Cap"; "Harrison Admitted Deed."

ENDNOTES

8   Trial transcript, testimony of T. L. Baum; "Kenneth Beasley Kidnapping Case." It is not clear what caused the confusion over the name; the reporters might have wanted to conflate the name of the defendant with that of a black man to whom he was selling wine.

9   *Charles N. Hunter and Race Relations in North Carolina*, by John H. Haley, University of North Carolina Press, Chapel Hill, 1987, pp. 107-8.

10   *Ibid.*

11   *Tar Heel* booklet, testimony of T. L. Baum.

12   *Ibid.*

13   *Ibid.*

14   *Ibid.*

15   Trial transcript, testimony of T. C. Woodhouse; *Tar Heel* booklet, testimony of T. C. Woodhouse.

16   *Ibid.*; "Kenneth Beasley Kidnapping Case"; "Witnesses Saw Boy in Blue Cap"; "Harrison Admitted Deed."

17   *Ibid.*

18   Trial transcript, testimony of T. C. Woodhouse; *Tar Heel* booklet, testimony of T. C. Woodhouse.

Chapter 13: Laying Out the Alibis

1   "Kenneth Beasley Kidnapping Case"; "Endeavor to Prove Alibi; Defense in Kidnapping Case," *Charlotte Observer*, March 17, 1907, p. 1; "Harrison Tries to Prove Alibi," *N&O*, March 17, 1907, p. 9.

2   *Tar Heel* booklet, testimony of E. G. Swain.

3   "Kenneth Beasley Kidnapping Case"; "Endeavor to Prove Alibi"; "Harrison Tries to Prove Alibi."

4   Trial transcript, testimony of Norris Walston.

5   "Kenneth Beasley Kidnapping Case"; "Endeavor to Prove Alibi"; "Harrison Tries to Prove Alibi."

6   There may well have been a "negro skating rink" in Elizabeth City at the time. Starting in the 1890s, roller skating became a trend among America's youth, and skating rinks were popular hang-

out spots in towns all over the country. "Young St. Louis on Roller Skates Enjoys Fad So Intensely That Dancing and Other Forms of Winter Amusement are Neglected," *St. Louis Republic*, Nov. 12, 1905, p. 1; "When the World Takes to Wheels," *San Francisco Sunday Call*, Feb. 25, 1906, p. 11. A bit later, in 1916, Charlie Chaplin made one of his popular slapstick films, *The Rink*, in which he played a waiter in an upscale restaurant who goes skating on his lunch hour, to much comedic effect.

7 Trial transcript, testimonies of Dan Harrison, Sanders, and Parker; "This Booklet Contains the Evidence of the Beasley-Harrison Kidnapping Case," *Tar Heel*, 1907; "Kenneth Beasley Kidnapping Case"; "Endeavor to Prove Alibi"; "Harrison Tries to Prove Alibi."

8 *Ibid.*

9 "Kenneth Beasley Kidnapping Case"; "Endeavor to Prove Alibi"; "Harrison Tries to Prove Alibi."

10 *Tar Heel* booklet, testimony of Lee Thomas.

11 *Ibid*, testimony of J. W. Fisher.

12 *Ibid.*

13 Ms. Forbes also testified to that effect.

14 *Tar Heel* booklet, testimonies of Joe and Thomas Harrison; "Kenneth Beasley Kidnapping Case"; "Endeavor to Prove Alibi"; "Harrison Tries to Prove Alibi."

15 *Ibid.*

16 *Ibid.*

17 Copyright 1885, W. A. Evans and Brothers. The sheet music cover has an illustration of a heavyset, dark-skinned African-American woman apparently in the act of walking out on her husband, carrying a carpetbag in one hand and her equally dark-skinned child by his pants in her other hand.

18 W. A. Williams, Publisher, Warnock, OH, 1892.

19 At the Washington State Republican Convention in Tacoma in 1908, the party adopted a resolution calling for a prohibition local option. Afterward, a delegate called for everyone to join in singing "the famous old temperance song." "Republicans Are for Local Option: Convention Sings 'Where Is My Wandering Boy To-Nite' as It Votes for the Plank," Associated Press, May 14, 1908

20   *Tar Heel* booklet, testimony of Hoge Harrison; "Kenneth Beasley Kidnapping Case"; "Endeavor to Prove Alibi"; "Harrison Tries to Prove Alibi."
21   *Ibid.*
22   *Dead and Gone*, p. 96.
23   Trial transcript, testimony of Margaret Gallop.
24   *Dead and Gone*, pp. 96-97.

Chapter 14: Was the Answer in Norfolk?

1   Trial transcript, testimony of Margaret Gallop; *Norfolk, Portsmouth, Berkeley Directory*, 1904, 1905, Hill Directory Co., Norfolk, Newport News, Richmond.
2   *Atlas of Norfolk, Portsmouth, Berkeley, Virginia, and Vicinity: Including Lamberts Pointe, Norfolk on the Roads, South Norfolk, Pinners Pointe, West Norfolk, Town of Hampton Roads, etc.*, Sam W. Bowman, Norfolk, 1900.
3   Lost Norfolk, by Amy Waters Yarsinke, History Press, Charleston, SC, 2009.
4   "Survey for S. A. Woodward," Union Trust and Title Corporation records, Field Book 36B, p. 90.
5   Deed Book 137A, p. 318, and Deed Book 183A, p. 555, Norfolk County Public Registry.
6   Trial transcript, testimony of Margaret Gallop.
7   *Sea of Gray: The Around-the-World Odyssey of the Confederate Raider Shenandoah*, by Tom Chaffin, Hill and Wang, New York, 2006.
8   City of Norfolk online property tax listings, www.norfolk.gov. The house address currently is 405 Duke Street, although Duke Street, like Granby, has been renumbered. According to the Bowman atlas of 1900, it was 192 Duke Street.
9   Conversation with Ella Swain, assistant director, Hunter House Victorian Museum, Nov. 1, 2017.
10   Deed Book 39, p. 315, Norfolk County Public Registry.
11   *The History of Norfolk, Virginia*, by H. W. Burton, 1877, pp. 27, 38, 112.
12   Lucy Biggs died in 1909 at age seventy-nine. Norfolk tax

listings indicate that as of 1911, the Glisson House was still titled in the name of her estate.

13   *Norfolk, Portsmouth, Berkeley Directory*, 1906, 1907.

14   *Norfolk: The First Four Centuries*, by Thomas C. Parramore, with Peter C. Stewart and Tommy L. Boger, University Press of Virginia, Charlottesville, 1994, pp. 232-33.

15   *Ibid.*, p. 256.

16   *Ibid.*, p. 256, citing *New York Voice*, June 7, 1894, p. 1.

17   "Illustrated Standard Guide to Norfolk and Portsmouth and Historical Events of Virginia, 1607 to 1907," www.archive.org.

18   *Norfolk: The First Four Centuries*, pp. 267-68.

19   *The Independent Man*, p. 10.

Chapter 15: One Lady Must Be Lying

1   Anyone following the trial in the press would have had a hard time keeping the Woodhouses straight. At least one paper, the *Daily Industrial News* of Greensboro, NC, confused T. C. with J. J. in describing their testimonies. "Swears He Saw Harrison with the Beasley Boy," March 19, 1907, p. 1.

2   *Tar Heel* booklet, testimony of J. J. Woodhouse.

3   *Ibid.*; trial transcript, testimony of J. J. Woodhouse; "Endeavor to Prove Alibi."

4   *Ibid.*; trial transcript, testimony of John Aydlett.

5   *Tar Heel* booklet, testimony of J. J. Coogan.

6   Princess Anne County no longer exists. In the early 1960s, it was consolidated into the current city of Virginia Beach.

7   Trial transcript, testimony of D. F. Burfoot; *Tar Heel* booklet, testimony of D. F. Burfoot.

8   "Swears He Saw Harrison with the Beasley Boy."

9   *Ibid.*; trial transcript, testimony of E. W. Ansell; *Tar Heel* booklet, testimony of E. W. Ansell.

10   Trial transcript, testimonies of Bennett Walker and Irving Gallop.

11   Trial transcript, testimony of T. N. Davenport; *Tar Heel* booklet, testimony of T. N. Davenport.

12   Trial transcript, testimonies of Stephen Gordon and Cleve Newbern; *Tar Heel* booklet, testimonies of Stephen Gordon and Cleve Newbern.
13   Trial transcript, testimony of Thomas C. Woodhouse; *Tar Heel* booklet, testimony of Thomas C. Woodhouse.
14   "Swears He Saw Harrison With the Beasley Boy."
15   *Tar Heel* booklet, testimony of Cassie Beasley.
16   *Kidnapped*, p. 25.
17   *Josephus Daniels*, p. 182, citing *The Mind of the South*, p. 86.
18   *Tar Heel* booklet, testimony of Cassie Beasley; "Endeavor to Prove Alibi."
19   *Ibid.*; trial transcript, testimony of Cassie Beasley.
20   "Lawyers Get on Harrison's Alibi," *N&O*, March 20, 1907, p. 1; "Crowds at the Trial; Able Argument on Both Sides of the Case," *Goldsboro Weekly Argus*, Goldsboro, NC, March 28, 1907, p. 1.
21   *Ibid.*
22   "Harrison Lynched, Says Gov. Aycock," *N&O*, Aug. 28, 1907, p. 1.
23   "Lawyers Get on Harrison's Alibi"; "Crowds at the Trial."
24   "Harrison Lynched, Says Gov. Aycock."
25   *Ibid.*
26   *Ibid.*
27   *Tar Heel* booklet, Judge Allen's charge to the jury.
28   *Ibid.*
29   "Harrison Denies Guilt; In His Cell, the Convicted Kidnapper Protests His Innocence," *N&O*, March 24, 1907, p. 34.

Chapter 16: Eloquent Machinations

1   *Pasquotank County Superior Court Minute Docket, 1901-1908*.
2   Charles Brantley Aycock Collection, North Carolina State Archives; letter from W. D. Pruden to Justice William R. Allen, Apr. 13, 1912, and letter from Justice William R. Allen to W. D. Pruden, Apr. 16, 1912.
3   *Tar Heel* booklet, post-trial motions.

4   *Dead and Gone*, pp. 97-98.
5   *Ibid.*, p. 98.
6   *Ibid.*, p. 98; *Tar Heel* booklet, post-trial motions.
7   *Tar Heel* booklet, post-trial motions.
8   *Dead and Gone*, pp. 98-99.
9   *Pasquotank County Superior Court Minute Docket, 1901-1908*; *Tar Heel* booklet, post-trial motions.
10 "Kidnapped Boy in Arkansas?" *Raleigh Times*, March 22, 1907, p. 1; "Harrison Gets the Law's Limit," *Farmer and Mechanic*, March 26, 1907, p. 3.
11 "Truth of the Trains," by Katie Miles, *Constructing the Past 1*, Issue 1, 2000, p. 52.
12 *A Place Called Subiaco: A History of the Benedictine Monks in Arkansas*, by Hugh Assenmacher, Rose Publishing Co., Little Rock, 1977.
13 *Orphan Train Riders: Their Own Stories*, vol. 1, compiled by Mary Ellen Johnson, ed. by Kay B. Hall, Gateway Press, Baltimore, 1992.
14 "Senator Beasley's Trip Fruitless," *Dispatch*, Lexington, NC, Apr. 10, 1907, p. 1.
15 Camden County is located directly between Currituck and Pasquotank.
16 Brief of Defendant-Appellant, *State v. Harrison*, Aycock & Daniels, Aydlett & Ehringhaus.
17 *Ibid.*
18 "Harrison Lynched, Says Gov. Aycock; Appeal of Man Convicted in Beasley Kidnapping; Prejudice Alleged," *N&O*, Aug. 28, 1907, p. 5.
19 The case has inspired at least one book, a "nonfiction novel," *The Mystery of Beautiful Nell Cropsey*, by Bland Simpson, University of North Carolina Press, Chapel Hill, 1993. The old Cropsey home, where the mystery began, still stands on the bans of the Pasquotank River and has been featured in recent Elizabeth City Halloween ghost walks, with costumed re-enactors regaling tourists with the story.
20 *The Devil's Tramping Ground and Other North Carolina Mystery Stories*, by John Harden, University of North Carolina Press, Chapel

Hill, 1949, pp. 11-23.
21   *Ibid.*
22   *State v. Wilcox*, 131 N.C. 707, 42 S.E. 536 (1902).
23   The press also noted the similarities between the cases. The *News & Observer*, reporting on the noisy crowd attending Harrison's trial, said, "The Wilcox trial a few years ago can almost be called a tame affair when compared to it." "Lawyers Get on Harrison's Alibi," March 20, 1907, p. 1.
24   "Harrison Lynched, Says Gov. Aycock."
25   *Pasquotank County Superior Court Minute Docket, 1901-1908*.
26   *State v. Harrison*, 145 N.C. 408, 59 S.E. 867, 870 (1907).

Part IV: Resolutions

Chapter 17: At His Own Hands

1   *North Carolina State Prison*, by William G. Hinkle and Gregory S. Taylor, Arcadia Publishing, Charleston, SC, 2016, pp. 11, 23.
2   *Ibid.*, p. 7; *One Dies, Get Another: Convict Leasing in the American South, 1866-1928*, by Matthew J. Mancini, University of South Carolina Press, Columbia, 1996, p. 202.
3   *North Carolina State Prison*, pp. 8, 11.
4   *One Dies, Get Another*, pp. 202-7.
5   Also by way of illustration, in 1871, North Carolina had a total of 389 prison inmates. Some 264 of them are recorded to have been illiterate, and 108 were in their teens. *Ibid.*, p. 202.
6   *North Carolina State Prison*, p. 45.
7   For example, according to a State Productivity Statement for 1892, North Carolina inmates harvested 1,022 bales of cotton, 29,500 bushels of cottonseed, 3,800 bushels of peanuts, 3,800 bushels of corn shucks, and 40,000 pounds of wheat straw for the year. *Ibid.*, pp. 61-62.
8   *Ibid.*, pp. 31-32, 63, 65, 74.
9   *Illustrated Standard Guide to Norfolk and Portsmouth and Historical Events of Virginia, 1607-1907*, published for 1907 Jamestown Exposition by Standard Lithography and Publishing Co., pp. 21-23.

10   "Josh Harrison's Suicide," *Norfolk Virginian-Pilot*, Sept. 19, 1907, p. 1; "Suicide Carried His Secret to the Grave," *Norfolk Ledger-Dispatch*, Sept. 19, 1907, p. 1.
11   Ibid.
12   Ibid.
13   "Harrison's Last Plea," *Washington Post*, Sept. 20, 1907, p. 3; "Harrison Left a Letter," *Charlotte Observer*, Sept. 20, 1907, p. 1; "Blew Out His Brains," *Greensboro Patriot*, Greensboro, NC, Sept. 25, 1907, p. 5.
14   Ibid.
15   "The Harrison-Beasley Mystery," *N&O*, Sept. 20, 1907, p. 4; "The Harrison-Beasley Mystery," *North Carolinian*, Raleigh, Sept. 26, 1907, p. 4.

Chapter 18: Theories of Lost Boy Cases

1   "Snowden Keeps History Alive," by Cindy Beamon, *Daily Advance*, Elizabeth City, Apr. 9, 2013.
2   Interview with Barbara Snowden, Apr. 26, 2014; interview with Travis Morris, June 13, 2016.
3   *Analysis of Lost Person Behavior: An Aid to Search Planning*, by William G. Syrotuck, Amer Publications, Westmoreland, NY, 1977.
4   Ibid.
5   Ibid.; *Managing the Lost Person Incident*, by Kenneth A. Hill, National Association For Search and Rescue, Chantilly, VA, 1998; "The Psychology of Lost," by Kenneth A. Hill, in *Lost Person Behavior*, ed. by Kenneth A. Hill, National Search and Rescue Secretariat, Ottawa, ON, 1999, pp. 1-15.
6   Ibid.; "Just in Time Training, Wilderness Missing Person Search Procedures," Nebraska Emergency Response.
7   *Managing the Lost Person Incident*; "The Psychology of Lost."
8   "The Problem of Lost Children," by Edward H. Cornell and Kenneth A. Hill, in *Children and Their Environments: Learning, Using, and Designing Spaces*, ed. by Christopher Spencer and Mark Blades, Cambridge University Press, Cambridge and New York, 2005.

9   Dennis was by most accounts a special education student whose mental acuity may have lagged behind his age by a year or so.

10   "Search in the Smokies for Lost Boy, Dennis Martin, Produces Lessons for Future Searches," by Jim Balloch, *Knoxville News Sentinel*, June 28, 2009, citing *Lost! A Ranger's Journal of Search and Rescue*, by Dwight McCarter and Ronald Schmidt, Graphicom Press, Yellow Springs, OH, 1998.

11   *Ibid.*

12   In *Dead and Gone*, p. 96, Wellman suggests that the Poplar Branch road was within sight of Currituck Sound, and that if Harrison had abducted Kenneth and then taken to the road in his buggy, he might have been spotted by fishermen or hunters in boats that day. Actually, that is not the case. The roadway did not, and still does not, come closer than a quarter-mile to the shore, and at no point is it within sight of the water. It was separated from the sound by expanses of trees and farm fields, some of which still exist today.

13   "Currituck Sound, NC Environmental Restoration—Investigations," U.S. Army Corps of Engineers, Wilmington District, Apr. 8, 2013.

14   *Ibid.*; "The Biology of Drowning," by C. Garland, Western Pennsylvania Search and Rescue Development Center, 2009.

15   Currituck County Public Registry.

Chapter 19: All Misgivings Relieved

1   *Dead and Gone*, p. 101.

2   Notwithstanding the strange ransom demand from Rocky Mount, which Beasley must have concluded by then was a hoax.

3   *Cemetery John: The Undiscovered Mastermind of the Lindbergh Kidnapping*, by Robert Zorn, Overlook Press, New York, 2012, pp. 224-25.

4   *W. L. B. Dunton, by his guardian, S. M. Beasley v. Farmers Manufacturing Co.*; *Currituck County Superior Court Minute Docket*.

5   "Beasley and Vann Nominated," *Weekly Economist*, Aug. 26,

1904, p. 1.
6 Currituck County Superior Court Minute Docket.
7 The term *guano* is often associated with the excrement of seabirds. But in the early 1900s, it was a general term for plant fertilizer, which could also be derived from other sources, such as minerals and processed fish. *A Historian's Coast*, pp. 114-18.
8 Currituck County Superior Court Minute Docket.
9 *Ibid.*
10 *Ibid.*
11 *Dead and Gone*, pp. 101-2.
12 Trial transcript, testimonies of Thomas Harrison and Joe Harrison.
13 *Dead and Gone*, p. 101.
14 Interview with Sam Walker, Apr. 26, 2014.

Part V: Reckonings and Reassessments

Chapter 20: History in Transition

1 *Charles Brantley Aycock*, pp. 336-39.
2 *Ibid.*, pp. 337-38, citing "A Perilous Departure; Ex-Governor Aycock Explains Why He Said Supreme Court Forgot Law, " *Morning Star*, Wilmington, NC, Oct. 31, 1909.
3 *Ibid.*, p. 341; *Prohibition in North Carolina, 1715-1945*, pp. 168-69.
4 *Charles Brantley Aycock*, pp. 341-43, citing letters from Aycock to Henry Groves Connor and Judge William R. Allen, the presiding judge in the Harrison trial.
5 Charles Brantley Aycock Collection, 1880-1959, letter to Clarence H. Poe, Jan. 27, 1910.
6 *Charles Brantley Aycock*, pp. 345-46; *Josephus Daniels*, pp. 208-9.
7 Charles Brantley Aycock Collection, 1880-1959, letter to Clarence H. Poe, March 29, 1911.
8 *Charles Brantley Aycock*, p. 346.
9 *Ibid.*, p. 162, citing *N&O*, July 7, 1900.

ENDNOTES

10   Charles Brantley Aycock Collection, 1880-1959, copy of form letter from J. J. Laughinghouse, Oct. 7, 1911.

11   Charles Brantley Aycock Collection, 1880-1959, letter to J. R. Rodwell, Jan. 18, 1912.

12   *Charles Brantley Aycock*, p. 349, citing *It's a Far Cry*, by Robert W. Winston, Henry Holt and Co., New York, 1937, p. 246.

13   Charles Brantley Aycock Collection, 1880-1959, letters to Aycock from Zeno Brown (March 7, 1912), John Sentelle (March 9, 1912), and Robert B. Glenn (March 26, 1912).

14   *Charles Brantley Aycock*, pp. 360-61.

15   Charles Brantley Aycock Collection, 1880-1959, letter to H. G. Chatham, Apr. 1, 1912.

16   *Charles Brantley Aycock*, pp. 361-62, citing *Age Herald*, Birmingham, AL, Apr. 5, 1912, and *N&O*, Apr. 5, 1912.

17   He was assisted by his right-hand-man, Aus Watts, who served as collector of internal revenue for the western part of the state, and then as statewide revenue commissioner until his resignation in disgrace in 1923.

18   *The Paradox of Tar Heel Politics*, pp. 38-39, 47.

19   *Ibid.*, pp. 59-60.

20   *Acceptance and Unveiling of the Statue of Charles Brantley Aycock*, 72nd Cong., 1st sess., H. Doc. 343, GPO, May 20, 1932.

21   "McCrory Signs Bill to Put Graham Statue in U.S. Capitol," *Asheville Citizen-Times*, Oct. 2, 2015.

22   *Democracy Betrayed*; "Gov. Aycock and the Tug-of-War Over NC History," by Timothy B. Tyson, *N&O*, March 13, 2015.

23   Article by Valerie Strauss, *Washington Post*, May 18, 2016.

24   "Confederate Graves, Gov. Charles Aycock Marker Vandalized in Raleigh," *Charlotte Observer*, Jan. 3, 2016.

Chapter 21: To the Four Winds

1   "Biographical Summary of Thomas Jordan Jarvis, 1836-1915," by Jonathan D. Sarris. The former Aycock Hall was rechristened Legacy Hall in 2015 after a series of protests in which "the Black Student Union and other student groups at ECU advocated

for the name change and dubbed this week as 'Judgment Week.' " Selective judgment, one might say. "ECU to Remove Former Gov. Charles B. Aycock's Name from Dorm," by Jane Stancill, *N&O*, Feb. 20, 2015.

2   *Legendary Locals of Elizabeth City*, by Marjorie Ann Berry, Arcadia Publishing, Charleston, SC, 2014, p. 73.

3   *The Independent Man*, pp. 15-17.

4   Saunders's most famous moment came in 1926, when he published *The Book of Ham*. It was a harsh critique of the Reverend Mordecai Ham, a traveling Baptist minister who was anti-black, anti-Semitic, and anti-Catholic, yet also a mentor to the young Billy Graham. Ham had publicly accused Julius Rosenwald, the Jewish philanthropist who financed construction of black schools throughout the South, of building black houses of prostitution in Chicago. Saunders's book refuted the accusations in detail, although many did not want to hear it.

5   "Proposal Could Preserve Tales of Pioneer Journalist," by Jay Price, Associated Press, *Wilmington Star-News*, Dec. 12, 2003.

6   *The Independent Man*, pp. 27-29.

7   *Ibid.*, pp. 23-24.

8   Deed Book 148A, p. 169, Norfolk City Public Registry.

9   The farm in Poplar Branch was purchased by the Griggs family, whose descendants still reside on part of it today. Deed Book 51, p. 150, Currituck County Public Registry.

10   "Had His Foot Mashed Off," *Tar Heel*, July 30, 1910, p. 4; "Another Sad Incident in Unfortunate Family," *Tar Heel*, Aug. 12, 1910, p. 1.

11   *Ibid.*

12   U.S. Decennial Census, 1910; World War I draft registration card; U.S. National Cemetery Interment Control Form.

13   U.S. Decennial Census, 1930 and 1940; shipping registries for *S.S. Empress of India* (1929), *S.S. Guayaquil* (1927), and *S.S. Mary* (1928).

14   World War II draft registration card.

15   "Kenneth Beasley, Long-Missing Kidnapped Boy, Reported Found," *Asheville Citizen-Times*, Dec. 28, 1913, p. 6; "Kenneth Beasley Reported Seen," *Daily Journal*, New Bern, NC, Dec. 19, 1913, p.

Endnotes

1.
16   U.S. Decennial Census, 1920, 1930, 1940.
17   Will Book 19, p. 185, Norfolk City Clerk of Court.
18   "From the Archives: Central State Hospital," *Richmond Times-Dispatch*, May 9, 2016.
19   *City of Norfolk v. Ethel Beasley*, file no. CH05-2013, Office of the Clerk of Norfolk Circuit Court.
20   World War I draft registration cards, death certificates, marriage certificate.
21   World War I draft registration card.
22   *The Heritage of Currituck County 1985*, entry by Mary Alyce Sumrell, p. 278.
23   *Ibid.*
24   "Currituck Native of World War I Fame Dies," *Dare County Times*, Manteo, NC, Apr. 16, 1943, p. 1.
25   U.S. Decennial Census, 1910; Deed Book 48, p. 218, Currituck County Public Registry.
26   U.S. Decennial Census, 1920.
27   "Poplar Branch," by Vickie Brickhouse, *Journal of Currituck County Historical Society*, 1977.
28   U.S. Decennial Census, 1940.
29   "Jarvis Portrait Unveiled," *Asheville Citizen-Times*, Nov. 12, 1945, p. 9.

BIBLIOGRAPHY

Books

Assenmacher, Hugh. *A Place Called Subiaco: A History of the Benedictine Monks in Arkansas*. Little Rock, AR: Rose Publishing Co., 1977.

Bates, JoAnna Heath, ed. *The Heritage of Currituck County North Carolina 1985*. Winston-Salem, NC: Albemarle Genealogical Society in cooperation with Currituck County Historical Society and Hunter Publishing Co., 1985.

Berg, A. Scott. *Wilson*. New York: G. P. Putnam's Sons, 2013.

Berry, Marjorie Ann. *Legendary Locals of Elizabeth City*. Charleston, SC: Arcadia Publishing, 2014.

Bledsoe, Jerry. *Death Sentence: The True Story of Velma Barfield's Life*, Crimes, and Execution. New York: Penguin Group, 1998.

Burton, H. W. *The History of Norfolk, Virginia*. Norfolk, VA: Norfolk Virginian, 1877.

Butchko, Thomas R. *On the Shores of the Pasquotank: The Architectural Heritage of Elizabeth City and Pasquotank County, North Carolina*. Elizabeth City, NC: Museum of the Albemarle, 1989.

Cash, W. J. *The Mind of the South*. New York: Vintage Publishing, 1941.

Cecelski, David. *A Historian's Coast: Adventures Into the Tidewater Past*. Winston-Salem, NC: John F. Blair, Publisher, 2000.

Cecelski, David, and Timothy B. Tyson, eds. *Democracy Betrayed: The Wilmington Race Riot of 1898 and Its Legacy*. Chapel Hill, NC: University of North Carolina Press, 1998.

Chaffin, Tom. *Sea of Gray: The Around-the-World Odyssey of the Confederate Raider* Shenandoah. New York: Hill and Wang, 2006.

Christensen, Rob. *The Paradox of Tar Heel Politics*. Chapel Hill, NC: University of North Carolina Press, 2008.

Chudacoff, Howard P. *Mobile Americans*. New York: Oxford University Press, 1972.

Clegg, Claude A., III. *Troubled Ground: A Tale of Murder, Lynching, and Reckoning in the New South*. Urbana, IL: University of Illinois Press, 2010.

Coker, Joe L. *Liquor in the Land of the Lost Cause*. Lexington, KY: University Press of Kentucky, 2007.

Craig, Lee A. *Josephus Daniels: His Life and Times*. Chapel Hill, NC: University of North Carolina Press, 2013.

Crespino, Joseph. *Strom Thurmond's America*. New York: Hill and Wang, 2012.

Daniels, Josephus. *Editor in Politics*. Chapel Hill, NC: University of North Carolina Press, 1941.

Elliott, Jeffrey M. *Fantasy Voices: Interviews with American Fantasy Writers*. Borgo Press, 1982.

Fass, Paula S. *Kidnapped: Child Abduction in America*. New York: Oxford University Press, 1997.

Ferling, John. *Almost a Miracle: The American Victory in the War of Independence*. New York: Oxford University Press, 2007.

Gerard, Philip. *Down the Wild Cape Fear: A River Journey through the Heart of North Carolina*. Chapel Hill, NC: University of North Carolina Press, 2013.

Hagen, Carrie. *We Is Got Him: The Kidnapping That Changed America*. New York: Overlook Press, 2011.

Hairr, John. *North Carolina Lighthouses and Lifesaving Stations*. Charleston, SC: Arcadia Publishing, 2004.

Haley, John H. *Charles N. Hunter and Race Relations in North Carolina*. Chapel Hill, NC: University of North Carolina Press, 1987.

Hanchett, Tom. *Sorting the New South City: Race, Class, and Urban Development in Charlotte, 1875-1975*. Chapel Hill, NC: University of North Carolina Press, 1998.

Harden, John. *The Devil's Tramping Ground and Other North Carolina Mystery Stories*. Chapel Hill, NC: University of North Carolina Press, 1949.

Harlan, Louis R. *Separate and Unequal: Public School Campaigns and Racism in the Southern Seaboard States, 1901-1905*. Chapel Hill, NC: University of North Carolina Press, 1958.

Hill, Kenneth. *Lost Person Behavior*. Ottawa, ON: National Search and Rescue Secretariat, 1999.

———. *Managing the Lost Person Incident*. Chantilly, VA: National Association for Search and Rescue, 1998.

Hinkle, William G., and Gregory S. Taylor. *North Carolina State Prison*. Charleston, SC: Arcadia Publishing, 2016.

James, Bill, and Rachel M. James. *The Man from the Train: The Solving of a Century-Old Serial Killer Mystery*. New York: Simon & Schuster, 2017.

Johnson, Mary Ellen. *Orphan Train Riders: Their Own Stories*. Edited by Kay B. Hall. Vol. 1. Baltimore, MD: Gateway Press, 1992.

Kantrowitz, Stephen. *Ben Tillman and the Reconstruction of White Supremacy*. Chapel Hill, NC: University of North Carolina Press, 2015.

Klotter, James C. *William Goebel: The Politics of Wrath*. Lexington, KY: University Press of Kentucky, 1977.

Krakauer, Jon. *Under the Banner of Heaven: A Story of Violent Faith*. New York: Doubleday, 2003.

Larsen, Lawrence, and Barbara Cottrell. *The Gate City: A History of Omaha*. Lincoln, NE: University of Nebraska Press, 1997.

Lebsock, Suzanne. *A Murder in Virginia: Southern Justice on Trial*. New York: W. W. Norton & Co., 2003.

Mancini, Matthew J. *One Dies, Get Another: Convict Leasing In the American South, 1866-1928*. Columbia, SC: University of South Carolina Press, 1996.

Matthews, Donald R., ed. *North Carolina Votes: General Election Return by County*. Chapel Hill, NC: University of North Carolina Press, 1962.

McCarter, Dwight, and Donald Schmidt. *Lost! A Ranger's Journal of Search and Rescue*. Yellow Springs, OH: Graphicom Press, 1998.

McCleave, Mansel. *Hunger Pains in Our Heads: The Story of the Non-Violent Student Sit-In Movement and the Black Struggle for Equality*. Birmingham, AL: Tavine'ra Publishing, 2008.

Newkirk, Vann R. *Lynching in North Carolina: A History, 1865-1941*. Jefferson, NC: McFarland & Co., 2009.

Newton, Michael. *The Encyclopedia of Kidnappings*. New York: Facts on File, 2002.

Oney, Steve. *And the Dead Shall Rise*. New York: Vintage Books, 2003.

Orr, Oliver H., Jr. *Charles Brantley Aycock*. Chapel Hill, NC: University of North Carolina Press, 1961.

Parramore, Thomas C., with Peter C. Stewart and Tommy L. Boger. *Norfolk: The First Four Centuries*. Charlottesville, VA: University Press of Virginia, 1994.

Ross, Christian K. *The Father's Story of Charley Ross, the Kidnapped Child Containing a Full and Complete Account of the Abduction of Charles Brewster Ross From the Home of His Parents in Germantown, With the Pursuit of the Abductors and Their Tragic Death; The Various Incidents Connected With the Search For the Lost Boy; The Discovery of Other Lost Children, Etc. Etc. With Facsimiles of Letters From the Abductors*. Philadelphia: John E. Potter, 1876.

Saunders, Keith. *The Independent Man: The Story of W. O. Saunders and His Delightfully Different Newspaper*. Washington, DC: Saunders Press, 1962.

Spence, James R. *Watering the Sahara: Recollections of Paul Green from 1894 to 1937*. Edited by Margaret D. Bauer. Raleigh, NC: Office of Archives and History, NC Department of Cultural

Resources, 2008.

Spencer, Christopher, and Mark Blades, eds. *Children and Their Environments: Learning, Using and Designing Spaces*. Cambridge and New York: Cambridge University Press, 2005.

Stephenson, Frank, Jr. *Carolina Moonshine Raiders*. Murfreesboro, NC: Meherrin River Press, 2001.

Syrotuck, William G. *Analysis of Lost Person Behavior: An Aid to Search Planning*. Westmoreland, NY: Amer Publications, 1977.

Wellman, Manly Wade. *Dead and Gone: Classic Crimes of North Carolina*. Chapel Hill, NC: University of North Carolina Press, 1954.

Wells, Susan Barringer. *A Game Called Salisbury: The Spinning of a Southern Tragedy and the Myths of Race*. West Conshohocken, PA: Infinity Publishing, 2007.

White, Carroll. *Norfolk: A Pictorial History*. From the "Those Were the Days" collection, edited by Linda G. Fates. Virginia Beach, VA: Donning Co. Publishers, 1975.

Whitener, Daniel Jay. *Prohibition in North Carolina, 1715-1945*. Chapel Hill, NC: University of North Carolina Press, 1945.

Winston, Robert W. *It's a Far Cry*. New York: Henry Holt and Co., 1937.

Wright, Gavin. *Old South, New South: Revolutions in the Southern Economy since the Civil War*. New York: Basic Books, 1986.

Yarsinke, Amy Waters. *Lost Norfolk*. Charleston, SC: History Press, 2009.

Young, Perry Deane. *The Untold Story of Frankie Silver*. Asheboro, NC: Down Home Press, 1998.

Zorn, Robert. *Cemetery John: The Undiscovered Mastermind of the Lindbergh Kidnapping*. New York: Overlook Press, 2012.

Articles

Ansell, Henry B. "Recollections of a Life Time and More." 1907. Southern Historical Collection, University of North Carolina at Chapel Hill.

Barnes, Billy. Interview with Paul Green, March 5, 1975, #B-0005-1, Southern Oral History Program Collection #4007, Southern Historical Collection, University of North Carolina at Chapel Hill.

Bessler, John D. "The Public Interest and the Unconstitutionality of Private Prosecutors." *Arkansas Law Review* 47, No. 3 (1994): 511.

Brickhouse, Vickie. "Poplar Branch." *Journal of the Currituck County Historical Society* (1977): 171.

Davis, Ronald L. F. "Creating Jim Crow: In-Depth Essay." www.jimcrowhistory.org.

Garland, C. "The Biology of Drowning." 2009. Western Pennsylvania Search and Rescue Development Center.

Green, John B., III. " 'A New Court House of Brick': A Documentary History of the Currituck County Courthouse, Currituck, North Carolina," with an addendum, "Establishing a Date For the Currituck County Jail." 1998. Prepared for the County of Currituck, North Carolina, and the Currituck County Historical Society, New Bern, NC.

Hagen, Carrie. "The Story Behind the First Ransom Note in American History." *Smithsonian* (Dec. 9, 2013).

Jones, Gordon Cowley. "The Introduction of Modern Education into Currituck County, North Carolina." *Journal of the Currituck County Historical Society* 1, No. 2 (Aug. 1971): 62.

"Just in Time Training, Wilderness Missing Person Search Procedures." Nebraska Emergency Response.

Kelly, Fred. "Little-Known Stories about Well-Known People." *The State* 39, No. 11 (Nov. 1, 1971): 25.

Kelly, Susan Stafford. "Party on the Line: Recalling Southern Bell and Carolina Telephone." *Our State* (Feb. 26, 2014).

Miles, Katie. "Truth of the Trains." *Constructing the Past* 1, issue 1 (2000): 52.

Morrill, Dan L. "Jim Crow Comes to Mecklenburg County." University of North Carolina-Charlotte, www.cmhpf.org.

Nash, Jay Robert. "Patrick Crowe: The Friendly Kidnapper." *Jay Robert Nash's Annals of Crime*, www.annalsofcrime.com.

Peterson, Garneth Oldenkamp. " 'A Really Spectacular and Truly

Named Desperado': Pat Crowe and the Cudahy Kidnapping Case." *Nebraska History* 57 (1976): 331.
"Pioneer Electrical Weekly of America, The." *Electrical Review* 43, no. 17 (Oct. 24, 1903): 608.
"Rise and Fall of a Moonshine Capital, The." *Our State* (Feb. 28, 2011).
Semuels, Alana. "Segregation Had to Be Invented." *The Atlantic* (Feb. 17, 2017).
Walker, Carrie Parker. "Some Memories of Currituck County, North Carolina, 1908-1957." *Journal of the Currituck County Historical Society* 1, no. 2 (1974): 43.

Newspapers

Age Herald, Birmingham, AL.
Atlanta Journal.
Asheville Citizen-Times, Asheville, NC.
Asheville Register, Asheville, NC.
Caucasian, Clinton, NC.
Charlotte Observer, Charlotte, NC.
Chatham County Herald, Siler City, NC.
Chatham Record, Pittsboro, NC.
Concord Daily Tribune, Concord, NC.
Daily Economist and *Weekly Economist*, Elizabeth City, NC.
Daily Industrial News, Greensboro, NC.
Daily Journal, New Bern, NC.
Daily Standard, Raleigh, NC.
Dare County Times, Manteo, NC.
Dispatch, Lexington, NC.
Fayetteville Observer, Fayetteville, NC.
French Broad Hustler, Hendersonville, NC.
Goldsboro Weekly Argus, Goldsboro, NC.
Greensboro Patriot, Greensboro, NC.
Knoxville News-Sentinel, Knoxville, TN.
Landmark, Statesville, NC.
Morning Post, Raleigh, NC.

Morning Star, Wilmington, NC.
New York Herald.
New York Times.
New York Voice.
News & Observer, Raleigh, NC.
Norfolk Ledger-Dispatch.
Norfolk Virginian-Pilot.
North Carolinian, Raleigh, NC.
Philadelphia Inquirer.
Raleigh Times.
Richmond Times-Dispatch.
Roanoke Beacon, Plymouth, NC.
St. Louis Republic.
Tar Heel, Elizabeth City, NC; "This Booklet Contains the Evidence of the Beasley-Harrison Kidnapping Case, Judge Allen's Charge to the Jury, The Verdict of the Jury, and The Sentence of Joshua Harrison to the Penitentiary," 1907. Cited herein as "the *Tar Heel* booklet."
Union Republican, Winston, NC.
Washington Post.
Weekly High Point Enterprise, High Point, NC.
Wilmington Messenger, Wilmington, NC.
Wilmington Star-News, Wilmington, NC.
Windsor Ledger, Windsor, NC.
Winston-Salem Journal, Winston-Salem, NC.

Archives and Libraries

Charles Brantley Aycock Collection, North Carolina State Archives.
Currituck County Public Registry, Office of the Register of Deeds.
Currituck County Record of Elections, 1894, 1896, 1898.
Currituck County Superior Court Minute Dockets, Office of the Clerk of Court.
Norfolk County Public Registry (deeds), Norfolk Circuit Court.
Norfolk, Portsmouth, Berkeley Directory, 1904, 1905, 1906, 1907,

published by Hill Directory Co., Norfolk, Newport News, Richmond.
Pasquotank County Superior Court Minute Dockets, Office of the Clerk of Court.
Public Laws of the State of North Carolina, Sessions 1903 and 1905.
Record of Marriages, Book A (1851-1867), copied from the Register of Deeds Office, Currituck County, 1998, Albemarle Genealogical Society.

Personal Interviews

Griggs, Charles. Nov. 14, 2015.
Morris, Travis. June 13, 2016.
Sawyer, Roy. July 26, 2014.
Snowden, Barbara. Apr. 26, 2014.
Swain, Ella. Nov. 1, 2017.
Walker, Sam. Apr. 26, 2014.

Online and Miscellaneous

Acceptance and Unveiling of the Statue of Charles Brantley Aycock, 72nd Cong., 1st sess., H. Doc. 343. GPO, May 20, 1932.
Adams, Susan H. *Statement Analysis: What do Suspects' Words Really Reveal?* Federal Bureau of Investigation, Oct. 1996.
Atlas of Norfolk, Portsmouth, Berkeley, Virginia, and Vicinity: Including Lamberts Pointe, Norfolk on the Roads, South Norfolk, Pinners Pointe, West Norfolk, Town of Hampton Roads, etc. Norfolk, VA: Sam W. Bowman, 1900.
Bureau of Census. *Twelfth Census*. U.S. Dept. of Commerce.
Currituck Sound, NC Environmental Restoration—Investigations. U.S. Army Corps of Engineers, Wilmington District, Apr. 8, 2013.
"Descendants of Zorababel Harrison." Genealogy compiled by Walter Gallop, June 21, 2007.

"Documenting the American South." Biography of Thomas J. Jarvis. www.unc.edu.

From Cape Henry to Currituck Beach Including the Albemarle and Chesapeake Canal. U.S. Coast and Geodetic Survey map, 1913.

Graham, Frank Porter. Speech before Joint Session of the North Carolina General Assembly on occasion of the unveiling of the Howard Chandler Christie portrait of Governor Charles B. Aycock, Apr. 9, 1951.

Illustrated Standard Guide to Norfolk and Portsmouth and Historical Events, 1607 to 1907. Published for 1907 Jamestown Exposition by Standard Lithography and Publishing Co. www.archive.org.

Lowry, Robert. "Where Is My Wandering Boy Tonight?" Words and music. Warnock, OH: W. A. Williams, 1892.

Rosenfeld, M. H. "Good-Bye, My Honey, I'm Gone." Words and music. W.A. Evans and Brothers, 1885.

Schools vs. Saloons: Governor Jarvis on the Eternal Conflict That Is Raging Between the School-Room and the Bar-Room, That Is the Reason for the Election in May. Speech originally published by Edwards & Broughton Printing Co., Raleigh, NC, 1908; Documenting the American South, http://docsouth.unc.edu.

Soil Map, North Carolina, Camden and Currituck Counties. Baltimore, MD: A. Hoen & Co., 1923.

State v. Harrison, 145 NC 408, 59 S.E. 867 (1907).

State v. Harrison, Brief of Defendant-Appellant, Aycock and Daniels, Aydlett and Ehringhaus.

State v. Harrison, Record on Appeal.

State v. Wilcox, 131 N.C. 707, 42 S.E. 536 (1902).

"Survey for S. A. Woodward." Union Trust and Title Corporation Records, Norfolk, VA.

"Thomas Jordan Jarvis, 1836-1915." *Documenting the American South,* docsouth.unc.edu.

U.S. Decennial Census. www.census.gov.

U.S. Department of Veterans Affairs. U.S. National Cemetery Interment Control Forms.

BIBLIOGRAPHY

U.S. Department of War. Draft Registration Cards.
www.intotodaysdollars.com
Young v. United States ex rel. Vuitton et Fils S.A., 481 U.S. 787 (1987).

IILLUSTRATION CREDITS

Illustrations are photographs unless otherwise identified.

xii   Map / MATT DAVIS, THE MAP SHOP, CHARLOTTE, N.C., From "Curricuck Beach To New Inlet" Nautical Chart, 1913, OFFICE OF COAST SURVEY, NATIONAL OCEANIC AND ATMOSPHERIC ADMINISTRATION

6   Sam and Cassie Beasley / COURTESY OF SAMUEL WALKER.

10   Schoolhouse - Odd Fellows Hall / AUTHOR PHOTO

14   Beasley home / COURTESY OF CURRITUCK COUNTY (N.C.) HISTORICAL SOCIETY

16   Nina Harrison / COURTESY OF SAMUEL WALKER

26   Joshua Harrison home / COURTESY OF CURRITUCK COUNTY HISTORICAL SOCIETY

36   Kenneth and Ethel Beasley / COURTESY OF SAMUEL WALKER

46   Lithograph, Charles Brewster Ross / LIBRARY OF CONGRESS, PRINTS AND PHOTOGRAPHS DIVISION

58   Edward Cudahy, Jr., and sisters / DOUGLAS COUNTY (NEB.) HISTORICAL SOCIETY

70   Newspaper headlines / "Hundred Now in Search of the Lost Boy," *NEWS AND OBSERVER*, Raleigh, N.C., Feb. 16, 1905; "Complete Story of Lost Beasley Boy," *WEEKLY ECONOMIST*, Elizabeth City, N.C. Feb. 17, 1905; "$500 Reward for Lost Boy," *NEWS AND OBSERVER*, Feb. 28, 1905; "Search Abandoned," *NEWS AND OBSERVER*, Feb. 26, 1905; "Kidnapper Put Behind the Bars," *NEWS AND OBSERVER*, Sept. 8, 1906; "A Sensation in Currituck Court," *THE NORTH CAROLINIAN*, Raleigh, Sept. 13, 1906; "Harrison Makes Complete Denial," *NEWS AND OBSERVER*; Sept. 11, 1906.

72   Old Currituck Courthouse / COURTESY OF KEITH VINCENT, COURTHOUSEHISTORY.COM

72   Currituck County Jail / AUTHOR PHOTO

77   Article: *WASHINGTON POST*, SEPT. 8, 1906

78   Lynching vistims / *SALISBURY EVENING POST*, AUG. 6, 1906

86   Pritchard, Butler, Russell, Daniels / COURTESY OF THE NORTH CAROLINA OFFICE OF ARCHIVES AND HISTORY. White, Simmons / COURTESY OF THE NORTH CAROLINA COLLECTION, UNIVERSITY OF NORTH CAROLINA CHAPEL HILL LIBRARIES

102   Drawing, Prohibition referendum / RALEIGH *NEWS AND OBSERVER*, MAY 26, 1908

114   Thomas J. Jarvis / LIBRARY OF CONGRESS, NATIONAL PHOTO COMPANY COLLECTION

130   Headline / *THE FARMER AND MECHANIC*, RALEIGH, MARCH 19, 1907

134   Article: *THE WASHINGTON POST*, MARCH 16, 1907

139   Headlines / "Lawyers Get on Harrison's Alibi," *THE NORTH CAROLINIAN*, Raleigh, March 21, 1907; "Harrison's Alibi is Attacked by the Prosecution," *ASHEVILLE CITIZEN-TIMES*, March 19, 1907; "Harrison Tries to Prove Alibi," Raleigh *NEWS AND OBSERVER*, March 17, 1907; "Harrison Had a Fretful Child," *RALEIGH TIMES*, March 18, 1907.

Illustration Credits

151   Norfolk boardinghouse / AUTHOR PHOTO

158   Postcard, Pasquotank County Courthouse / COURTESY OF KEITH VINCENT, COURTHOUSEHISTORY.COM

168   Headlines / *THE FARMER AND MECHANIC*, RALEIGH, MARCH 26, 1907

170   Article / *NEW YORK TIMES*, MARCH 21, 1907

180   Article / RALEIGH *NEWS AND OBSERVER*, AUGUST 28, 1907

184   Penitentiary / STATE ARCHIVES OF NORTH CAROLINA

192   Headlines / "He Prefers Death to Term in Prison," *RICHMOND (VA.) TIMES-DISPATCH*, September 19, 1907; "An Abductor Suicides," DAILY PRESS, Newport News, Va., September 19, 1907; "Harrison a Suicide," *ROANOKE BEACON*, Plymouth, N.C., September 27, 1907; "Blows Out His Brains in Preference to a 20 Years Sentence," *THE WEEKLY HIGH POINT (N.C.) ENTERPRISE*, September 25, 1907.

199   Map / OPENSTREETMAP.ORG

202   H.S. Ward / LIBRARY OF CONGRESS, NATIONAL PHOTO COMPANY COLLECTION

216   Charles Aycock / STATE ARCHIVES OF NORTH CAROLINA

221   Cartoon / RALEIGH *NEWS AND OBSERVER*, JULY 7, 1900

228   Lithograph, S.M. Beasley / RALEIGH *NEWS AND OBSERVER*, AUG. 24, 1899

232   Sam Beasley headstone / AUTHOR PHOTO

238   Joshua Harrison headstone and cemetery / AUTHOR PHOTO

INDEX

Photographs in italics

Adams, Spencer, 220-21
Alabama Educational Association, 223
Allen, William R., 122, 135-36, 165, 167, 172, 204; background in state legislature, 121; denies Harrison's post-trial motions, 174; friendship with Aycock, 121; instructions to jury, 167-68; selected as judge for Harrison trial, 121; sentences Harrison to prison, 174
Ansell, W. E., 25, 162-63, 207
Anti-liquor (prohibition) movement: anti-black rhetoric, 104-11; dispensary reforms, 104-5; fears of black criminality, 106; impact of 1893 financial panic on, 104-5; local ordinances passed by General Assembly, 105-7; promoted by Aycock and Simmons, 105-7; Raleigh referendum of 1900, 105; statewide referendum of 1908, *107*, 110, 218; white and black cooperation in 1870s and 1880s, 104
Atlanta Constitution, 88
Atlantic Collegiate Institute, 14
Aycock, Charles B., 13, 85, 139, 141, 148, 162, 165, *216*, 229; accusations of alcoholism, 220-23; argues appeal for Harrison, 176-80; closing argument at trial, 166-67; considers U.S. Senate campaign, 220; court cases tried by, 1905-6, 120-21; cross-exam of witnesses in Harrison trial, 128-29; death, 223; disputes over school funding, 119-20; education speech at 1904 Democratic Convention, 119-20; educational reforms, 12, 82; elected governor in 1900, 12, 220-21; family background, 93; grave desecrated, 227; leader in White Supremacy Campaign, 94; legal practice after Harrison trial, 217-18; legal practice post-governorship, 118; name removed from monuments, 225-26; opposition to lynching, 82-83; post-trial motions, 172-73; racial appeals during Harrison trial, 135-36; racial rhetoric on campaign trail, 134-35; reasons for taking Harrison case, 118-21; reflections on white supremacy, 219; reluctance to seek office after 1908, 219; reputation restored in 1930s, 225; response to Wilcox lynching threat, 178; retained to represent Harrison, 118; Statuary Hall memorial, 225; supports statewide prohibition in 1908, 218; threat to resign governorship, 119
Aydlett, Edwin F.: career after Harrison trial, 230-31; cross-exam of eyewitnesses, 128-29; defense of Jim Wilcox in Nell Cropsey case, 179;

legal representation of Sam Beasley, 208; nominates Beasley for State Senate, 208; political power broker in Elizabeth City, 116; represents Harrison in debt collection suit, 208-9; retained by Harrison in kidnapping trial, 74, 116
Aydlett, John, 160

Barco, Caleb, 25
Barnard, John E., 76
Barnum, P. T., 56
Barrington, John, 98
Baum, Thomas L., 140-41, 144, 207; alleged to have threatened defense witness, 141-42; cross-exam by Aycock, 134-36; testifies to hearing Harrison confess to kidnapping, 133-34
Beasley, Cassie Walker, 7, 13, 15, 17, 20, 211, 213; comparisons with Ross parents, 164-65; death, 234; grief and frail health, 25, 43, 67, 164; life in Norfolk after trial, 234; testifies at Harrison trial, 164-66; visited by Ann Harrison, 147-48, 165
Beasley, Ethel, 36, 234-35
Beasley, Louis Moran, 14, 23, 124; death, 234; service in Merchant Marine and Quartermaster Corps, 233-34
Beasley, Samuel M., 7, 8, 17-18, 116, 135, 148, 164, 207, 229; accepts likelihood of son's death, 43, 123; alleged attempt at ransom negotiation, 136-37, 205; attitude toward lynching, 77; business and political background, 13; compared with Ross, Cudahy parents, 67-68; death and gravesite, 232-33, 232; efforts to ban liquor business, 73-74; election results in 1898, 99; endorsed by White Men's Union in 1898, 99; and Harrison's suicide, 190; home and farm, 13-14; informed of son's disappearance, 22-23; legal dealings with Edwin Aydlett, 208; life in Norfolk after trial, 231-32; marriage and children, 13-14; offers reward for son's return, 37-38, 40; opposes Harrison's motion for change of venue, 75-76; and search for Kenneth, 123-24; sponsors 1903 Currituck liquor ordinance, 107-8, 124-25; sponsors 1905 amendment to 1903 ordinance, 108-9, 124-25; testimony at Harrison trial, 123-26; threat made by Harrison, 124-25; travels to Arkansas in search of Kenneth, 174-75
Beasley, William Kenneth, 14-15, 27, 36, 37, 57, 67, 69, 79, 131, 193, 203; comparison with Warburton, Martin disappearances, 198-99; disappearance from schoolhouse, 20-25, 110; false rumors of safe return, 24, 40; first speculation of kidnapping, 24-25; last day at school, 17-20; likely scenario for abduction, 210-11; neighbors organize search for, 22-24, 142; other suspects in disappearance, 203-4; personality, 21, 41-42; physical appearance and photo, 36, 37-39; pocketknife, 18, 126, 177; ransom hoax in Rocky Mount, NC, 41, 126; theories as to disappearance, 194-201; theories as to fate, 213
Bellamy, John D., 95
Berry, John L., 133, 162; eyewitness to boy in buggy, 127-28
Biddle Institute, 89
Biggs, Asa, 155
Biggs, Kader, 154-55
Biggs, Lucy, 155
"Black Second" congressional district, 89-90
Bond, William M., 139, 143; later career as superior-court judge, 229; retained as special prosecutor, 117
Branch, "Hurricane," 23
Brown, Bertha, 218
Brown, George H., 181
Brown, J. C., 9
Buffalo City, NC, 108
Burfoot, Dennis J., 151-62, 174
Butler, Marion, 86, 92

Callahan, James, 63, 68; arrest, trial, and acquittal in Cudahy kidnapping, 64-65
Cartwright, Johnson, 39
Cash, W. J., 93, 165

INDEX

Cecelski, David S., 225
Charlotte Messenger, 89
Chatham, Hugh G., 223
Cherry, R. Gregg, 237
Christensen, Rob, 85
Clark, Walter, 220
Clement, Hayden, 176-77, 180
Cleve, William, 236, 237
Clinton, Henry, 89
Coates, Ta-Nehisi, 226
Cohoon, Walter L.: career as newspaper publisher and disputes with W. O. Saunders, 230-31; closing argument at trial, 166; retained as special prosecutor, 117
Connor, Henry Groves, 120
Coogan, J. J., 161
Craig, Locke, 218, 219; and disenfranchisement amendment, 100; elected governor in 1912, 94; role in White Supremacy Campaign, 94
Cropsey, Nell, 178-79
Crowe, Pat, 68, 73, 109; capture and return to Omaha, 66; compared with Ross kidnappers, 63; criminal background, 63-64; escape from Omaha and subsequent crimes, 64, 65-66; public adulation for, 66; revenge motive toward Cudahy, 63-64; shootout with police, 65-66; threat to kill Eddie Cudahy after kidnapping, 64; trials and acquittals, 66; writing and public-speaking tour, 67
Cudahy, Edward Jr. "Eddie," *58*, 59-67, 213; abduction, 60, 62-63; coverage of kidnapping in NC and VA press, 67; kidnappers cite Ross case in ransom letter, 60; ransom demand for, 60; released after ransom paid, 62; testifies in Crowe trials, 66
Cudahy, Edward Sr., 68; antitrust suit against, 66; owner of Cudahy Packing Co., 60; pays ransom for son, 60-61; resented by public as robber baron, 64, 65, 66, 68
Currituck County: history and geography, 1-2; population, 7-8, 33; pre-trial publicity and alleged prejudice against Harrison, 73, 75-77, 177; school construction and funding, 11-12
Currituck Jail, 71, *71*
Currituck Courthouse, 71-72, *72*
Currituck Sound: dimensions and hydrology, 200; drowning statistics, 200-201; fishing and hunting, 8-10, 201
Currituck Telephone Co., 20

Daniels, Frank, 118, 217
Daniels, Josephus: coordinator of White Supremacy Campaign, 93, 95; and disenfranchisement amendment, 100; editor of *News & Observer*, 93; as Methodist layman, 105, 115; photograph of, *86*; promotes Raleigh anti-liquor referendum, 105; publishes stories alleging abuse of power by blacks, 95; and Red Shirt campaign, 97; reports on Wilmington Insurrection, 98; as secretary of navy, 224
Davenport, T. N., 163
Donahue, J. J., 60
Douglass, Joseph, 54, 126, 189; confession in Ross case and death in Long Island shootout, 55
Doxey, W. A., 127
Dudley, Mathias, 140
Dunton, William, 208

Ehringhaus, John C. B., 231
Elizabeth City, NC, 14, 23, 145; destruction in Civil War, 33-34; growth in 1890s and 1900s, 121; racial tensions in 1898 election, 98

Financial panic of 1893: impact on anti-liquor movement, 104-5; and racial politics, 90-92
Fisher, J. W., 134, 143-44
Forbes, Isaac, 32
Forbes, Julia, 145
Fulton, Rebecca L., 96
"Fusion" alliance of Republicans and Populists, 91-92

Gallop, E. B., 127

Gallop, Harold, 236
Gallop, Hodges M., 34-35
Gallop, Irving, 19, 163, 211
Gallop, Maggie Harrison: death, 236; at Glisson House, *150*, 154-56; marriage and children, 34-35; pre-deceased by her three sons, 236; reaction to father's death, 190; residences in Norfolk, 151-57, 236; suspected of helping father conceal Kenneth, 148-49, 212; testifies at father's trial, 148-49; at 203 Granby Street house, 151-53, 156
Gardner, O. Max, 225
Gerard, Philip, 96
Germantown, PA, 47-48
Gladstone Hotel, 188
Glenn, Robert B., 218, 222-23; attempts to stop lynchings, 84-85; elected governor in 1904, 94; role in White Supremacy Campaign, 94; school funding disputes, 120; support for disenfranchisement amendment, 100
Glisson, Oliver, 154
Glisson House, *150*, 154-56
"Good-Bye, My Honey, I'm Gone," 146
Gordon, Stephen, 163
Grady, Henry Woodfin, 88, 89
Great Smoky Mountains National Park, 197-98
Green, Paul Eliot: boyhood recollection of lynching, 79-80; literary background, 80-81
Griggs, Charles, 30
Griggs, Mack, 25
Griggs, Martha Newbern, 76
Griggs, Robert Lee, 76, 77
Gudger, J. M., 222

Hall, George, 85
Harris/Harrison, Charlie, 134
Harrison, Ann Jarvis, 18, 33, 125, 165, 173; death, 237; marriage to Joshua Harrison, 30; reaction to husband's death, 190; testifies at husband's trial, including account of visit to Beasley home, 147-48
Harrison, Benjamin, 33
Harrison, Dan, 142
Harrison, Joe: accused of taunting Kenneth's parents, 145-47; testifies at father's trial, 145
Harrison, Joshua, 18, 29, 68, 69, 115, 118, 185, 193, 203, 212; alibi for day and week of Kenneth's disappearance, 74, 143-48; alleged attempt at ransom negotiation, 136-37; alleged threat against Samuel Beasley, 124-25, 132, 133; allegedly claims to know where Kenneth could be found, 132-33; ancestry, 29; appeal to NC Supreme Court, 177-81; assault accusations against, 34; bond hearing, 73, 75-77; charged with dealing liquor in 1904 and 1905, 109-10; children, 34; civil superior-court case, 72; content of suicide note, 189; convicted of kidnapping, 168-69; debts and collection issues, 208-9; early suspicions of, 25, 42-43; escape to Norfolk, 188; gravesite, 237-38, *238*; home, *26*; hostile courtroom atmosphere alleged by, 177-78; indicted for kidnapping, 72, 103; marriage, 30; motion for change of venue, 75; personal appearance, 34; personal demeanor during trial, 123; possibility of ransom deal, 207-10; post-trial motions, 171-74; property disputes with family, 33-34; protests innocence after conviction, 169; seen by witnesses in Norfolk after disappearance, 160-62; seen by witnesses riding in buggy with boy, 127-28; sentencing and appeal bond posted, 174; state moves to increase appeal bond, 180-81; suicide, 188-89; suspected of bootlegging, 73-74, 108, 109; threats of lynching against, 75-77; trial for murder of Caleb Owens, 30-31; trial for murder of William Harrison, 32-34, 74; visit to Beasley home after Kenneth's disappearance, 125-26
Harrison, Marvin Hoge, 145; later life, 235; testifies at father's trial, 143-44, 147
Harrison, Nina Pocahontas, 25, 34, 125, 155; absent from father's trial, 212;

INDEX

and disappearance of Kenneth, 19-20; donates Jarvis portrait to NC History Museum, 237; family background, 18; hired as teacher, 19; marriage and children, 236; personal tribute and description of Kenneth, 41-43; possible involvement in kidnapping, 210-13; return to Poplar Branch, 237

Harrison, Thomas: life after trial, 235-36; testifies at father's trial, 145

Harrison, Walter, 31

Harrison, William, 29, 33; alleged murder by son Joshua, 32-34

Harrison, Zorababel, 29

Hauptmann, Bruno Richard, 206

Haygood, Atticus G., 89

Highway 158, 1-2, 237

Hill, Benjamin H., 88

Hill, Kenneth A., 196-97

Holden, William W., 186

In Abraham's Bosom, 80-81
Independent, 116, 157, 230-31

Jacobs, Thornwell, 106
Jarvis, Bannister, 30, 237
Jarvis, Thomas B., 32
Jarvis, Thomas Jordan, 25, 73, *114*, 155, 173; career after Harrison trial, 229-30; Civil War service and early legislative career, 30, 116; defeated for re-election to U.S. Senate in 1894, 92; defends Harrison in court, 111, 115-16; finishes construction of state penitentiary, 186; in Harrison's previous murder trials, 32-34; political background as governor, senator, diplomat, 18-19; portrait, 237; speech at 1904 Democratic Convention, 120; supports statewide prohibition, 110-11, 218

Jarvisburg, NC, 12, 18, 34

Jennings, Minuard P., 18, 195, 210; and disappearance of Kenneth, 20-21, 23; resides in Beasley home, 126-27; testifies at trial, 126-27

Jury selection (in Harrison trial), 122-23

Kidnapping statutes: Nebraska, 65; North Carolina, 69; Pennsylvania, 55-56, 65
Kitchin, William W., 85, 220, 221; elected governor in 1908, 219

Laughinghouse, Joseph J., 221-22
Leibowitz, Sam, 206
Lindbergh kidnapping, 206
Littlefield, Milton S., 186
Logan County, AR, 176
Long Point School, Jarvisburg, NC, 12-13
Lost children, behavioral patterns of, 195-96
Lost Colony, The, 80
Lowry, Robert, 146
Lumsden, John, 218
Lynchings, *78*, 81-85; of George Rittle, Moore County, 1900, 82; of Henry Jones, Chatham County, 1898, 81-82; of James and Harrison Gillespie, Rowan County, 1902, 83-84; of John V. Johnson, Anson County, 1906, 84; of Silas Martindale, Moore County, 1901, 82; statistics in North Carolina and throughout South, 81

Manly, Alexander: newspaper office destroyed in Wilmington Insurrection, 97; publishes inflammatory editorial, 95-96
Manly, Charles, 95-96
map, *xii, 199*
Maple Swamp, 1; dimensions and topography, 22, 196, 198
Martin, Dennis, 197-98
McLean, Angus, 230
Meekins, Isaac "Ike": career after Harrison trial, 230; closing argument at trial, 166; political background, 116; retained by Harrison, 116
Meggs, Edward, 19
Morris, Chester R., 194
Morris, Travis, 194
Morrissette, Millard, 133, 207; eyewitness to boy in buggy, 127-28
Mosher, William, 126; compared with Cudahy kidnappers, 63; criminal background, 54; death in Long Island shootout, 55; physical deformity, 54

Nelson, George, 176

"New South" boosterism, 88-90
Newbern, Grover C., 163
Newbern, John, 32, 74
Newbern, Virginia Harrison, 74, 76
Newbern, Walter Jr.: owner of Newbern's Landing, 74; pledges bond for Harrison, 76
Newbern, Walter Sr.: owner of Newbern's Landing, 74; pledges bond for Harrison, 76
Newbern, Worth, 74, 76
News & Observer, 24, 37, 39, 41, 73, 93, 95, 98, 103, 127, 144, 162, 166, 213, 221. *See also* Daniels, Josephus
newspaper headlines, *70*, *77*, *130*, *133*, *138*, *168*, *170*, *180*, *192*
Nixon, W. T., 141
Norfolk Southern Railway, 9, 23, 121, 156
Norfolk, VA: called "wickedest city in the United States," 156; Granby Street district, 152-53; Hell's Half Acre (Tenderloin District), 156-57; industry, 9, 156; number of boardinghouses, brothels, 157; police corruption and liquor trade, 157; rumors of Kenneth's being sighted, 39-40; West Freemason Street neighborhood, 153-55
North Carolina Farmers Alliance, 91, 92
North Carolina State Penitentiary, *184*, 185-87, 221

Odd Fellows Hall, Poplar Branch, NC, 10-11, *10*, 13, 14, 18, 19-20, 108
Omaha Daily News, 63
Omaha, NE, 59-60
Omaha World-Herald, 63
Orphan Train Movement, 175-76
Owens, Caleb, 31, 205
Owens, Lydia, 31
Owens, Patrick, 31

Parker, John, 142
Pasquotank County Courthouse, 121-22, *158*
Philadelphia Inquirer, 54
Philadelphia Public Ledger, 50-51, 53
Pierce, J. J.: claims to have seen Kenneth in Norfolk, 39-40; testimony at Harrison trial, 131-32

Poe, Clarence, 220
Poplar Branch community, 1, 7-8, 198
Poplar Branch Landing, 8-10
Poplar Branch Road, 8-9, 14, 200
Porter, Ethel Beasley, 14; death, 235; life in Norfolk after Harrison trial, 234-35; photo and physical appearance, 38-39
Poyner, John W., 127, 136; search for Kenneth, 21-22
Pritchard, Jeter C., *86*, 92
Pruden, William D., 172; closing argument at trial, 166; retained as special prosecutor, 117

Race and politics, 87-101, *221*
Ransom, Matthew, 92
Reconstruction of 1870s and 1880s, 88
Red Shirt brigade, 97
Rodwell, J. R., 222
Rosenfeld, M. H., 146
Ross, Charley, *46*, 47-57, 67, 126, 167; abduction, 48-50; Cudahy kidnapping planned as copycat crime, 60; kidnapper's confession, 55; ransom demand for, 51; search for, 51-56
Ross, Christian, 48, 49, 68, 175; dilemma of whether to pay ransom, 52-54; financial problems, 52; ongoing search and reward offers, 56; press speculation into personal life, 54-55; reports son missing, 50
Ross, Sarah, 48, 56, 164, 175
Ross, Sophia, 48
Ross, Walter, 48, 49, 50; identifies kidnappers' bodies, 55
Royster Guano Company, 208
Russell, Daniel L., *86*, 97; background, 92; elected governor in 1896, 92; nearly lynched in 1898 campaign, 85, 88

Sanders, W. A., 142
Saunders, Keith, 116, 157
Saunders, W. O., 116, 157; disputes with Edwin Aydlett, Walter Cohoon, 230-31
Sawyer, J. Haywood, 139, 145, 146; retained as special prosecutor, 117
Sawyer, Roy, 30
schoolhouse, Currituck County, *10*, 10-

11, 17-22. *See also, Odd Fellows Hall*
Sentelle, John, 222
Silver Tones songbook, 147
Simmons, Furnifold M.: candidate in Black Second district, 94-95; coordinator of White Supremacy Campaign, 94; and disenfranchisement amendment, 100; elected to U.S. Senate in 1900, 95; photograph, *86*; re-election defeat, 1930, 224; U.S. Senate career, 218-19, 223-24
Sivells, Lemuel, 127-28
Sloane's Maternity Hospital, NY, 176
Smith, William C., 89
Snowden, Barbara, 194
St. Vincent's Hospital, 189, 232
Stephenson, Frank Jr., 108
Subiaco Abbey, AR, 176
Swain, E. G., 140
Syrotuck, William G., 195

Tar Heel, 134-35
Thomas, Lee, 143
Tillman, Ben, 96, 97
Turner, J. L., 132; eyewitness to boy in buggy, 127-28
Turner, Nat, 72
Tyson, Timothy B., 225

Waddell, Alfred Moore, 97
Walker, Bennett "Benny," 19-20, 21, 163, 211
Walker, Carrie Parker, 12-13
Walker, Nathan, 13
Walker, Sam, 213
Walker, William H., 8
Walling, George Washington, 53, 54, 55
Walston, Norris, 141
Warburton, Andrew, 196-97
Ward, Hallet Sydney, 123, 135, 139, 149, 165, 172, 188, *202*, 217; closing argument at trial, 167; at Harrison's bond hearing, 75-77; later elected to Congress and State Senate, 229; nicknamed "Hot Shot" and "Hot Stuff," 117; opposes defense motion for change of venue, 75-76; personal reflections on Harrison case, 211-13; political background in State Senate,

117; and post-trial motions, 173; and testimony of Sam Beasley, 123-26
Watts, Alston D. "Aus," 106, 111
Weekly Economist, 40, 73, 99
Wellman, Manly Wade: author of *Dead and Gone*, 28-29; journalistic treatment of Beasley case, 29, 42, 124, 148-49, 193, 211, 217; personal and literary background, 28
Westervelt, William, 54; trial and conviction in Ross case, 56
Whalehead Lifesaving Station, 35
"Where Is My Wandering Boy Tonight?" 146
White, George H., *86*
White, John, 160
White Supremacy Campaign of 1898, 93-101. *See also,* Race and politics
Wilcox, Jim, 178-79
Williams, Ella, 9
Wilmington Daily Record, 95, 96
Wilmington, NC: black middle-class Fusionist government of 1896, 95; November 1998 insurrection, 97-98
Winston, Robert, 217, 222
Women's Christian Temperance Union, 147
Woodhouse, Daniel W., 127, 136; search for Kenneth, 21-22
Woodhouse, J. J., 174; claims to have seen Harrison in Norfolk after Kenneth's disappearance, 159-61, 162
Woodhouse, James M., 31
Woodhouse, Thomas C., 159-60, 205, 207; claims to have communicated ransom negotiations, 136-37; criminal charges against, 209-10; prostitution allegation, 163-64; testimony at Harrison trial, 136-37; witness against Harrison on liquor charges, 209-10
Woodhouse, Wilson, 9
Wright, Daniel, 97
Wright, Ernest, 19-20
Wright, Silas, 97

Young, S. J., 9

About the Author

For CHARLES OLDHAM, *The Senator's Son* is his first published book, but it is the product of several lifelong passions. Charles was born and raised in Sanford, North Carolina, the son of a community college professor and a math teacher. His parents instilled in him a natural curiosity, and a love for reading. Early on, Charles had a special interest in history and politics, most especially that of North Carolina, where his family roots go back more than two centuries. He also has a keen eye for mysteries, for searching out the details of a story that needs to be explored. It is a talent that led him to become an attorney.

Charles graduated from Davidson College, and from law school at the University of Georgia. Afterward he practiced law in Sanford for a time, including a term as president of the Lee County Bar Association. He now lives in Charlotte, where for ten years he had a solo legal practice focused on criminal defense and civil litigation.

In his spare time, he can be found doing just about anything outdoors, especially hiking and camping. Charles also loves spending time with his family in the summer at their favorite vacation spots, including Ocean Isle Beach and Lake Junaluska in the mountains.

CharlesOldhamAuthor.com

Books That Endure

BEACH GLASS Books

BeachGlassBooks.com